Environmental Federalism

The Political Economy Forum

Sponsored by the Political Economy Research Center (PERC)
Series Editor: Terry L. Anderson

Environmental Federalism

EDITED BY
TERRY L. ANDERSON AND PETER J. HILL

ROWMAN & LITTLEFIELD PUBLISHERS, INC.
Lanham • Boulder • New York • Oxford

ROWMAN & LITTLEFIELD PUBLISHERS, INC.

Published in the United States of America
by Rowman & Littlefield Publishers, Inc.
4720 Boston Way, Lanham, Maryland 20706

12 Hid's Copse Road
Cummor Hill, Oxford OX2 9JJ, England

British Library Cataloguing in Publication Information Available

Library of Congress Cataloging-in-Publication Data

Environmental federalism / edited by Terry L. Anderson and Peter J. Hill.
    p. cm. — (Political economy forum)
    Includes bibliographical references and index.
    ISBN 0-8476-8570-5 (cloth : alk. paper). — ISBN 0-8476-8571-3
(pbk. : alk. paper)
    1. Environmental policy—United States. 2. Environmental policy—
United States—States. 3. Environmental protection—United States. 4.
Environmental protection—United States—States. 5. Federal govern-
ment—United States. 6. Decentralization in government—United States.
I. Anderson, Terry Lee, 1946– . II. Hill, Peter Jensen. III. Series.
GE180.E582 1997   97-19208
 363.7'056'0973—DC21   CIP

ISBN 0-8476-8570-5 (cloth : alk. paper)
ISBN 0-8476-8571-3 (pbk. : alk paper)

Printed in the United States of America

♾™The paper used in this publication meets the minimum requirements
of American National Standard for Information Sciences—Permanence of
Paper for Printed Library Materials, ANSI Z39.48–1984.

Contents

Tables and Figures

Tables

Figures

Acknowledgments

As with every other volume in the Political Economy Forum Series, the final product is a team effort that goes beyond the authors and editors. The captain of that team is Dianna Rienhart, who is responsible for PERC's desktop publishing process. She is the one who pays attention to detail and thus makes sure all the i's are dotted and t's are crossed. Her cocaptains are Michelle Johnson and Monica Lane Guenther, who assist with word processing, proofreading, and general project management.

Financial support for this forum and the papers came from Dunn's Foundation for the Advancement of Right Thinking, the E. L. Wiegand Foundation of Reno, Nevada, and the George F. Bennett Endowment at Wheaton College. Without their investment in knowledge, the research represented in this volume would not have been possible.

We thank the authors for their cooperation in writing the papers and exposing their ideas to constructive criticism from participants at PERC's Political Economy Forum held on June 13–16, 1996. The final product between these covers owes much to the intellectual debate held at that forum. The following individuals participated in the Political Economy Forum: Daniel K. Benjamin (PERC and Clemson University), Donald J. Boudreaux (Clemson University), David Brady (Stanford University), Karol Ceplo (Clemson University), Louis De Alessi (University of Miami), William Dennis (Liberty Fund Inc., Indianapolis), Sally K. Fairfax (University of California, Berkeley), Robert Fleck (Montana State University), David D. Haddock (Northwestern University), Andrew Hanssen (Montana State University), Dean Lueck (North Carolina State University), Fred McChesney (Emory University), Roger E. Meiners (PERC and University of Texas, Arlington), Thomas Merrill (Northwestern University), Andrew P. Morriss (Case Western Reserve University), Robert H. Nelson (University of Maryland), Seth Norton (Wheaton College), Randy T. Simmons (PERC and Utah State University), Richard L. Stroup

(PERC and Montana State University), Barton H. Thompson Jr. (Stanford University), Gordon Tullock (University of Arizona), and Ian Wills (Monash University, Australia).

Terry L. Anderson
Peter J. Hill

Introduction

Environmental Federalism: Thinking Smaller

Terry L. Anderson and Peter J. Hill

Change is in the air. After a century of growing national control, Americans are rethinking the role of the federal government vis-à-vis the states. This reconsideration has led to welfare reform and to a nationwide debate over education. Now it is beginning to focus on environmental policy, too.

Dissatisfaction with Washington-imposed environmental policy is well known.

- Local government officials are outraged by unfunded mandates—regulations imposed from Washington but paid for locally. For example, Montanans must clean up the naturally occurring arsenic in the Madison River because arsenic levels coming from geysers in Yellowstone Park exceed national standards. Yet, according to Environmental Protection Agency (EPA) estimates, a person would have to consume two liters of untreated water from the source *and* eat 6.5 grams of fish every day for seventy years to increase his or her risk of cancer by 1 in 10,000.

- A recent poll found that 72 percent favor state and local determination of the best ways to control air pollution. The poll also discovered that 65 percent believed "that state or local government would do a better job than the federal government in dealing with environmental concerns" (Adler 1996, 4).

- Towns such as Aspen, Colorado, and Triumph, Idaho, are locked in an unending battle with the EPA because it claims that hazardous waste sites (places that have old mine tailings) must be cleaned up even though the communities do not feel the risks warrant the disruptions (Stroup 1996).

- Federal regulations to protect endangered species and wetlands have forced property owners to stop farming, logging, and building on their property (Lund 1995).

- Costs of complying with national environmental regulations have risen from $53 billion in 1980 to over $150 billion today, a figure representing 2 percent of the nation's gross domestic product (Hopkins 1992).

Recognizing the excesses, Washington officials have attempted to address them through a "reinventing government" program. This approach has failed to downsize government or reduce regulations. In fact, just the opposite has occurred. Since 1993, the number of regulations proposed or issued by the Environmental Protection Agency has increased by 20 percent. Of the 430 regulations in the "pipeline" in April 1996, forty-six are expected to cost business at least $100 million annually. Only nine are receiving scrutiny under the "reinventing government" agenda. Hence, thirty-seven regulations will have an economic impact in excess of $3.7 billion per year (Crews 1996, 13–14).

These federal regulations are also costly to state and local governments. The Clean Water Act, the Clean Air Act, the Safe Drinking Water Act, and other laws require states and municipalities to meet national environmental standards at significant expense to local taxpayers but do not provide the funds to do so. These unfunded mandates, not all of which are environmental, are projected to cost $54 billion between 1994 and 1998 (Crews 1996, 17). Reinventing government is not working.

In search of an alternative, the Political Economy Research Center devoted its June 1996 Political Economy Forum to the issue of environmental federalism. This volume includes the papers from that forum plus another piece previously published that is relevant to the issue.

Prior to the 1970s, natural resources and environmental policy were governed mainly by common law, state laws, or federal agencies managing land and water from the ground up. This changed in the 1970s as environmental groups began to insist on tougher laws against pollution and began to argue that forests and grasslands were more valuable for recreation and wilderness than for commodity production.

Such activism fostered national rather than state or local regulation for several reasons. First, confidence in the federal government was high. If the federal government could fight a War on Poverty and land a man on the moon, why shouldn't it be able to solve environmental problems (Shaw 1996)? Second, by making the environment a matter of the national "public interest," environmentalists could trump state and local laws without concern for the costs. Claiming "third-party effects" and "free-rider" problems, environmental groups could get what they wanted by diffusing the costs over millions of taxpayers while concentrating the benefits on their interest group. Third, activists feared that state and local governments would dilute environmental laws in a "race to the bottom" wherein states compete with one another for business by relaxing environmental laws. Fourth, industry lobbyists also tended to favor federal control because they could do one-stop shopping in Washington instead of in fifty state capitals. Fifth, national environmental laws allowed industry to grandfather existing polluters when environmental laws were passed, thus raising another hurdle for new competitors. Sixth, the push toward national control has recently been bolstered by the view that all things in the environment are interconnected.[1] If the environment is one giant web of interconnections, then local action is too narrow and must be inferior to centralized coordination. Indeed, environmental activists have shifted focus again, seeking international, not just national, regulations to deal with global issues such as endangered species, climate change, or ozone depletion. These are powerful arguments that won the day in Washington and gave us the all-encompassing environmental laws that people are now beginning to question.

The history of growing intervention by the national government over the past three decades can be juxtaposed against federalism, which has deep roots in American life. In his chapter, David Haddock notes that the original colonists always referred to their union as *these* United States, emphasizing the fact that the individual states were united but not a unitary national state. Known as federalism, the system of "united states" allowed competing sovereign states to pursue their own policies for most issues. The role of the national government was to promote free trade, provide national defense, dispose of the public domain, and settle disputes between states.

Haddock contrasts federalism, under which the power emanates from the state rather than from the national government, with the current system of political centralization under which the national government delegates powers to state and local governments acting as the agent of the former. This "delegation model" typifies current environmental regulations.

Although the system of federalism created by the Constitution generated unprecedented economic growth, Haddock points out it also contained the seeds of its own demise by gradually increasing the demand for national control. As trade, migration, and pollution crossed state boundaries, there were increasing calls for uniform national regulations.

The centralization described by Haddock clearly has come with high costs. It has reduced the number of experiments with alternative policy options and generated one-size-fits-all policies that may be appropriate for some places but not for others. It has reduced the ability of citizens to monitor their governments. As decisions are further removed from constituents, it is more difficult to know whether political agents are acting in the public interest or on behalf of special interests. Because citizens cannot easily "vote with their feet" by moving to a different jurisdiction, the national government has obtained monopoly power over environmental regulation that reduces the options of citizens and raises the cost of services.

Decentralization and federalism offer ways to reduce these costs by providing experiments with different policies, by making it easier for citizens to monitor their political agents, and by giving citizens alternative jurisdictions from which to choose the policies they desire. Haddock's framework suggests the following principle as a guide for pursuing environmental federalism: *To minimize the costs of monitoring regulatory agencies, authority should devolve to the lowest level of government that also allows for control of pollution or other spillover effects.*

The remaining chapters in this volume examine the possibility of federalism under this principle. Although environmental policy in the past three decades has been dictated mostly from Washington, there is a rich history of states' success in solving resource and environmental problems. Such successes are illustrated in the management of public lands, wildlife, pesticides, and water.

Research by Leal (1995b) has shown that state forest management is more efficient than federal forest management. He found that Montana state forests earn $2.16 for every $1 they spend, while neighboring national forests earn only $0.51 for every $1 spent. A major reason for the difference is the higher costs of national forest timber sales. Leal's comparison of labor costs and labor hours in central Montana showed that the Gallatin National Forest required more than two and a half times the number of hours of labor to prepare a thousand board feet for sale and harvest than did the state office. Leal also reviewed grazing land management in Montana and found that management costs for Montana's state lands are approximately $0.82 per acre, compared to $3.79 per acre for Bureau of Land Management lands (Leal 1995a). If Montana were to manage BLM lands for $0.82 per acre and to collect the same revenues currently received by the BLM, it would net $48 million per year, compared with the BLM's annual loss of approximately $5 million.

Because states do a better job of managing their lands than do federal agencies, devolution of land management to the states should be a welcome reform. Robert Nelson, however, points out that even though the management of these lands causes losses to the U.S. Treasury, the losses represent money spent within the states. Even if states made money from a transfer of BLM lands, a transfer of the lands would mean loss of the large infusion of funds associated with the presence of BLM lands now coming from the federal treasury. This would mean "significant losses of jobs and income for many state residents." To compensate for this loss of federal funds, says Nelson, a state would have to earn between $25 million and $75 million in net revenues from lands that are now losing $10 million to $40 million per year under BLM management.

The institutional arrangements for creating greater flexibility and responsiveness in public land management are varied. Sally Fairfax examines one, state trust lands, where the mandate to manage for revenue should constrain bureaucratic malfeasance. Her focus is on efforts by environmental groups in western states to bid on grazing leases for the explicit purpose of not grazing. She finds, however, that bureaucracies responsible for managing the state lands often refuse to recognize these higher bids. Fairfax therefore raises the question of whether the trust concept increases bureaucratic accountability. She concludes that the trust concept may be helpful, but entrenched interests at the state level can thwart improved resource management.

Dean Lueck and Jonathan Yoder explain why wildlife management has been the domain of states but why that is changing. Lueck and Yoder point out that wildlife management is complicated by the costs of coordinating among the various landowners, private or governmental, over whose property wildlife may range. If the range is confined to a single parcel of private land (either naturally or by fencing), there are few coordination problems. If species range over territories larger than a single private landowner, wildlife management can be more complicated because of the transaction costs of coordinating management among the many landowners. This provides a rationale for state control. Only if species range over territories larger than a state is there reason to consider regional, federal, or even international control. Waterfowl are the quintessential example. Ducks and geese nest in Canada, migrate across the United States, and winter in Mexico. No individual landowner can coordinate habitat management over this range, and even single states are powerless to regulate management across state or international borders.

Nonetheless, in recent years, the authority of national government over wildlife has expanded beyond migratory species through the Endangered Species Act (ESA). Under the ESA authority, states have lost control of some wildlife management decisions. Grizzly bears, for example, can no longer be hunted in Montana because they are listed as an endangered species.

The argument for national control of endangered species rests on two premises: people derive value (called existence value) from knowing that a species exists, even though they will never consume or view it, and voluntary support for preserving species will be deficient because of the free-rider problem. Because individual owners of land or water cannot capture the benefits of this existence value, they will not take the value into account when making decisions that affect habitat. If existence value extends beyond state boundaries (as presumably it does), the argument is that the national government should intervene. However, as Lueck and Yoder discuss, this argument ignores many of the costs of national bureaucratic regulation, not the least of which is perverse incentives created by uncompensated takings.

Andrew Morriss applies the principle of federalism to pesticide management. This is an interesting case because some impacts of pesticide use are purely local, but other impacts cross state lines. For example, local impacts include wind or water carrying a pesticide to a neighbor's property, or the actual use of the pesticide may involve risks for the applicator. On the other hand, if pesticide residues enter the food chain, people far from the original place of use can be affected. Because of this dual nature of pesticide externalities, Morriss notes that pesticide regulation in the United States is "the product of cooperation between state and federal governments."

A dual regulatory system has distinct advantages. State regulation can better respond to location-specific needs. Because the types of pesticides used and the method of use can vary considerably by crop or region, flexibility is necessary to meet the demands of agricultural users for pest control under a variety of conditions and uses. National regulation, on the other hand, offers a way of controlling effects that may cross boundaries. As with so many environmental regulations, however, Morriss documents a shift toward increasing national control.

Early pesticide regulation at both the state and national levels was primarily concerned with the effectiveness of pesticides. Products that fell short of manufacturer claims had to be removed from the market. In 1947, however, the Federal Insecticide, Fungicide, and Rodenticide Act (FIFRA) changed the regulatory focus from efficacy to product harm. It demanded a more rigorous registration system and labeling of contents and instructions for use. Even then, Morriss tells us, this and each successive version of FIFRA "was built upon an existing regulatory scheme which depended largely on state-level regulations."

The power of the federal government increased substantially in 1970 when authority for pesticide regulation was transferred from the Department of Agriculture to the newly created Environmental Protection Agency. In 1972, the EPA banned DDT for most uses, and the Federal

Environmental Pest Control Act (FEPCA) revamped virtually every part of FIFRA to focus on the environmental impacts of pesticide residues. National registration under EPA rules is time-consuming and expensive. In 1975, 46,000 pesticides were awaiting federal reregistration; by March 1986, the EPA had not completed even one final reassessment of any pesticide's active ingredient and had conducted only preliminary assessments of about 20 percent of the registered active ingredients. By 1993, only 8 percent of the active ingredients had been reregistered under the new rules.

Morriss explains how the burdensome EPA regulations plus fears by agricultural users that environmentalists would "slam shut the door on pesticide use" allowed the states to regain some regulatory control. As a result, the mix of federal and state regulation has moved pesticide regulation in the direction of a solution consistent with the principle of federalism. Morriss's data show that the states have not entered into a race to the bottom. His data indicate that further devolution of the regulation and registration process to the states would be appropriate because of the problems of a one-size-fits-all national regulatory regime.

The history of water policy shows that states managed their water resources effectively until the federal government intervened to expand its control. In his chapter, Barton Thompson identifies four periods of U.S. water policy: the Gestation Period, 1849 to 1901; the Embryonic National Period, 1902 to 1914; the National Empire Period, 1914 to 1968; and the Environmental Period, 1968 to the present. During the Gestation Period, from 1849 to 1901, local miners and farmers forged water policies that met their specific needs. Generally these policies centered around the prior appropriation doctrine, which was codified by state legislatures. The Embryonic National Period began in 1902 when the role of the federal government in water allocation expanded significantly; this federal role matured with the massive water storage and delivery systems built during the National Empire Period. Even then, however, the role of the national government in western water allocation was limited through much of the twentieth century. It was not until the Environmental Period, which Thompson identifies as beginning in 1968, that the national government really began to dominate state water policy. This occurred through the national regulation of water quality.

One might surmise that this takeover occurred because states were not dealing effectively with clean water issues, but the evidence does not support this interpretation. Karol Ceplo and Bruce Yandle conclude that "prior to 1970, state management of water quality involved a mixture of statutes and common law" that provide "a positive history of responding to water-related problems." They find "significant diversity" among the states. Building on a common-law base, state water quality agencies quite often grew out of the agencies that managed water rights and water supply. States such as Arizona, California, and Oregon have "long-developed elaborate administrative mechanisms to control and prevent water pollution," while others, such as New Mexico, have done less. Ceplo and Yandle contend that states showed themselves capable of creating appropriate programs to manage pollution. Certainly there is no evidence of a general race to the bottom.

David Schoenbrod also finds no indication of a race to the bottom. He provides a history of the centralization of environmental policy and of the problems created by this centralization. Though federal involvement is rationalized on the premise that pollution crosses state lines, most of the efforts of the EPA have been directed at intrastate pollution. Moreover, the states were responding in the 1960s to increased public awareness of environmental problems before the federal government intervened.

Elevating natural resource and environmental regulations to the national level may have had some benefits. Spillover effects, such as pollution across state boundaries, can be taken into account. But this elevation has come with high costs. A one-size-fits-all policy has left too many problems unsolved and has led to a bureaucracy that is largely unaccountable to the American public.

There is growing doubt about whether the growth in national control should be sustained. For most natural resource and environmental problems, devolution is an alternative that can reduce costs and align results with the demands of citizens. While private ownership offers the ultimate degree of devolution, a government role may be appropriate when there are environmental effects that markets cannot fully handle. Devolution to local and state governments would leave it to governments at these levels to decide the boundary between public and private.

The examples of environmental federalism discussed in this volume provide a starting point for reversing the rising power of the national government and returning authority to states and individuals. They suggest ways to begin the process of decentralization. As our Founding Fathers understood, national regulations should be a last, rather than a first, resort.

Note

1. See Johnson (1997). Writing in *PERC Reports*, Charles T. Rubin (1994) noted: "We would do little conceptual violence to 'environmentalism' if we simply replaced the word 'environment' with the word 'everything,' and likewise spoke of 'everythingists' and 'everythingism.'"

References

Adler, Jonathan H. 1996. Green but Anti-Government. *CEI Update* 9(8): 4–5.

Crews, Clyde Wayne, Jr. 1996. *Ten Thousand Commandments: A Policy Maker's Snapshot of the Federal Regulatory State.* Washington, DC: Competitive Enterprise Institute, September.

Hopkins, Thomas D. 1992. *Regulatory Policy in Canada and the United States.* Rochester, NY: Rochester Institute of Technology.

Johnson, Ronald N. 1997. Ecosystem Management and Reinventing Government. In *Breaking the Environmental Policy Gridlock*, ed. Terry L. Anderson. Stanford: Hoover Institution Press, 22–52.

Leal, Donald R. 1995a. State Would Benefit from BLM Land. *Great Falls Tribune*, December 6.

———. 1995b. Turning a Profit on Public Forests. *PERC Policy Series*, PS-4. Bozeman, MT: Political Economy Research Center.

Lund, Hertha L. 1995. Property Rights Legislation in the States: A Review. *PERC Policy Series*, PS-1. Bozeman, MT: Political Economy Research Center.

Rubin, Charles T. 1994. Environmentalism as "Everythingism." *PERC Reports.* Bozeman, MT: Political Economy Research Center, December, 4–5.

Shaw, Jane S. 1996. Environmental Regulation: How It Evolved and Where It Is Headed. *Real Estate Issues* (April): 4–9.

Stroup, Richard L. 1996. Superfund: The Shortcut That Failed. *PERC Policy Series*, PS-5. Bozeman, MT: Political Economy Research Center.

Chapter 1

Sizing Up Sovereigns: Federal Systems, Their Origin, Their Decline, Their Prospects

David D. Haddock

Public choice theory warns of the dangers of dissipation through rent-seeking, an activity that can readily be observed in the workings of any government. Yet it is also clear that some governments have dissipated their citizens into far worse straits than others. Few First World citizens, for instance, are prepared to renounce their motherland for, say, Liberia, but many Liberians would eagerly make the reverse move despite the inevitable white-on-black discrimination that would be encountered on occasion.

Many explanations are offered to account for such First World–Third World differences, but most of them fail even a cursory empirical test. Consider the following common assertions in conjunction with their rather obvious but rarely pondered empirical weaknesses:

1. First World nations are resource-rich, but Third World nations are resource-poor. Japan is resource-poor while her citizens are affluent and largely satisfied with their homeland. But even though Russia is resource rich—perhaps the richest nation on earth—the exodus of her impoverished citizens has become a major political issue in Western Europe.

I began this project while at the International Center for Economic Research, Torino, Italy. I am grateful to Marty DeBoer, Edmund Kitch, Laura Lin, Daniel Polsby, and participants in PERC's 1996 Political Economy Forum for helpful conversations and to the Stanford Clinton Sr. Faculty Fund of Northwestern University for partial financial support.

2. First World countries invest in a lot of human capital, but Third World nations do not. India and Russia each train vast numbers of college and postgraduate students, a high proportion of whom try to utilize their human capital abroad. On the other hand, many Germans and Scandinavians leave school before college and live productive, satisfied lives near their birthplace. Even though the argument may seem well founded as a generalization, the actual cause and effect are reversed. First World families, enjoying higher wealth, are better able to offer their children college educations (though many find college inappropriate for their plans and capabilities) and the college-educated are unlikely to leave their homeland in part because of the high expected rewards to human capital there. Third World families more rarely can afford higher education even for talented children, but a high proportion of the college-trained emigrate to the First World. The greater First World potential for advantageous use of one's human capital both induces its creation and attracts it from abroad.[1]

3. First World nations are large markets but Third World nations are small markets. This assertion is a tautology once allowance for population differences is made—if the per capita size of a market is large, it is defined to be a First World nation. In absolute size mainland China is a larger market than most Western European nations (it is about the size of Italy), but on a per capita basis it is way below any of them—indeed, it is way below Taiwan, Hong Kong, or any other major extraterritorial Chinese enclave. China is potentially the largest market on earth, but its people are poor; Liechtenstein and Luxembourg, though tiny, are rich per capita.

4. First World nations are industrialized but Third World nations are agrarian. Denmark, New Zealand, and, yes, even the United States are quite agrarian by world standards. Some Latin American nations have a substantial industrial base, as do Iraq, India, and Pakistan.

Apparently one must account for the difference between the First and Third Worlds in some other way. Drawing on recent work of North (1990), Weingast (1995), and McGuire and Olson (1996), this chapter argues that a big part of the variation among national performance arises from a difference in institutions. The United States, Japan, Western Europe, and so on have somehow evolved a set of institutions that foster progress and retard exploitation by (or rather via) the sovereign. To be sure, democracy has a bearing (Reynolds 1995; McGuire and Olson 1996), but democracy by itself is plagued by rational ignorance and rational apathy, and some elected governments seem to go very wrong— the Nazi Party, for example, came to power via the ballot box. In some of the more progressive lands, including our own, an additional important institution is federalism. Though it is dangerous to assume that the sovereign's central objective is to benefit citizens, a properly formulated federalism and the intersovereign competition it engenders can align many sovereign and citizen objectives. In that environment sovereign actions create an illusion that the sovereign's prime motivation is to benefit citizens.

It is unsurprising that federalism, an institution of such surpassing importance to our nation, has generated a massive body of scholarly literature. However, the unsystematic character of nearly all of that literature is surprising. Each particular work excitedly focuses on some single attribute or implication of federalism, but the authors rarely delve deeply into issues of consistency with other literature. As always, some works can be dismissed for vagueness and thus irrefutability, while others can be dismissed for illogic. But a number seem intuitively sensible given their narrow confines. Consider, for example, works focusing on the improved ability of an overlapping range of federated sovereigns to exploit varying optimal scales of various government functions (e.g., Mueller 1996, 82). Consider those that point to the way federalism strengthens "voting with the feet" (e.g., Tiebout 1956). As will be argued below, however, there is substantial tension between optimal governmental scale and voting with the feet.

After discussing what federalism will be taken to mean here, the chapter briefly overviews the origins of U.S. federalism, arguing that the institution was chosen as the best way to navigate among diverse concerns of a new and fearful nation while retaining the established privileges of the elites of each of the states. The Founding Fathers designed, or more likely stumbled onto, a structure that appropriately (if accidentally) left a few matters to the national government, always where that level could provide the best scale of operation, but reserved most issues for the state governments, including many that would seem to require a much larger scale of operation than most states could achieve. As a largely unintended and unanticipated result, the federal structure fostered interstate migration of resources, nourished strong economic performance, and ultimately enhanced the freedoms of many whose lot had been beside the point in the view of the constitutional drafters or, indeed, those whom the drafters had intended to retain in servitude.

Federalism has gradually eroded over the years. A successive array of problems that are too large for states to deal with efficiently has been attacked instead at a national level. That has increased the importance of majority-rule voting by ballot at the expense of individualistic voting by feet. But concentrating the regulatory apparatus at the national level defuses the interstate competition that helps control government. That danger has been perceived slowly because the original strong federal system was so successful; over the generations people lost their fear of government because the government seemed so benign. But the government is unlikely to remain benign if the federal bounds on government continue to be loosened. There is little other reason for the government to act benignly.

If in fact many problems cannot be handled effectively by states but intersovereign competition is one of the citizens' main protections against sovereign abuse, what can be done? Instituting other layers of sovereign between the states and the national government, and perhaps below the state level as well, would increase our government's sensitivity to citizen preferences (Haddock 1996). A more direct but less thorough substitute will arise if the North American Free Trade Agreement (NAFTA) or the General Agreement on Tariffs and Trade (GATT) evolves into a very limited image of a national government, something resembling the U.S. government in its early years. That would force NAFTA and/or GATT members to compete more vigorously for the good opinion of their subjects. The ongoing transformation of the European Common Market into the European Union shows, however, that a budding super-sovereign fights to severely limit the powers that are retained by the constituent states, and a NAFTA or GATT that acquires enough teeth may well behave similarly.

This chapter is a paean neither to smaller government nor to larger government. Rather, it is a dream of a different government, one that best restores our heritage of federalism without simultaneously ignoring the new problems that new days have brought.

Unitary States, Federal States, and the Home of the Not-So-Free

Most sovereign states are unitary, meaning that by law all political power resides at the national level. Subordinate levels hold power as agents of the national government. Those delegations of authority are at will— at any time the national sovereign can terminate it unilaterally, and the agent state's acquiescence is legally irrelevant.

It is, of course, a matter of relevance whether the national government has the actual (as opposed to legal) ability to force recalcitrant agent states to relinquish their powers. That is a straightforward extension of Axelrod (1984), Hirshleifer (1995), Schelling (1960), Umbeck (1981), and others. If the national government can effectively assert some powers over the supposedly subordinate states but cannot terminate other powers, the government, though unitary de jure is federal de facto.

A few sovereign states are as a matter of law part of a federal net-work. One level of a federation possesses specified sovereign powers but lacks those that are reserved to the other level(s). Delegations of authority among the layers can be legally altered from the status quo only in accord with some process intended to elicit mutual agreement among the affected levels, or something very close to it. Another way of looking at this feature is to note that each of the several sovereigns in a federal system have vetoes over changes in the distribution of powers among them.[2] Again, the ability of each level of sovereign to defend its powers is relevant; if the national sovereign cannot exert its enumerated powers (e.g., the United Nations) it is hardly sovereign at all; if the smaller units (e.g., states in the United States or provinces in Canada) cannot prevent national overreaching, the nation is unitary de facto even if it is federal de jure.

Thus as the concepts are intended here, some states are federal though claiming to be unitary. Weingast (1995) argues, for example, that the Magna Carta implicitly recognized that England was once a federal state de facto because the king could not as a military matter force his will regarding many county matters upon the local barons. Conversely, other states claim to be federal but are not, the late Soviet Union being one case in point, India being another. Both those national governments have declared that "emergencies" caused them to dismiss subordinate governments and assume direct control over local matters. Indeed, the U.S. federal structure pretty clearly was inoperative temporarily in the post–Civil War South.

Some unitary states perform admirably in terms of human rights, economic performance, legal order, and control of the military, but many others fail miserably on several or all counts. In contrast, the performance of truly federal states is almost always impressive. I believe that there is much in common between the histories of the United States and most other important federal states. If so, it is worth considering the lessons our national history teaches.

The sovereign states of what is now the United States, of course, originated from thirteen of the continental British colonies along the Atlantic seaboard of North America. Early in our history the national government was consistently referred to as "*These* United States," emphasizing the plurality of the state sovereigns rather than the singularity of the national sovereign.[3]

The colonies had been established in many different ways, but none was part of any federal system, and it is fair to say that none aspired to equality of opportunity. The Massachusetts Bay Colony welcomed Puritans, who had suffered discrimination in England, but it did not care to enfranchise "heretics," whose religious views deviated even slightly from their orthodoxy. Peaceable Quakers who settled in Puritan areas were sometimes hounded by accusations of Satan-worship and witchcraft because of their non-Puritan worship. And the Puritans seemed unable to tolerate even minor variations of belief among themselves. A disgruntled breakaway group, after all, left to found Rhode Island.

The institution of slavery again refutes the notion that the American colonies were intended to foster equality of opportunity. Slavery was initially legal in all colonies (and the motherland). And, what is more, moral qualms played but a minor role in its abolition in the North. Only after most northern slaves had been pulled southward by high slave prices in the booming tobacco region did any state become interested in abolition, and then typically in a very gradual process, one lasting decades before the last slave was emancipated. That sluggard's pace permitted slaves to be sold out of state rather than freed. Citizens who competed with slave-powered enterprises supported true abolitionists trying to force the practice out of the state. Freedmen who had not been "sold down the (Mississippi) River" to the New Orleans slave market during the abolitionary transition were legally discriminated against, along with apprentices, Indians, women, virtually any non-English speaker, and many other groups.

Georgia was a convict colony and made no pretense of democratic equality (nor, perhaps, should they have under those circumstances). Even the relatively benign Pennsylvanians were principally intent on maintaining a land hospitable to Quakers, which meant a land constraining some non-Quaker preferences (which, of course, very often included a desire that Quakers be suppressed).

Our heritage of an open, welcoming, American melting pot, then, sprang somehow from a society determined to be about as welcoming as the modern United States is toward illegal immigrants, and as culturally diverse as the population of the British Isles would permit, at least the non-Celtic parts. What spontaneous social engine drove the remarkable transformation of the country into "the land of the free, the home of the brave," one of the wealthiest the world has ever seen? The answer tells much about the strengths of federalism, and the pitfalls to be avoided as this nation, or any federal union, faces ever more complex and widespread externalities.

The Origins of American Federalism

Following Lord Cornwallis's capitulation at Yorktown these united states were riven by fear: fear of the British who were still entrenched nearby in their Canadian colonies and the Bahamas; fear of the Spanish who held Florida; fear of the French on Caribbean footholds, still smarting from the loss at British and colonial hands of their mainland holdings. In retrospect we realize that over the long haul the European powers were on their way out of America, unwilling to tolerate the continual net drain on their treasuries. But that was unclear to either the Americans or most Europeans of that day.

More fear was closer at hand, fear of the aboriginal nations to the west who resisted encroachment on tribal lands. Closer still—fear of each other! And perhaps most fearsome of all, fear of some national government that might usurp the powers and privileges of the stable state oligarchies that had carried over from colonial times.

Unfortunately the various fears were mutually inconsistent, given the military technology of the time. A nation-state strong enough to defeat the European superpowers of the day would seem to have the ability, and modern public choice theory would say the incentive, to overwhelm the state oligarchies. But if the states remained completely independent, Spain might move across the Florida border to pick off colonies one by one beginning with Georgia. Or England might do something similar from New Brunswick, Quebec, or Ontario. And what if North Carolina, say, concluded a treaty with Spain under which they were to help the Spaniards take Georgia and the Spaniards were to help them forcibly unite the Carolinas. What if New York, Connecticut, and Massachusetts combined to blockade Rhode Island in order to stop competitive lobster fishing? Surely Virginia and Maryland could not be counted on to come to the aid of that little state. Or, turning the tables, suppose New York, Massachusetts, and Rhode Island blockaded Connecticut? Such scenarios may seem farfetched today, but they did not seem implausible at the end of the eighteenth century when the states had no postcolonial history on which to base predictions, and colonial history revealed some strife between neighbors. Indeed, within a single life span, the Civil War would vindicate such fears despite the precautions undertaken by constitutional drafters.

Similarly, prisoners-dilemma and free-rider problems plagued the states as they faced the Indians. Why should Pennsylvania, for example, try to control its citizens' encroachments on tribal lands when encroachment by New Yorkers or Virginians might lead to the same hostilities along the western border? But on the other hand, if New York and Virginia could be counted on to put down any uprising, why should Pennsylvania risk the lives of its native sons to help? Since each state could think the same, there might be plenty of opportunities for Indian wars but hardly any organized defense against them.

The Articles of Confederation were intended to sneak between those various fears. A modern analogue, perhaps, would be NATO. But under the Articles the central government was more a debating club among the states than a sovereign with powers it could exercise. The national government could neither tax nor raise a military force except by soliciting state contributions. Each state could either accept or reject the solicitation. Despite their fears of an overarching government, these thirteen united states ultimately designed our present Constitution, as amended, in an effort to control the impending national government while still allowing it to make preparations against their even greater fears of the Europeans and Indians.

The Constitution was intended to leave in place most powers and privileges of the various state oligarchies, while simultaneously creating a military fabric capable of dealing with European powers and Indian nations alike. Until the Civil War, the nation had only a tiny peacetime standing army, but it had the ability to call up (as opposed to begging for) state armies (or militias) during time of national emergency. Lest even that arrangement prove too dangerous to states' rights, an amendment laying down a private right to keep and bear arms had to be promised before agreement to ratify the document could be obtained; people were to be prepared to defend themselves from the European powers, from the Indians, and from their own government.

To reduce the likelihood of conspiracies between a state and a foreign or Indian nation, relations with those entities were reserved for the national government.[4] Notice that rather than the states functioning as agents of the national government, the national government was functioning, in fact if not in law, almost as an agent of the state governments. That feature was still clear as late as the Dahlonega gold rush (the first gold rush in our national history) when Georgia decided to deal with the Cherokee nation directly (and harshly), then ignored a Supreme Court decision that held that Georgia could behave in no such way.[5] The upshot, of course, was not humiliation for Georgia but removal of the Cherokee to a newly devised "Indian Territory." It is remarkable that the prestige of the Supreme Court survived the affront.

During the present century we are familiar with allegations that the national government has encroached on states' rights, but as *Cherokee Nation v. Georgia* underlines, there is a bilateral power struggle within a federal system as each level attempts to exercise powers that have been reserved for another level.

Under the U.S. Constitution the military was controlled in fourteen parts (more as other states were admitted to the Union), one by each state and an ordinarily small one by the national government. No one or even several of those together were powerful enough to take the offensive against the others if the others drew together in a defensive league. Further, there was implementation of the famous "balance of powers" at the national government level; the president is not a prime minister selected by the legislature, he is an independent political actor with his own unique political constituency shared by no other important member of government.[6] The Supreme Court justices, though selected by the president with the concurrence of the Senate, are independent by lifetime tenure, nondiminution of salary, and a difficult impeachment process. But why is it that only the Senate must concur, not the House of Representatives? The answer is that originally the Senate represented the state governments, while, like the president, the House more closely represented the voters directly. "The Senate of the United States shall be composed of two senators from each State, chosen by the Legislature. . . ."[7] That arrangement persisted until the passage of the Seventeenth Amendment in 1913.

In effect, what we are accustomed to think of as a three-part legislative/executive/judicial balance of power in the national government is actually in four parts, because the action or acquiescence of the House and the Senate are each required for most national actions, and their actions often are poorly correlated. Since 1913 the political constituencies and the voting records of the House and the Senate have overlapped sufficiently to make it easy to ignore the difference. But during the nation's early decades, it was difficult for the national government to undertake any action if a couple of state senators strongly opposed. As an added check, the national government's financial powers were still severely constrained, though not as severely as under the Articles of Confederation.[8]

A final remarkable and important feature of the Constitution was to reserve the regulation of interstate commerce to the national government. In effect, the Constitution created a common market. Entities such as the European Union, NAFTA, and GATT attempt to create common markets. But even when successful they take decades to reach full fruition. The United States common market, in contrast, came into existence virtually overnight. Why the difference?

Ordinarily when government interventions such as tariffs, quotas, or subsidies are in place for a period, private investments are altered to take advantage of them. If removal of the interventions is suggested, therefore, a ready-made concentrated interest group is in place to resist, or barring that to insist on a gradual transition with compensation. But English tariffs, quotas, and subsidies in America were usually intended to benefit homeland interests, often at notable cost to the colonies. American victory in the Revolutionary War disenfranchised those concentrated British interest groups. As a consequence, the emerging nation was able to institute a common market quickly because few enfranchised interest groups opposed it, though the brief period under the Articles of Confederation had revealed the dangers.

In my view, the rapid and little opposed institution of our domestic common market provides one of the strongest evidences of the widespread desirability of free trade; with few enfranchised interest groups already dependent on trade restrictions, legally requiring free trade among the states was no obstacle to a union of sovereigns who were otherwise highly suspicious of each other and of the proposed national government.

Government in the Public Interest (Sort of)

Thus upon formation of these United States there was little notion that the natural or expected course of government was to serve "the public interest," whatever that is taken to mean. Instead, government was viewed with trepidation, a dangerous though sometimes convenient inevitability. History dictated such a view. Sovereigns quite blatantly placed their own interests well above citizen interests, paying attention to the latter only to the extent that their own interests were likely to be compromised.[9] Perhaps eighteenth-century England came closest to being an exception, but its record was so lackluster that emigrants willingly endured hardship and danger by forsaking England for a primitive America. Indeed, even today the notion of a publicly interested government would seem ludicrous to a vast part of the world's population.

Yet the English sovereign and some of her former colonies often have behaved toward the bulk of their citizens in a relatively benign fashion.[10] How did that great leap occur? What role was played by the federal structure emanating incidentally from the Magna Carta and imitated overtly by these United States?

From the viewpoint of the citizenry, federal hierarchies are said to have two advantages over centralized sovereigns. The more obvious claim is a direct application of neoclassical production theory; federalism permits greater specialization and division of labor among levels of the hierarchy in conjunction with more appropriate scales of operation for various governmental undertakings. The national army could be large when it needed to be, as in time of war, but small when that was more efficient. The states could conduct operations that are more appropriately small in scale. That focus argues for a functional distribution of powers among the federal levels according to the span of various problems. Thus one might hear "The national government should only deal with externalities that transcend state boundaries. Problems of a smaller span should be handled by state or local governments."[11] But considering the vast differences in the technology of producing government services, and the orders of magnitude of the growth of the U.S. economy, the appropriate degree of vertical disintegration of governmental operation must have changed over the more than two centuries of our national existence. Why then has the basic structure of our federal system remained so stable?

Weingast (1995) notes a more subtle advantage of federalism that is related to opportunism as formulated by the new institutional economics. The following recommendation from Machiavelli's *The Prince* will set the stage:

> a prudent ruler ought not to keep faith when by so doing it would be against his interest, and when the reasons which made him bind himself no longer exist. If men were all good, this precept would not be a good one; but as they are bad, and would not observe their faith with you, so you are not bound to keep faith with them. Nor have legitimate grounds ever failed a prince who wished to show colourable excuse for the non-fulfillment of his promise. (152, ch. 18)

Talk about self-fulfilling! Machiavelli is discussing the attractive side of sovereign power from the sovereign's viewpoint—by its (or his or her) nature a sovereign cannot be forced to abide by earlier promises that are no longer in the sovereign's interest. But this sovereign coin has an ugly side too: "the greater the sovereign's ability to impel submission by citizens . . . the less the sovereign's ability to induce voluntary cooperation. This paradox turns the sovereign's power into the sovereign's handicap" (Haddock 1994).

If properly structured, Weingast argues, federalism can mitigate that "sovereign's paradox" if lower levels in the hierarchy are given most regulatory powers, including that over their own economies, while the national level is limited to external relations and to preserving free trade among the units of the lower levels. If states cannot impose tariffs, quotas, and the like, especially faithless sets of state regulations will be frustrated by interstate competition (Tiebout 1956).[12] Weingast's suggestion argues for a devolution of most powers to the lower levels of the federal hierarchy, and makes reference to neither optimal scale nor specialization and division of labor. According to that view, federalism is a useful tool when constructing self-enforcing agreements between sovereigns and the private citizens who otherwise find the sovereign so threatening.[13]

Thus seen in isolation, each of the purported advantages of federalism seems very plausible to an economist. But taken together they seem almost inevitably mutually contradictory—one can simultaneously endow high levels of the federal hierarchy with all technologically appropriate government functions while limiting the top level to oversight only if oversight is the only technologically appropriate government function at a high level.

Despite appearances, that does not mean total war between the viewpoints; some government functions can safely be scaled appropriately because a rational self-interested sovereign's incentives are to carry out some activities in a way that is also in the public interest (McGuire and Olson 1996).

Contract law is an example. Because of the vast range of present and potential circumstances under which contracts may be concluded, most stipulations of contract law are defaults that apply only if the parties have not agreed to alter them. Any sovereign that made the defaults compulsory would seriously damage the governed economy, and thus the sovereign's own tax base. In consequence, in order to be protected by the law, a contracting party only needs to (1) learn applicable contract law, and (2) negotiate around any unwanted stipulations. That process is least costly if a single form of contract law can be resorted to over and over so that only that one form has to be learned, and every recorded decision under it becomes a precedent for all future contracts.[14]

So the tension between the alternative formulations of federalism would seem to focus on matters where the sovereign's interests run counter to those of most citizens. For instance, as noted above, the sovereign and the citizen share an interest (for different reasons to be sure) in maximizing the economy's tax base, but they have incompatible preferences about the tax rate that is applied to the base. Assuming that the burden cannot be forced onto other taxpayers, a citizen would be willing to pay those taxes necessary to finance government projects that are worth more to him than they cost him in taxes. But since the sovereign, though subject to no tax, also benefits in many ways from the projects, the sovereign's incentives are to push government expenditures so long as government projects have any positive value at the margin to the sovereign. In other words, the sovereign's incentives are to expand projects to a point at which the marginal value is well below the marginal tax cost, in fact to a point where the marginal value to a typical citizen is negative.

Consequently, the Constitution as originally approved strongly constrained the national government's ability to finance projects, meaning that a substantially greater proportion of government outlays came from the states than do now. The drafters recognized that both the state and national sovereigns would have ample incentive to "overtax" (from the drafters' perspective), but that the states would be more severely constrained by interstate competition than the nation would be by international competition. Thus, not only were government projects more concentrated in the states, there was a smaller government in total.

The Tiebout effect does not completely protect resource owners, and in fact does nothing to protect some of them. The protection of interstate competition is complete only if resources are perfectly mobile, and is of hardly any aid to owners of completely immobile resources (Epple and Zelenitz 1981). During the early national period most resources were reasonably mobile over a moderate time span. Land was the most notable exception, for the amount of long-run immobile capital was minor. Early voting laws linked suffrage to property ownership, so the electorate consisted almost entirely of landowners. Today that is viewed as a highly illiberal aspect of our history, but the Tiebout effect offers a more agreeable explanation. Nonowners of property would be well protected by interstate competition for their relatively mobile resources. Property owners, however, would be subject to exploitation by the sovereign, and by other citizens to the extent that the others could engineer transfers from the property owners to themselves. That problem was mitigated by permitting property owners to determine the makeup of the sovereign.

In brief, if mobile resource owners were abused, many of them would move out of the state; if immobile resource owners were abused, they could be expected to vote the rascals out of office. If, alternatively, the vote were universal, the interests of the electorate would be much more heterogeneous, likely expanding the sovereign's marching orders (and discretion). Achieving a coherent government time path would become highly problematic (Arrow 1970). And the cost of informing oneself of governmental actions would increase with the range and inconstancy of projects, which, by encouraging greater rational ignorance, would decrease voter understanding of government policy. Moreover, with an enlarged electorate the likelihood that one voter could influence an election's outcome would fall, and that would increase the proportion of voters who failed to vote altogether, in other words, exacerbating the voters' paradox.

The Erosion of Federalism

Many factors are claimed in the literature to have shifted power away from the states and toward the national government—the large peacetime standing army that remained in place after the Civil War (Anderson and McChesney 1994), the Supreme Court insinuating national authority over local affairs under the interstate commerce clause, the New Deal rising phoenixlike from the ashes of the Great Depression, and on and on. Whatever its source, that shift eroded federalism as devised by the nervous drafters of the Constitution. One or more of those factors may well be on point, but here I will focus on two other generally consistent hypotheses that flow more directly from the historical account above.

First, from the seed of fear, the federal system grew into a relatively weak and diffuse national government empowered to deal only with matters much too large for states to handle on their own, states with near total governance power over their internal affairs, a common market among those states creating interstate competition that led the states "as though by an invisible hand" to advance the public interest despite the sovereigns' interests. In one sense the system worked too well; it so advanced the public interest in comparison with most other nations of the time that over the generations many people ceased reflecting carefully on what had made the United States different from so many other nations. But that state of affairs coupled with the economics of information ultimately fostered "the fallacy of the publicly interested government" that was so prevalent through much of the twentieth century. Many people now seem to believe that our government advances the public interest because that is the sovereign's interest.[15] By removing citizen suspicion of the noncompetitive national government, the fallacy curbs resistance to increased centralization of government operations, which erodes the federal structure. That is a dangerous outcome if the national sovereign's interests are actually to monopolize sovereign power and the interests of many state sovereigns are well served by that transfer. Americans of the late eighteenth century would have been extremely worried.

But how could state sovereigns ever be advantaged by relinquishing power to the national government? The Tiebout effect holds only if the states are forced to compete with each other. If one competitor expands (or contracts) inappropriately, resources move elsewhere. But if all competitors expand or contract in unison, there is little incentive for resource movement. The national government in such a scenario is a cartel's joint sales office. Consider the funding of block grants to states from national taxes, for example. Consider the sizable national subsidies to higher education, even to state-owned schools that educate a largely local student body. Consider the national taxes that fund the bulk of construction costs for "national" highways, even those (the majority) that are used predominately by local traffic. If Illinois taxed its citizens to pay for more highways than were desired, some citizens might move to Indiana—unless the taxes in Indiana are at a similar overblown level because they are actually homogenized national taxes that are transferred back to the states to finance "national" highways.

Second, new problems gradually evolve that, like national defense, seem to transcend the authority of the states, leading to pressure for regulation at a higher level of the federal hierarchy, i.e., national regulation. For instance, potential competition for mobile resources kept the early postcolonial states in line, but the actual amount of interstate commerce in commodities was relatively minor. As it grew, interstate regulatory issues grew apace. Indeed, commerce of any sort was minor compared to what it has become, with a great deal of output coming from home production and most jobs being self-employment or family-employment; as interdependency increased, the opportunities for interfamily disputes (e.g., antitrust disputes) increased with it. Little pollution crossed colonial borders; today we hear constantly of "acid rain" and the "greenhouse effect" with impacts far from the source. Water was plentiful in the East and so water property rights issues were muted; as the West was settled, and as the rate of water usage nationwide increased, cross-boundary disputes over water rights grew. One could greatly lengthen such a list, but surely the point is made.

There have been opposing reactions to the growth of interstate problems. Some commentators have called for the national government increasingly to supplant the states in order to internalize the growing interstate problems. Others essentially deny that any significant new interstate problems are there to be internalized. Neither approach is likely to convince skeptics because each is inappropriate. To claim that there has been no increase in the magnitude of externalities that cross state lines is preposterous. To deny that it is more difficult to internalize them when dealing with multiple sovereigns rather than one is, if not preposterous, at least nonobvious.

On the other hand, to call for national intervention whenever an externality crosses a state line is to commit the fallacy of the publicly interested government. It is the federal system that makes the sovereign appear relatively publicly interested despite the private interests of those in government. To the extent that national intervention erodes federalism it simultaneously erodes the intersovereign competition that forces sovereigns to behave "as if" in the public interest. Why then would one expect a national regulation to appropriately handle the new problems?

It is quite possible to be better off suffering unregulated externalities than to labor under a grasping, inept, or apathetic regulator. Every day one can hear some television journalist recounting a performance failure of some private sector activity, and then noting with urgency that "the industry is completely unregulated." Every day one can hear the same journalist reporting some scandalous breach of duty by some government operative. But one never hears the journalist note that the one problem can only be avoided by incurring the other, and that a sober cost-benefit analysis is actually what is called for rather than a panic-stricken demand that (in each case) corrective measures be undertaken right now! The interesting question involves the range of realistic institutional alternatives and how they would alter the mix of government actions between those that are in the public interest and those that are not (Demsetz 1969). It is of little moment whether an institutional alteration leads to less, more, or merely different government.[16]

A Revival of Federalism

Though the fallacy of the publicly interested government held sway through much of this century, the fallacy now seems (for a time at least) to be beating a slow retreat. Perhaps the benefits of a fuller federalism can be recovered. But it is necessary to keep in mind that we are now facing a trade-off between state governments that are too small to handle some important problems versus a national government that is too undisciplined to handle the problems properly. The optimal solution to a trade-off will ordinarily be an interior one where the marginal losses from reallocating powers would be equal in the opposite directions. In other words, some advantages of specialization/division-of-labor/scale would be sacrificed in order to curtail sovereign ability to use sovereign powers inappropriately, but a modest potential for government dissipation would persist because it would be too costly to remove it all. Costs are to be balanced, not eradicated. Can the benefits of a federal union be recovered while the range of interstate problems continues to expand?

As I discussed elsewhere (Haddock 1996), the case for centralization has been badly overstated. Gathering all an externality's participants within a single regulatory unit does indeed provide benefits, and the larger the framework the more likely that result becomes. But many interstate externalities are far from nationwide, so the benefit is exhausted before regulation becomes national. Moreover, pointing to the benefits while ignoring concurrent costs is inappropriate, for ideal regulation would maximize net rather than gross benefits. Many of the gross benefits could be preserved through properly devolved regulation, while substantial costs could be avoided.

Ideal regulation inevitably differs from place to place and oscillates within any one. Centralized regulation, in contrast, tends toward homogeneity and stability because of predictably poor data gathering and weak incentives for remote agents to act in their principals' interest. Furthermore, complete internalization is theoretically inappropriate. Because increased internalization through regulation concomitantly increases information and agency costs between the public and their regulators and increases distortions from government monopoly power, it should proceed only until its incremental benefits match the incremental costs. The federation of the early United States worked quite well with only thirteen strong units facing the national unit. Are fifty weak units an improvement? Perhaps three (or even more) levels of sovereign are called for: a national sovereign that is strictly confined to truly national problems where sovereign and citizen interests are mutually consistent, state sovereigns to deal with the smaller-scale problems that they handle best, and a dozen or so competing regional sovereigns lying in the federal hierarchy between the states and the nation with the regions having near-total authority over the mutually inconsistent sovereign/subject interests. Indeed, I believe that some government functions could advantageously be handled by sovereigns that are smaller than states (Haddock 1996). The chain of command required to reach a regional sovereign would be substantially shorter and more accessible than that of the national sovereign. And if one did not like the regional sovereign's responsiveness, it would be easier to leave that realm than to leave the nation as a whole. Frey and Eichenberger (1996) argue that for some government functions federated sovereigns needn't even be geographical entities, but simply governmental entities with established protocols by which subjects can join one or leave another by declaration rather than movement. For those functions, perfect resource mobility would be closely approached because it would require no costly physical movement.

Perhaps GATT or an expanded NAFTA will ultimately provide a different solution to the same problem. But that would not be the sort of federal system envisioned if GATT or NAFTA were allowed to become strong central governments, "government" as we have come during the present century to understand that term. Like the early national government of the United States, those organizations would serve the desired function only if they guaranteed operation of a common market and perhaps regulated a few institutions of mutually consistent sovereign/subject interest such as contract law, while each member state functioned with unfettered discretion within their own borders, but without discretion over the movement of resources across their borders.

Conclusion

If, as Weingast (1995) argues, it was the federal system in the United States that frustrated the sovereign's natural tendency to view citizens as mere instruments of sovereign satisfaction, why has the public permitted the erosion of federalism? This chapter argues that the erosion was speeded by the fallacy of the publicly interested government and by the willingness of state sovereigns to have the national government act as a cartelizing agent. But that is merely the time-path; the erosion was made inevitable by the expansion over time of various legitimate regulatory problems that genuinely exceeded state abilities. If so, we would be well advised to reformulate the federal structure in a manner that takes account of those new problems.

For many governmental functions the reformulation is simple. Some governmental functions are appropriately small-scale; for these, the states can be permitted to handle them as they wish, with interstate competition controlling abuses. For some governmental functions the sovereign's interests coordinate with that of the citizens and whatever scale is appropriate can be selected. Sovereign abuse is a danger under a federal system only for conflicting sovereign–subject interests that are properly dealt with on a large scale. For those, there is no perfect solution. Some technical efficiency should be sacrificed in the interests of controlling the sovereign's paradox, but some modest danger of abuse must be tolerated in the interests of efficiency.

A reformulation could be accomplished either by creating a new level(s) of sovereign, and/or incrementally through the evolution of GATT or NAFTA into a common market manager but hardly anything more. The European Union, driving headlong to "harmonize" the legal systems of its constituent nations, seems to be ignoring this important lesson. The Tiebout effect does not and cannot function unless the constituent legal systems are not harmonized; one cannot vote with one's feet if all the candidates on the ballot are the same.

Notes

1. Third World nations that find a way to credibly offer rewards to human capital investments rather quickly achieve near–First World human capital levels and soon enough become thought of as effectively First World nations. Many east and southeast Asian nations provide examples.

2. The various levels of a federal system may agree ex ante that under specified circumstances they will abide ex post by something resembling compulsory arbitration. Thus in the United States an individual state cannot veto loss of a particular power that is enumerated in the Constitution if an amendment has passed the national Congress and a specified supermajority of the states have agreed to give up that power. Such defenses against free-riding and holdouts can be misused, but they are reminiscent of voluntarily accepted private agreements such as condominium covenants. Each state accepted the arbitrationlike procedure upon entry into the Union.

3. That emphasis was a natural continuation of the colonial outlook. In the Continental Congress of 1776, for example, Richard Henry Lee of Virginia

moved "that these," not the, "united colonies are and of right ought to be free and independent states," plural.

4. Technically Indian nations were foreign nations—and under the law still have many aspects of that sovereignty. See *Santa Clara Pueblo v. Martinez*, 436 U.S. 49 (1978), for a recent and interesting application holding that one full-blood Indian who was born and raised on a reservation was not legally an Indian at all because her mother's tribe was patrilineal, her father's tribe was matrilineal, and the civil rights statutes of the United States do not protect anyone against gender discrimination by a sovereign Indian nation. Nevertheless, to make the Indians' foreignness abundantly clear, the Constitution as drafted explicitly mentioned relations with the tribes as a reserved power of the national government.

5. *Cherokee Nation v. Georgia*, 30 U.S. (5 Pet.) 1 (1831). Dahlonega was the Cherokee capital and the gold-bearing lands were entirely within the Cherokee reservation as established in 1785 by the Treaty of Hopewell. That treaty ended hostilities between Caucasians and the Cherokee nation, which had sided with England during the Revolutionary War. Direct state dealings with the tribes were not limited to Georgia. For example, New York amicably acquired land from the Oneida nation in 1795, a dealing whose ghost returned nearly two centuries later to haunt the state. See *County of Oneida v. Oneida Indian Nation*, 470 U.S. 226 (1985).

6. And originally the president did not even select the vice president; that office was held by the candidate with the second-highest vote total.

7. U. S. Constitution, art. I, sec. 3.

8. For instance, the national government could not directly tax incomes until passage of the Sixteenth Amendment in 1913.

9. McGuire and Olson (1996) deal specifically with the strength of sovereign interest in citizen interests under a variety of situations.

10. That, of course, is not a claim that the treatment is benign in any absolute sense. The chapter does not address that question.

11. Aranson (1990) labels such motivations utilitarian federalism.

12. The Tiebout effect does little to protect immobile resources such as land and minerals, a matter addressed below.

13. On the theory of self-enforcing agreements see Telser (1980) and Klein and Leffler (1981).

14. Thus, anything that fragments contract law will disadvantage those who for whatever reason are compelled to use the less popular forms (Haddock and Hall 1983, 1–18; Haddock 1994). That is to say, there are network externalities—one is better off using a form of contract law that everyone understands than to have to learn different ones and research different sets of precedents to prepare or litigate different contracts.

15. The economics of information (Stigler 1961) holds that investments in information impose opportunity costs, and as a result people do not learn things that are "not worth knowing," things that cost more to learn than the expected value of the knowledge to the investor (as contrasted with the society). If the government *seems* to be acting in the public interest, and if a prisoner's dilem-

ma makes individual (as opposed to mass) inquiry largely fruitless, why not substitute a myth about a publicly interested government for the heavy lifting required by careful contemplation? Unless you happen to be one of the rare nuts who just enjoy bench-pressing heavy ideas, that is individually optimal even though the rational ignorance engendered may be socially destructive.

16. Considering the frequency with which market-oriented scholars taunt government-oriented ones with the Nirvana fallacy, it is interesting to examine the actual words Demsetz used in the article that introduced that concept. Demsetz says, if one "does not analyze the workings of the empirical counterparts of such words as 'government' and 'nonprofit,' his conclusion can be clarified by restating it as follows: 'The previous discussion leads to the conclusion that for optimal allocation . . . it would be necessary to remove the nonoptimalities.' The same charge, of course, can be levied against those who derive in a similar way the opposite policy conclusion, one that calls for a reduction in the role played by government" (Demsetz 1969, 3).

References

Anderson, Terry L., and Fred S. McChesney. 1994. Raid or Trade? An Economic Model of Indian–White Relations. *Journal of Law and Economics* 37 (April): 39–74.

Aranson, Peter H. 1990. Federalism and the Economic Order. *Cato Journal* 10: 17–38.

Arrow, Kenneth J. 1970. *Social Choice and Individual Values.* New Haven: Yale University Press.

Axelrod, Robert. 1984. *The Evolution of Cooperation.* New York: Basic Books.

Demsetz, Harold. 1969. Information and Efficiency: Another Viewpoint. *Journal of Law and Economics* 12: 1–22.

Epple, Dennis, and Allan Zelenitz. 1981. The Implications of Competition among Jurisdictions: Does Tiebout Need Politics? *Journal of Political Economy* 89: 1197–217.

Frey, Bruno S., and Reiner Eichenberger. 1996. FOCJ: Competitive Governments for Europe. *International Review of Law and Economics* 16: 315–27.

Haddock, David D. 1994. Foreseeing Confiscation by the Sovereign: Lessons from the American West. In *The Political Economy of the American West*, ed. Terry L. Anderson and Peter J. Hill. Lanham, Md.: Rowman and Littlefield, 129–45.

———1996. Must Water Regulation be Centralized? In *Water Marketing: The Next Generation*, ed. Terry L. Anderson and Peter J. Hill. Lanham, Md.: Rowman and Littlefield, 43–61.

Haddock, David D., and Thomas D. Hall. 1983. The Impact of Making Rights Inalienable: *Merrion v. Jicarilla Apache Tribe*. *Supreme Court Economic Review* 2: 1–41.

Hirshleifer, Jack. 1995. Anarchy and Its Breakdown. *Journal of Political Economy* 103: 26–52.

Klein, Benjamin, and Keith B. Leffler. 1981. The Role of Market Forces in Assuring Contractual Performance. *Journal of Political Economy* 89: 615–41.

Machiavelli, Nicolò. 1532. *Il Principe*. Reprinted in *Great Books of the Western World*, vol. 23 (1952). Chicago: Encyclopaedia Britannica.

McGuire, Martin C., and Mancur Olson Jr. 1996. The Economics of Autocracy and Majority Rule. *Journal of Economic Literature* 34: 72–96.

Mueller, Dennis C. 1996. *Constitutional Democracy*. New York: Oxford University Press.

North, Douglass C. 1990. *Institutions, Institutional Change and Economic Performance*. Cambridge: Cambridge University Press.

Reynolds, Glenn Harlan. 1995. Is Democracy Like Sex? *Vanderbilt Law Review* 48: 1635–61.

Schelling, Thomas C. 1960. *The Strategy of Conflict*. Cambridge: Harvard University Press.

Stigler, George J. 1961. The Economics of Information. *Journal of Political Economy* 69: 213–25.

Telser, Lester G. 1980. A Theory of Self-Enforcing Agreements. *Journal of Business* 53: 27–44.

Tiebout, Charles M. 1956. A Pure Theory of Local Expenditures. *Journal of Political Economy* 64: 416–24.

Umbeck, John R. 1981. Might Makes Rights: A Theory of the Formation and Initial Distribution of Property Rights. *Economic Inquiry* 19: 38–59.

Weingast, Barry R. 1995. The Economic Role of Political Institutions: Market-Preserving Federalism and Economic Development. *Journal of Law, Economics, and Organization* 11: 1–31.

Chapter 2

Public Land Federalism:
Go Away and Give Us More Money

Robert H. Nelson

In July 1995, Representative James Hansen (R-Utah), chairman of the National Parks, Forests and Lands subcommittee of the House Resources Committee, introduced legislation to transfer ownership of the Bureau of Land Management (BLM) lands to any state requesting such a transfer. A companion bill was introduced in the Senate by Craig Thomas (R-Wyoming). BLM lands represent 24 percent of the land area of the eleven westernmost lower forty-eight states, half of the total federal acreage in these states.[1]

Among the federal lands, the BLM lands are on the whole the least nationally distinctive. They were the last to be set aside for retention in long-term federal management, a consequence of the Taylor Grazing Act of 1934 (Calef 1960). As a result of BLM and other ownership of federal lands in the West, the federal government today is closely involved with land-use planning, decisions to build physical infrastructure, wildlife management, and many other decisions that elsewhere in the United States would be state and local responsibilities.

The proposed legislation to offer BLM lands to the states was a logical application of the devolution philosophy that the Republican majority in the 104th Congress was advocating in many areas of government. Indeed, there are many observers on all sides of the political spectrum who believe that the federal system has overreached its grasp (Rivlin 1992). A 1995 report of the National Academy of Public Administration recommended that in general "EPA and Congress need to hand more responsibility and decision-making authority over to the states and localities. . . . The principle is simple: one size does not fit all. Those states that are capable and willing to take over functions from the federal government should have full operational responsibility" (National Academy of Public Administration 1995, 2).

Resources for the Future reported in 1996 that while environmental risk assessment remains mired in controversy at the federal level, at the state level new risk approaches are being tried that make the process "more democratic, more inclusive, more closely tied to locally defined public values, more honest about its own limitations, and, hence, more likely to be productive" (Minard 1996, 6). Dave Foreman (1996, 4), the founder of Earth First!, a group never traditionally associated with advocacy of a greater state role, commented that "I believe the federal government has usurped far too many powers from the states."[2]

The Supreme Court has begun to signal new directions in American federalism. Since at least the New Deal, the Court has helped to sustain the growth of the powers of the national government relative to the states. Recent decisions suggest, however, that "the Rehnquist court wants the federal government to start leaving the states alone" (Biskupic 1996, A17). Indeed, according to Yale Law Professor Paul Gewirtz, "What we're seeing from the judicial branch is an across-the-board restriction on national government power on every front and a bolstering of state sovereignty" (quoted in Biskupic 1996, A17). These developments so alarmed the editorial board of the *New York Times* (1996, A20) that it described a new "reactionary" trend manifested in a "revolutionary [Supreme Court] interpretation of federalism."

On the surface, therefore, it might have seemed that legislation to offer to transfer the BLM lands to the states would have generated much legislative interest, even if actual passage remained unlikely in the 104th Congress. Nothing would have been required of any state; a transfer would have occurred only if the state officially sought it. Yet the legislation went nowhere. State governments themselves showed little interest—in contrast, for example, to insistent state demands that welfare and Medicaid responsibilities should be transferred to them. Environmental groups were, as expected, opposed. Perhaps more surprisingly, ranchers, miners and other groups with commodity interests in the BLM lands also were lukewarm.

This outcome, to be sure, was not altogether unexpected to those familiar with public land history. Western groups have often agitated against the role of the federal government, but then supported federal authority as the protector of their own interests. In the early part of this century, western cattlemen generally supported the creation of the Forest Service as a means of fending off homesteaders and migrant sheep herders. As public land historian Louise Peffer relates,

There was a minority opinion in the West which, though not completely crystalized at the beginning of the century, was more in harmony with the overall program of the [Pinchot] conservationists than with the prevailing western attitude. The cattlemen using the public range were uneasy over the eagerness of western politicians to have the land pushed piecemeal into private ownership. . . . Government conservationists gave support to the stockmen's case by recognizing forage crops as an important resource and by favoring some means by which those crops, and incidentally the graziers, would be protected. (Peffer 1951, 317)

In 1929, President Herbert Hoover suggested that the federal lands be transferred to the western states. Similar to the arguments heard today for the BLM transfer legislation, Hoover reasoned that

the federal government is incapable of the adequate administration of matters which require so large a measure of local understanding. We must seek every opportunity to retard the expansion of federal bureaucracy and to place our communities in control of their own destinies. . . . Western states have long since passed from their swaddling clothes and are today more competent to manage much of their affairs than is the federal government. (Quoted in Limerick 1995, 3)

The West, however, proved to be "almost unanimous in its condemnation" of Hoover's proposal, only in part because the federal government proposed to retain the most valuable part of the ownership bundle, the mineral rights (Peffer 1951, 209). Another factor was that "the powerful livestock interests" also opposed a transfer of the lands (Clarke and McCool 1996, 159).

In the late 1970s, ranchers and other participants in the "Sagebrush Rebellion" again demanded that federal lands be transferred to western states. As a candidate for president, Ronald Reagan endorsed the rebellion and its goals. Yet, once again, the West showed little interest in translating rhetoric into reality. At his confirmation hearing in January 1981, James Watt declared that as secretary of the Interior he did not intend to follow up on the transfer proposal. Instead, he favored efforts to improve federal land management, making it more responsive to the interests of the West, and thereby acting to "defuse" rather than implement the Sagebrush campaign. Westerners opposed Reagan administration proposals to sell off portions of federal lands—the pub-lic land "privatization" plan—even more vehemently (Nelson 1995, ch. 6 and 7).

History thus suggests that western demands for transfer of the BLM and other public lands may be mainly a tactical vehicle for pressuring federal administrators to comply with western wishes. They should not, one might well conclude, be taken at face value. Yet, without disputing the historical accuracy, it might be premature to accept this conclusion as definitive for the future as well.

In the past, centralization of land management authority at the federal level was consistent with the growing accumulation of federal power that took place in most areas of government over the course of the twentieth century. A growing role for the BLM was running with the tides of history. Today, however, the opposite may be true. As noted above, a basic rethinking is taking place with respect to the role of the federal government. This is part of a systematic reassessment of the legacy of the Progressive era goal of the "scientific management" of society (Wiebe 1995). It was this Progressive vision that provided a foundation for the development of the twentieth-century American welfare and regulatory state with power centralized at the federal level (Waldo 1984).

Since the 1970s, however, the deregulation movement has dismantled much of the Progressive governing apparatus once found in agencies such as the Civil Aeronautics Board, Interstate Commerce Commission, and other regulatory bodies. It was through these instruments that the federal government for many years asserted tight control over the operations of transportation, communications, banking, and other core American industries. Today, the prospect is being raised of a similar relinquishment of federal control over the operations of state and local governments (Nelson 1994, 1996a). Like the private industries that operated for many years under tight federal oversight, states and localities have tended to become mere operating divisions within one unified governing system, directing public and private affairs alike throughout the nation through the instrument of the federal government. President Bill Clinton's signing of legislation in August 1996 transferring major welfare responsibilities back to the states, reversing a growing nationalization of welfare since the New Deal, offered further evidence of the strength of this trend.

There are also indications today that more Westerners than in the past might in fact welcome a transfer of the BLM lands to state ownership—that demands for transfer of federal lands are not always a form of political posturing.[3] The quid pro quo of the past—the federal government does roughly what the West wants, and also pays for it, while the lands remain in federal hands—is being disrupted. The federal land management system has become so polarized and gridlocked that frequently it is not capable of serving western interests. The budget pressures of recent years have also left the federal government less able to continue the traditional bountiful flow of financial support.

Depending partly on future election results, the Congress and the president might be able to agree to offer BLM lands to the states. This will only happen, however, if western states push aggressively for such legislation. It may thus be timely for the western states to consider more closely where their real interests lie—whether in fact an assumption of ownership of BLM lands might serve their goals. Further, since there are many possible arrangements and options with respect to a transfer, what might be the terms and conditions required by western states, in order for them to be willing to accept the BLM lands?

This chapter examines whether a transfer of BLM lands would in fact serve the interests of a state accepting the lands. What is to be lost by a state in accepting the ownership of BLM lands? What is to be gained? Would such a transfer on balance be a good idea for a western state? How does all this depend on the specific arrangements proposed for the transfer?

To be sure, there are significant variations in the circumstances of individual states in the West. Thus, there need not be any one state answer. The states differ greatly, for example, in the added revenue potential, especially from leasable minerals, from assuming ownership of BLM lands. Besides minerals potential, the BLM lands differ among the states in the main types of surface uses and many other respects as well.

The West and the Senate

In exploring the question of federal versus state (or local) ownership of BLM lands, it would be naive not to recognize the important role played in this issue by the disproportionate political power that the West holds in the U.S. Senate. In total, eleven western public land states (Alaska, Arizona, Colorado, Idaho, Montana, Nevada, New Mexico, Oregon, Utah, Washington, and Wyoming) have only 9 percent of the population of the United States but 22 percent of the votes in the Senate. In the 104th Congress, Westerners chaired the Senate Appropriations Committee (Hatfield), Budget Committee (Domenici), Judiciary Committee (Hatch), Energy and Natural Resources Committee (Murkowski), Committee on Rules and Administration (Stevens), Veterans Affairs Committee (Simpson), and Indian Affairs Committee (McCain). When Republicans control the Senate, the West assumes a role in that body more traditionally associated with its dominance by southern Democrats.

On the other side of the U.S. Capitol, except for California, the presence of the West in the House of Representatives is limited. Alaska, Wyoming, and Montana have only one representative; Nevada and Idaho have two. In the eleven public land states noted above, the West has a total of thirty-nine representatives, equal to 9 percent of the House. These eleven states, by comparison, have 45 percent of the land area of the United States.

Yet, on the whole, the western numerical strength in the Senate is more than sufficient to compensate for the weakness in the House. The Congress operates by the rule of "you scratch my back today, and I will scratch yours tomorrow." Similarly, when the president wants to pass some legislation, western Senate votes are numerous and available for negotiation. This all translates into a large number of political chips held by western senators at any given time. From a national point of view, making some political concessions to the West may be rational and sound public policy making as well, because otherwise nationally important legislation might not be able to muster enough support to be enacted.

The constituents of western senators who stand to benefit from all this merely happen to be at the right place at the right time; they can call in a windfall that dates as far back as the Constitutional Convention of 1787 and the Connecticut "great compromise" that created a bicameral legislature. Moreover, in sparsely populated western states, it does not take a great deal of federal funds to have a major economic impact on the state. All this is relevant to the interest of western states in the BLM lands, because it is the presence of the public lands that provides many opportunities for federal spending in these states.

BLM Defends Its Role

The BLM is not shy about explaining the workings of the relationship the West has with the federal government. After the BLM transfer bill was introduced by Representative Hansen, the BLM hastened to remind Westerners that they should not get carried away to the point of losing sight of their real interests. In August 1995, the agency issued a study of "Public Rewards from Public Lands" (BLM 1995b). In the accompanying press release, BLM observed that there are "numerous benefits that all Americans receive from public lands which are managed by BLM." Getting closer to the heart of the matter, the BLM noted that

> states acquiring BLM-managed lands would lose millions of dollars in Federal funds by doing so. In the last fiscal year, the BLM spent the following amounts on programs that benefit states and local governments: $99.3 million on the payments in lieu of taxes (PILT) program; $10 million on range improvements; $235.7 million on wildland firefighting; $25.1 million on recreation resource management; and $53 million on oil and gas leasing. (BLM 1995a)

To make sure that each western state understood clearly just what was at stake, the BLM also provided state-by-state breakouts of the federal funds being channeled into the state through the intermediary of the BLM. As an example, Table 2.1 shows the details provided by BLM for the state of Colorado. The BLM spent $137 million in Colorado in 1994, partly because BLM's general service center for the West is located in

Table 2.1
Colorado Benefits from BLM Lands, 1994
(dollars)

Federal Collections from BLM-Management Lands and Minerals

Grazing Fees	$ 873,000
Recreation and Use Fees	106,000
Mining Claim Holding Fees	945,000
Miscellaneous Receipts	465,000
Sale of Land and Minerals	512,000
Mineral Royalties, Rents, and Bonuses	76,248,000
Total	$ 79,149,000

Direct BLM Financial Transfers to Colorado

Payment in Lieu of Taxes (PILT)	$ 6,368,000
Grazing Fees	147,000
Proceeds of Sales	20,000
Mineral Royalties, Rents and Bonuses	34,372,000
Total	$ 40,907,000

BLM Investments in Colorado

Management of Lands and Resources	$ 122,716,000
Land Acquisition	1,056,000
Range Improvements	401,000
Construction and Access	805,000
Fire Management/Firefighting	
Prescribed Fire/Presuppression	2,487,000
Firefighting and Rehabilitation	9,107,000
Service Charges, Deposits, and Forfeitures	476,000
Total	$ 137,048,000

Source: Bureau of Land Management (1995b).

Denver where it maintains a large payroll. In addition, payments of $40.9 million were made to Colorado from revenues earned from BLM-managed lands and minerals. These payments represented the state and local share under various statutory formulas by which the revenues from BLM and other public land activities are distributed.

The $79 million that the federal government earned in 1994 in revenues from BLM lands and minerals in Colorado was much less than the $178 million that the federal government transferred to the state. The net inflow of about $100 million of federal funds provided a significant economic boost to Colorado. So the BLM asked, why should Colorado want to take over the BLM lands, when it already has such a good deal. The BLM implicitly said that it is happy to continue the informal quid pro quo of long standing—BLM employees get good jobs in nice places where the cost of living is low (much of the federal spending in Colorado is for federal salaries, also providing a secondary economic gain for others in the state) and Colorado receives a large financial windfall.

The Western "Balance of Payments"

What is true of BLM lands is also true of national forest lands, Department of Energy research facilities, Bureau of Reclamation water projects, and many other federal activities in the rural West. The Kennedy School of Government at Harvard, in conjunction with Senator Daniel Patrick Moynihan of New York, prepares annual calculations of the total inflow of federal funds into each state, as compared with the total outflow for taxes and other forms of payment—the balance of payments (Friar and Leonard 1995).

In these calculations, the Mountain West fares particularly well. Thanks in part to Senator Pete Domenici's chairmanship of the Budget Committee, New Mexico has the most favorable balance of payments with the federal government of any state in the nation. Federal spending yielded the citizens of New Mexico a net inflow of federal funds equal to $3,255 per capita in 1994—much of which was received initially as salary payments to federal workers in New Mexico.

The states of the Mountain West as a whole had a favorable balance of payments with the federal government of $696 per capita, ranking this region second among the nine regions of the United States. The only region that did better in terms of net inflow of federal funds was the East South Central region (Alabama, Kentucky, Mississippi, Tennessee), partly reflecting the legendary legislative skills of southern Democrats of years gone by.

The West Coast states and Nevada do not experience the same scale of benefits. It may be that the relationship of these states with the federal government is dominated by their large urban centers that pay substantial taxes and do not receive the disproportionate benefits that accrue to many rural areas of the West (and South). California thus has a small negative balance of payments with the federal government, comparable in magnitude to Massachusetts.

The Interior Department

Although it cannot be said officially, the principal role of the U.S. Department of the Interior in practice is to ensure that the historic expectations of the western states continue to be realized. One agency, the Bureau of Reclamation, delivers cheap water and power across the West; the average subsidy to agricultural users has been 80 percent. The National Park Service administers more than 360 units, many of them park and recreation areas across the West that attract millions of tourists annually, helping to sustain rural economies. Park fees are less than 10 percent of the cost of running the national park system. The Fish and Wildlife Service administers other recreational areas that also serve hunters, hikers, bird-watchers, and millions of other outdoor enthusiasts at minimal costs to these users. Firefighting receives more than $500 million per year in the federal budget, most of this spent on the forests of the West. There are also direct cash transfers such as "payments in lieu of taxes" (PILT)—supposedly making up for lost property taxes on federal lands—which historically have provided about $100 million per year in federal moneys to western states. These agencies have facilities elsewhere, but the bulk of their lands and their responsibilities are in the West.

For the rural areas of the West, where federal lands dominate the landscape, it is not farfetched to say that these lands have a unique political system seen nowhere else in the United States. The limited amounts of private land are surrounded by a sea of federal land. In the extreme case of Nevada, where 83 percent of the state is federal land, a number of counties are well over 90 percent federal land. In such areas, the citizens in practice look to Washington, not the state capital, for much of their governance.

There is a de facto legislature for much of the rural West and a de facto executive branch, both located in Washington. The makeup of these branches is unlike anything found in standard political theory. For many practical purposes, the effective legislature for the public land areas of Wyoming consists of the one elected member of the U.S. House of Representatives, along with the two elected members of the U.S. Senate. In this informal governing system, the effective governor of the BLM lands of Wyoming is the secretary of the Interior—and for the national forests of Wyoming the chief of the Forest Service (the secretary of Agriculture traditionally has paid little attention to the national forests). These executive branch officials, like the territorial governors of old, are not elected but are appointed by the president.

As a result of this informal governance structure for public lands, the public officials actually elected at the state and local level in the rural West have less real responsibility than their counterparts elsewhere in the United States. The true authority over vast acreages within their jurisdictions lies in Washington. When politicians can make promises but have neither the power to deliver nor any obligation to raise the money to pay for them, it encourages a political climate of rhetorical excess rather than substantive discussion and action. A number of past western politicians have in fact become masters of a rhetorical style grounded in what Stegner (1987, 15) described as the characteristic attitude of the West: tell the federal government to "get out, and give us more money."

In some measure, the political and management structure for the public lands might be rationalized by Progressive era theories of governance. The Progressives in fact sought to minimize the role of democratic politics in the administrative tasks of government. As a technical undertaking, the management of the lands should be turned over to the experts. Mere "politicians" were likely to be driven by short-term considerations reflecting the pressures of "the special interests."

Why else might the West have so readily accepted the long-term absence of normal democratic prerogatives? Partly it is that the western legislators in Washington, unlike ordinary state and local legislators, can operate without any real budget constraint. They do not have to raise the funds to pay for the programs they deliver. Instead, these programs are paid for by the rest of the nation. The advantages of this arrangement have been so great that it has served the interests of western states to avert their eyes from the lack of any normal democratic political process. The perpetuation of this arrangement also serves the interests of the federal legislative representatives of the West, who typically win re-election by overseeing the delivery of federal services to their constituents. The public lands provide an abundance of such opportunities.

Fiscal Impacts of BLM Lands

In 1982, while working in the Office of Policy Analysis, located in the Office of the Secretary of the Interior, I undertook an analysis of the

1981 costs and revenues in the management of BLM lands (Nelson and Joseph 1982). Although the data are not current and inflation has been about 65 percent since 1981, in most respects the overall picture today would be altered little.

The users of the BLM lands pay little for this use, even while the federal government makes large expenditures on their behalf. As Table 2.2 shows, the full costs in 1981 of BLM livestock grazing management—incorporating overhead and other indirect costs as well as direct costs—equaled $125.5 million. This was about $12.50 per "animal unit month" (AUM) of grazing on BLM land. At the time, the BLM was collecting a grazing fee of $2.31 per AUM. Five years later, in 1986, the BLM estimated that the actual market value of livestock grazing on BLM land averaged $6.53 per AUM. Thus, not only were the administrative costs to the government much greater than the revenues collected by the government, the costs were also two to three times the estimated total market value of the grazing activity.

Table 2.2
BLM Rangeland Forage Costs by State, 1981
(thousands of dollars)

State	Direct Cost of Output	Indirect Costs	Total Output Cost
Alaska	$ 386.9	$ 4,516.4	$ 4,903.3
Arizona	4,248.9	5,132.0	9,380.9
California	2,753.7	5,179.5	7,933.2
Colorado	4,707.0	6,753.7	11,460.7
Idaho	4,950.4	9,191.0	14,141.4
Montana	5,482.2	6,468.3	11,950.5
Nevada	7,848.0	10,196.1	18,044.1
New Mexico	5,562.2	5,890.3	11,452.5
North Dakota	36.3	34.1	70.4
Oregon			
Public Domain	4,250.7	7,166.4	11,417.1
O&C Lands	331.4	386.1	717.5
Utah	6,284.1	7,020.2	13,304.3
Washington	121.1	156.3	277.4
Wyoming	4,840.4	5,478.9	10,319.3
Subtotal	$ 51,803.3	$ 73,569.3	$ 125,372.6
Other	53.3	55.9	109.4
Total	$ 51,856.6	$ 73,625.4	$ 125,482.0

Source: Nelson and Joseph (1982).

Indeed, in 1981 the capital value of purchasing a long-run grazing permit for one AUM was in the range of $50 to $100. This amounted to a total long-run capital value for all BLM grazing of $500 million to $1 billion (for the approximately 10 million AUMs of grazing on all BLM land). If government administrative costs for grazing had instead been redirected to buying out the grazing activity, it would have required only five to eight years to buy out all grazing on BLM lands. This is not to argue that such a buy-out would necessarily be desirable but to make the point that the administrative costs of BLM grazing were (and still are) greatly in excess of what can be economically justified by the returns from grazing.

It is unlikely that the states would be willing to continue this arrangement with the ranching community within the state, if they took over BLM lands. Indeed, on their own state lands, the states typically charge grazing fees at least two to three times the federal fee. For example, the state grazing fee in Colorado in 1994 was $6.42 per AUM; in Montana it was $4.09; and other western states have similar fees. The federal fee for 1996 was $1.35 per AUM.[4]

A second feature of interest in table 2.2 is the substantial portion of the costs of grazing administration that are derived from overhead. The indirect costs, in fact, represented 59 percent of the total BLM grazing management costs. BLM in most of its published estimates of costs omits any such allowance for overhead, showing only the direct expenditures ($51.9 million in 1981) and thus greatly underestimates the actual federal costs of livestock grazing (as well as forestry, recreation, and other BLM activities). There is little incentive for BLM to economize on the land-use planning, personnel management, contracting procedures, environmental impact statements, and many other process requirements that escalate the indirect costs of its management. In fact, there is an incentive to inflate these costs in order to increase budgets.

From the state perspective, much of this spending can be regarded as a benefit to be encouraged. All the BLM process activities provide high-paying jobs in rural western economies where such jobs are scarce. The incomes and spending of these BLM jobholders then spread as secondary impacts, in many areas making a significant contribution to the total economic base of a rural economy.

If a western state took ownership of the BLM lands, of course, higher spending would no longer be advantageous for its own sake. New state managers would probably act to slash the levels of overhead found in BLM budgets. On their own state trust lands, the states at present spend much less than the BLM without any apparent loss in management effectiveness. In their recent study of state management of trust lands, Souder and Fairfax conclude "that the trust mandate provides useful clues for a more fruitful balancing of environmental and industry priorities in public resource debates than is currently available in the power struggles over federal lands" (1996, 294).

Table 2.3 shows the aggregate revenue and cost picture for grazing and other outputs of the BLM lands. Besides grazing management, large losses are also incurred in public domain timber management (outside Oregon), recreation and wildlife, and hardrock (nonleasable) minerals.[5] The net losses on recreation and wildlife management—equal to $106 million in 1981—exceeded that of grazing management, partly reflecting the fact that almost no revenues were collected from recreational users. Again, this is a benefit to recreationists and others in a western state. If the states took over the lands, however, they would likely act to raise more revenue through fees and other charges collected from recreational users.

Table 2.3
Revenues and Costs from BLM Lands in 13 Western States, 1981
(millions of dollars)

Type of Public Land Output	Revenue	Cost
Timber		
Public Domain, except Oregon	$ 1.3	$ 11.8
Public Domain, Oregon	14.5	1.1
O&C Lands (Oregon)	200.0	48.3
Subtotal	$ 215.8	$ 61.2
Rangeland Forage	24.7	125.4
Recreation and Wildlife	0.9	107.1
Oil and Gas	754.3	72.8
Coal	40.1	45.0
Other Leasable Minerals	28.6	20.1
Nonleasable Minerals	2.4	11.3
Other	10.0	–
Total	$ 1,076.8	$ 442.9

Source: Nelson and Joseph (1982).

Minerals Revenue

The federal government owns approximately one-third of the coal reserves of the United States, the great majority of which are located in western states (Nelson 1983; Tarlock 1985). Federal coal represents almost 30 percent of total U.S. coal production. In 1994, Wyoming produced 237 million tons of coal, mostly from federal leases, equal to 23 percent of U.S. production and making Wyoming the leading coal-producing state in the nation. Total federal royalties from federal coal leases in 1993 equaled $264 million (Minerals Management Service 1994, 61).

The federal government also holds large oil and natural gas reserves in the West that are the source of approximately 5 percent of total U.S. production of oil and gas. Total federal royalties from onshore (excluding the outer continental shelf) oil and gas leases equaled $583 million in 1993, mostly from western states.

Unlike surface management, mineral leasing yields a large excess of revenues over costs. However, this is only in part a benefit to the federal government. Under the Federal Coal Leasing Amendments Act of 1976, the revenues from onshore federal mineral leasing are distributed 50 percent to the state in which the lease is located (minus a small adjustment for royalty collection costs), 40 percent to the federal Reclamation Fund for the support of federal water projects in the West, and 10 percent directly to the federal treasury.

The federal government actually receives considerably less than these percentages indicate because the royalty payments made by federal lessees are deducted from federal taxes owed under the corporate income tax. Such deductions can reduce total federal income tax collections by as much as 35 percent of the magnitude of the royalty payment. Assuming the Reclamation Fund is a benefit to the federal treasury (a generous assumption), the federal return can be as low as 15 cents per dollar of federal royalty collected.

The net return is even worse because the great majority of the administrative costs of federal mineral leasing are borne by the federal government. Hence, the Commission on Fair Market Value Policy for Federal Coal Leasing (1984, 329) recommended that "the Congress should reexamine the distribution formula for Federal coal leasing revenues to provide a more equitable treatment for the Federal government."

Given that mineral leasing is the main source of government revenue from BLM lands, there is little if any financial reason for the federal government not to transfer all BLM lands to the states. Indeed, on the whole, as will be discussed below, there would be a modest net fiscal gain to the federal government from such a transfer (free of charge).

If such a transfer were to occur, the states would have much potentially to gain. Assuming they got all the revenues going to the federal treasury and the Reclamation Fund, new mineral revenues would add perhaps $500 million per year to the coffers of all western states combined. In estimating the net fiscal impacts of a transfer of BLM lands, the heart of the matter will be the balancing of this $500 million state mineral revenue gain against the added administrative costs the western states would incur for accepting the management responsibilities. (It would also be important to factor in any new major sources of revenue the states might be able to develop.)

At present, the federal government spends more than $500 million to administer the BLM lands, thus creating a net loss from their management. The states thus would have to implement significant administrative economies, if they were to realize a fiscal benefit from a transfer. It seems quite likely that they would in fact be able to accomplish such cost cutting. However, the specific circumstances of individual states vary considerably, as will be discussed below.

BLM Forestry

As shown in table 2.3, BLM forestry on the public domain lands outside of Oregon is typical of most BLM surface uses. It generates few revenues and in comparison high costs, yielding a loss in 1981 of $10.5 million. Public domain forestry, however, is a minor part of the overall BLM activity in the West, except in Oregon.

Until the designation in 1990 of the spotted owl as a threatened species under the Endangered Species Act, the BLM forests in western Oregon, the so-called O&C lands, yielded financially lucrative harvests of timber. As shown in table 2.3, these 2 million acres in 1981 yielded a "profit" of $152 million. Again, the bulk of the net revenues leaves the federal system; in this case 50 percent of O&C timber revenues are distributed to the local counties where the timber is harvested. The federal government absorbs the full administrative costs, which in 1981 were about 25 percent of total timber revenues. Thus, on a net basis in 1981, the O&C counties received about 66 percent and the federal government received about 33 percent of O&C timber sale revenues.

More recently, however, there have not been any positive net revenues. Following the spotted owl listing, as timber harvests have plummeted by 75 percent or more from their former levels on O&C lands (and national forests as well), the BLM has incurred sizable losses. Part of the reason for this is that the Congress agreed to compensate the local Oregon counties for their significant losses in timber revenues under the spotted owl protection plan. This compensation—about $50 million in 1994—has been provided through direct appropriations to the counties from the federal treasury.[6]

Table 2.4 shows BLM's recent estimates of the large benefits now flowing to Oregon from the presence of all BLM lands, mostly attributable to the O&C lands (BLM 1995b). In 1994, BLM made direct financial payments of $101 million to the state and to the O&C counties in Oregon. The federal government collected $71 million in revenues from BLM-managed lands and minerals, which went to the federal treasury, but it spent $139 million managing the BLM lands in Oregon. Thus, the net financial inflows to Oregon associated with the presence of BLM lands equaled $169 million in 1994. On the other side of the ledger, this was the "loss" to the federal government. At present, unless the terms of a transfer allowed Oregon to raise timber harvests significantly, the state would very likely experience a negative fiscal impact from taking possession of BLM lands.

Overall Fiscal Impacts

Taking into account minerals, timber, grazing and other resources, table 2.5 shows the total revenues and total costs in 1981 for the BLM public domain lands in the West (excluding the O&C lands, which have a much different history and statutory basis, and are not considered part of the public domain). The basic picture today would look similar, although revenues have fallen somewhat in real terms and costs have kept up with inflation. In 1981 total revenues of $876 million from BLM lands and minerals were well above the total costs of $389 million. However, as shown in table 2.6, fully $377 million of the federal revenues were transferred to the states. This meant that, instead of a federal "profit" of $488 million, the actual federal net gain was only $111 million.[7]

If the BLM surface and mineral estate had been transferred to the western states, this $111 million would have gone to the states as well. This estimated net fiscal gain to the states from a land transfer is probably a lower bound because it assumes that the states would have replicated the BLM's low surface revenues and high management costs.

Moreover, the projected overall gain to the western states would have been very unevenly distributed, reflecting the highly skewed distribution of revenues from oil and gas, coal, and other mineral leasing. In fact, only New Mexico, North Dakota, and Wyoming would have been fiscal winners. Other states would have typically experienced a small negative fiscal impact in the magnitude of $5 million to $20 million per year.

The Congressional Research Service produced similar estimates of fiscal impacts for 1993. Table 2.7 shows net income accruing to the federal government from BLM lands in each state. The $111 million federal profit in 1981 had become a net fiscal loss of $113 million by 1993. This largely reflected declines in mineral revenues (in real terms) from 1981

Table 2.4
Oregon Benefits from BLM Lands, 1994

Federal Collections from BLM-Managed Lands and Minerals

Grazing Fees	$ 1,524,000
Recreation and Use Fees	119,000
Miscellaneous Receipts	291,000
Sale of Land and Minerals	3,969,000
O&C Land Grant Fund	60,075,000
Coos Bay Wagon Road Grant Fund	4,062,000
Mining Claim Holding Fees	943,000
Mineral Royalties, Rents, and Bonuses	113,000
Total	$ 71,096,000

Direct BLM Financial Transfers to Oregon

Payments in Lieu of Taxes (PILT)	$ 2,872,000
Grazing Fees	225,000
O&C Grant Lands	97,642,000
Proceeds of Sales	187,000
Mineral Royalties, Rents, and Bonuses	56,000
Total	$ 100,982,000

BLM Investments in Oregon

Management of Lands and Resources	$ 26,152,000
Land Acquisition	3,023,000
Construction and Access	1,071,000
Coos Bay Wagon Road Grant Lands	625,000
Management of O&C lands	85,263,000
Fire Management/Firefighting	
Prescribed Fire/Presuppression	8,236,000
Firefighting and Rehabilitation	13,126,000
Service Charges, Deposits, and Forfeitures	1,730,000
Total	$ 139,226,000

Source: Bureau of Land Management (1995b).

Table 2.5
Total Revenues and Costs from
BLM Public Domain Lands in 13 Western States, 1981
(thousands of dollars)

State	Total Revenues	Total Costs	Net Revenues
Alaska	$ 21,231.1	$ 69,447.2	$ - 48,216.1
Arizona	11,452.3	21,492.2	-10,039.9
California	56,428.6	35,610.4	20,818.2
Colorado	55,511.1	36,686.6	18,824.5
Idaho	10,017.5	29,367.5	-19,350.0
Montana	37,952.6	34,664.5	3,288.1
Nevada	27,123.9	35,031.6	-7,907.7
New Mexico	267,854.8	31,737.9	236,116.9
North Dakota	49,273.6	1,540.9	47,732.7
Oregon*	18,967.2	23,078.6	-4,111.4
Utah	52,401.0	33,131.1	19,269.9
Washington	515.7	1,306.8	-791.1
Wyoming	267,968.0	35,858.3	232,109.7
Total	$ 876,697.4	$ 388,953.6	$ 487,743.8

* Public domain lands do not include the O&C lands.
Source: Nelson and Joseph (1982).

to 1993. Hence, if the western states took possession of BLM lands, and replicated existing BLM revenue and management practices, they would now experience a small negative fiscal impact overall. However, with their large energy mineral resources New Mexico and Wyoming would still be big winners. For Colorado and Montana, states also having significant mineral resources, there would be little impact either way. Also similar to the results for 1981, other states would lose modest amounts, typically now in the range of $10 million to $40 million per year. Fiscal impacts of this magnitude are probably not large enough to be decisive factors in determining whether a state should accept or reject an offer of BLM lands.

The State Management Record

These fiscal results do not allow for the possibility that transferring BLM land to the states would create strong incentives for state land manage-

Table 2.6

Distribution of BLM Public Domain Land Revenues and Costs, 1981

(millions of dollars)

State	Total Cost	Revenues to Federal Government	Revenues to States	Net Revenues to Federal Government
Alaska	$ 69,447.2	$ 2,500.0	$ 18,731.1	$ -66,947.2
Arizona	21,492.2	6,376.7	5,075.6	-15,115.5
California	35,610.4	31,520.7	24,907.9	-4,089.7
Colorado	36,668.6	30,362.2	25,148.9	-6,324.4
Idaho	29,367.5	6,341.8	3,675.7	-23,025.7
Montana	34,664.5	24,848.7	13,103.9	-9,815.8
Nevada	35,031.6	16,196.0	10,927.9	-18,835.6
New Mexico	31,737.9	139,066.3	128,788.5	107,328.4
North Dakota	1,540.9	45,170.1	4,103.5	43,629.2
Oregon*	23,078.6	16,972.2	1,995.0	-6,106.4
Utah	33,131.1	30,720.0	21,681.0	-2,411.1
Washington	1,306.8	427.9	87.8	-878.9
Wyoming	35,858.3	149,914.2	118,053.8	114,055.9
Total	$ 388,953.6	$ 500,416.8	$ 376,280.6	$ 111,463.2

* Does not include the O&C lands.

Source: Nelson and Joseph (1982).

Table 2.7
Aggregate Returns to the U.S. Treasury from
BLM Land and Resource Management, FY 1993
(millions of dollars)

State	Net BLM Revenues	Net MMS* Revenues	Net Federal Revenues
Alaska	$ −83.164	$ 0.103	$ −83.061
Arizona	−38.444	0.087	−38.357
California	−48.681	19.869	−28.812
Colorado	−31.873	32.501	0.628
Idaho	−13.932	2.012	−11.920
Montana	−26.606	21.516	−5.090
Nevada	−47.341	7.397	−39.944
New Mexico	−40.973	133.184	92.211
Oregon	−48.383	0.062	−48.321
Utah	−42.093	29.546	−12.547
Wyoming	−44.830	194.872	150.042
Eastern States	−11.539	14.726	3.187
DC Office	−90.150	0.000	90.150
Total	$ −568.009	$ 455.875	$ −112.134

* The Minerals Management Service (MMS) collects the royalty revenues from mineral leases on BLM lands and bears a portion of the mineral management costs for these lands.
Source: Gorte (1995).

ment improvement and innovation. Indeed, recent studies suggest that state management has been superior to federal management (Souder and Fairfax 1996). The states earn more revenues from similar resources and incur lower costs compared with federal land agencies, and the lower costs do not seem to be at the sacrifice of environmental quality.

The state of Washington manages 5 million acres, somewhat more than half of which are heavily forested. The state forest lands are held in trust for a range of beneficiaries that include the University of Washington, Washington State University, the Washington Department of Corrections, and local county governments. The Washington Department of Natural Resources is legally obligated to manage the lands for the long-run gain of the beneficiaries. The forested portions of Washington's state trust lands in 1994 generated net revenues of more than $100 million. As a comparison, BLM's O&C lands cover a slightly smaller area of similarly high-quality land for timber purposes. In 1994, the federal government experienced a net loss of about $100 million on these comparable lands (BLM 1995b).

The Washington Department of Natural Resources recently commissioned an outside review of its management, conducted by the Natural Resources Law Center of the University of Colorado School of Law. Completed in June 1995, the report found that "the DNR's reputation as one of the leading public land management agencies in the country appears to be well deserved." Indeed, "its programs and practices set the standard for public land management at both the state and federal level." The Department of Natural Resources was not only earning sizable revenues but was voluntarily implementing "habitat protection requirements exceeding those that may in fact be required under federal or state regulatory law" with respect to endangered species. Much of the success of the Washington program derived from the trust status that imposed a "stewardship obligation of the highest order" and demanded "the utmost care in all actions that affect the present and future condition of the lands and their resources" (Independent Review Committee 1995, ex. sum.: 1, 10, and 12).[8]

Other states and local governments also own significant forest lands. In Montana the state forests are located near or adjacent to ten national forests managed by the U.S. Forest Service. The lands thus are similar in topography, types of trees, and other characteristics. In addition to timber management programs, both federal and state lands accommodate other public uses such as recreation, livestock grazing, and wildlife habitat improvement.

However, from 1988 to 1992, the national forests lost $42 million, while the state forests earned $13 million to benefit the public schools of Montana. As analyzed by Leal (1994 and 1995b), the primary reason for the poorer financial performance of the national forests was their much higher administrative cost structure. On the Gallatin National Forest, for example, it required 11.6 hours per thousand board feet for timber sale preparations compared with 4.5 hours for nearby state forest lands. Reflecting such differences, the total administrative cost equaled $175 per thousand board feet for national forests in one region of Montana compared with $52 for nearby state forest lands. The differentials were not this great in every region, but the costs of national forest timber management always exceeded costs of nearby state management by more than 50 percent. The high Forest Service costs partly reflect the burdens of land-use planning, environmental impact statements, and other procedural requirements that have grown rapidly in the past two decades. All this spending, however, does not seem to yield much benefit on the ground. Based on assessments by independent review bodies, Leal (1994, 26) concluded that "empirical evidence . . . indicates that the state does a better job of protecting watersheds from the impacts of logging than the Forest Service."

In response to the proposed federal legislation discussed at the beginning of this chapter, Idaho's Office of the State Controller (1995) undertook a study of the possible implications of a state takeover of the ownership of federal lands. In Idaho, the BLM manages 11.8 million acres, whose main revenue-generating use is livestock grazing; the Forest Service manages 20.4 million acres of which about two-thirds is used for timber harvesting. Existing state lands cover 2.4 million acres used for both grazing and logging.

As table 2.8 shows, the BLM and Forest Service lands both incurred large net losses. Total BLM revenues in 1994 were $7.7 million, far below management costs of $40.1 million. Forest Service total revenues were $102.5 million, also far below the costs of $196.2 million. Not included in these costs is an additional cost of $90.4 million spent by the federal government on fire suppression in Idaho.

The state of Idaho, by contrast, received revenues of $46.3 million in 1994, almost three times the state costs of $14.9 million. The state received gross revenues of $53.3 per acre from its timber lands, much greater than the Forest Service timber receipts of $8 per acre and the BLM receipts of $3.90 per acre. Idaho did spend significantly more for direct timber related activities on its timber lands, $7.60 per acre compared with $1.77 per acre for the Forest Service. The higher investment level is perhaps one reason why the revenues per acre received by the state were much higher. When Forest Service management costs for non-revenue producing activities such as dispersed recreation are added, however, the Forest Service total management costs per acre were about 50 percent higher than management costs for the Idaho Department of Lands. The BLM total management costs per acre were lower than the state costs, reflecting the largely low-intensity grazing use of the BLM lands.

All three of the land management agencies have specific cost accounts for timber and grazing. These accounts are significant underestimates because they do not make adequate allowance for administrative overhead that represents a major part of total agency spending. Yet, even using these minimum figures, the BLM grazing and timber programs and the Forest Service grazing program lost money. At the federal level, only the Forest Service timber program was profitable. For the state agency, by contrast, both grazing and timber programs generated significant positive net revenues.

If the state of Idaho took over BLM grazing lands and managed them

Table 2.8
Idaho Federal and State Land Management
Revenues and Costs, FY 1994
(millions of dollars)

Activity	Acres (thousands)	Revenues	Costs	Net Revenues	Revenues (per acre)	Costs (per acre)
BLM Grazing	11,633	$ 2.0	$ 6.4	$ 4.4	$ 0.17	$ 0.55
BLM Timber	322	0.4	1.3	-0.9	1.24	3.90
All BLM	11,859	7.7	40.1	-32.4	0.65	3.38
USFS Grazing	1,429	1.0	3.5	-2.5	0.69	2.44
USFS Timber	12,423	99.4	22.0	77.4	8.00	1.77
All USFS	20,438	102.5	196.2	-93.7	5.02	9.60
State Grazing	1,878	1.3	0.8	0.5	0.69	0.41
State Timber	780	41.6	5.9	35.7	53.33	7.60
All State	2,400	46.3	14.9	31.4	19.28	6.21

Source: Idaho Office of the State Controller (1995).

for the same revenues per acre and costs per acre as its own state grazing lands, the transfer of BLM grazing lands would yield Idaho an additional $2.1 million in net revenue per year. If the same assumptions are made with respect to the transfer of BLM timber lands, Idaho could earn an additional $14.7 million per year in net revenue. A transfer of BLM lands to the state, in short, is likely to yield positive net revenues from the lands for Idaho.

Based on the same types of calculations, a separate analysis of the revenue potential from a transfer of BLM lands to the state of Montana reached much the same conclusion (Leal 1995a). Montana has 5.2 million acres of state trust land. The surface management costs for the state are $0.82 per acre, as compared with the BLM costs of $3.79 per acre. If the state were to take over the BLM lands, it would spend $10 million per year in managing the lands, based on the historic experience of existing state lands. This would be much less than the $34 million actually spent by BLM in 1994. Assuming that the state collected the same revenues as the BLM does, $58 million in 1994, the net revenues under state management would come to $48 million. On the other side of the ledger are land-related federal transfers to Montana that amounted to $33 million in 1994. The net increase in revenues to Montana from taking possession of BLM lands in 1994 would have come to $15 million per year.

In October 1995, the Natural Resources Law Center of the University of Colorado (which also did the Washington State study) released an analysis of approximately 3 million acres of school trust lands managed by the State Board of Land Commissioners. Like state trust land management throughout the West, these lands earned a substantial profit for the beneficiaries. Total Colorado costs for management were $2.2 million, compared with revenues of $23.6 million. The net revenues of $21.4 million were distributed 45 percent directly to the school beneficiaries of the trust and 55 percent to a permanent fund that also benefits the schools indirectly through transfers of the income from financial investments made with the permanent fund (Natural Resources Law Center 1995).

While state trust lands in Colorado were yielding net income, the Natural Resources Law Center found that there were numerous ways in which the quality of management of state lands could be improved. The recommendations included that "the State Land Board should develop a comprehensive inventory of trust assets," in order to have a better basis for assessing management successes and failures. Other recommendations were that "market value should be obtained for agricultural leases"; that "the State Land Board should adopt a policy of public use of state lands"; and that the State Land Board "should inventory urban and transitional lands" with the idea that some of them might suitably be sold for attractive prices to accommodate urban development (Natural Resources Law Center 1995, xi, xiii, xv).[9]

The study of state trust lands in Colorado did not make any comparisons with BLM lands in the state. However, the Congressional Research Service study noted above found that the revenues from the 8.3 million acres of BLM lands in Colorado in 1994 were $77.6 million, while the costs of management were $39.4 million. Federal management yielded net revenues of $4.60 per acre, compared with net revenues of $7.13 per acre for state lands. If the BLM lands could be managed with the same revenues and costs as the state lands, Colorado could earn an additional $21.5 million per year in net revenue from a transfer of BLM lands (allowing for the loss of the existing state share of federal revenues).

In response to discussion in Nevada of the possibility of transferring BLM lands to state ownership, Eureka County commissioned a study of the potential impacts on the state of Nevada and on Eureka and other local counties in Nevada of such a transfer. Because Nevada has almost none of its original state grant lands remaining in state ownership, the Intertech Services Corporation (1994), which undertook the study, looked to Arizona, Idaho, New Mexico, and Utah.[10] As shown by the Intertech analysis, all four states earned positive net revenues on their state lands over the five years from 1989 to 1993, suggesting that Nevada could also gain from a federal land transfer.

Should a State Take BLM Land?

The above analysis suggests that most western states would be capable of earning positive net revenues from BLM lands, but this does not mean that each state would necessarily be better off financially. As noted above, federal spending in each state is a cost to national taxpayers but can well be regarded as a benefit within a state. From the state perspective, the more the federal government spends, the better off the state will be—as long as the form of spending is not actually harmful in some fashion to the state.

The net economic benefit from the presence of BLM lands thus will reflect the sum of federal revenue transfers plus the total federal spending in the state that would not occur in the absence of the BLM lands. On this basis, only Wyoming and New Mexico would be clear fiscal winners from a transfer of BLM lands. A typical western state might be able to make money from the BLM lands, but the state would lose the large infusion of funds associated with the presence of BLM lands now coming from the federal treasury. This would mean significant losses of jobs and income for many state residents. To compensate for this loss of federal spending in the state, a state would have to earn perhaps $25 million to $75 million in positive net revenues from state management of BLM lands. Given that most of these lands are now generating loses of $10 million to $40 million per year under BLM management, this would require a substantial economic turnaround. Evidence presented above suggests this is plausible, but by no means a certainty.

Of course, gains to western states depend on the continued willingness of national taxpayers to keep the funds flowing to the West. The current pressures to reduce federal spending may call this assumption into question. To the extent that the federal government should decide to withdraw from its historic role in the West, the fiscal benefits to a state in taking possession of BLM lands would become much greater. If the federal government were to demand, for example, that BLM management must generate revenues to cover its costs, the fiscal case for state ownership would become more compelling.

In any case, as noted above, the fiscal impacts are not in themselves large enough that they should necessarily determine a state position with respect to taking possession of BLM lands. There are broader and potentially more important considerations that might cause a state to accept a transfer of BLM lands. Historically, land management has been the most local of all government functions. The federal government in the West is performing tasks that elsewhere in the United States would be the responsibility of a state or local planning and zoning board. The federal government decides whether a new ski resort will or will not be built in a state. It decides whether further land will be used for parks and wilderness or for timber production. Federal officials decide whether new land will be made available for urban and rural development or will be kept free of such intensive uses and open for dispersed recreation.

The federal government, in short, shapes much of the landscape of most western states. As long as federal administrators follow state and local wishes, this may not be much of an infringement on state prerogatives. However, national interest group pressures and national politics have at times yielded results opposed by the majority of the state residents.

Transferring BLM lands to the states would represent a major change in the federal–state balance of power in the West. It would represent a declaration by the states in the West that they have decided to assume control over their own destiny—to grow up politically. In the end this consideration could prove to be as important as any of the fiscal calculations discussed above. One might recall that historically wars have been fought, many thousands have died, and national treasuries have been exhausted, all for the political control over much less land than is at stake in the public lands of the West.

Another reason for state control is that the land-use planning systems resulting from the public land legislation of the 1970s have promoted gridlock and polarization, rather than the more rational decision processes that their congressional sponsors envisioned (U.S. House 1993). Over the course of 1995, the forests and public land management subcommittee of the Senate Energy and Natural Resources Committee held nine hearings throughout the nation to assess the current conditions and possible future directions for the national forests. Witnesses reflected diverse backgrounds and political outlooks. Yet, as the chairman of the committee, Senator Frank Murkowski of Alaska, said near the conclusion of the process: "nobody is defending the status quo. . . . Nobody is maintaining that it is not broken. . . . There are different views of what is broken, what needs fixing, and how to fix it. But I have been overwhelmed by the universal dissatisfaction with the current status" (1996, 355).

A transfer of ownership of BLM lands to the states would offer the opportunity to rethink the institutional arrangements of western land management from first principles. The states would be less constrained by traditional ways of doing things and habits of thought that have hardened over many decades of federal administration, dating back to the Progressive era. They could apply common-sense solutions that federal administrators find difficult or impossible to implement in the current institutional maze of federal land management.

Impacts on Existing Users of BLM Lands

An aggregate analysis of fiscal impacts and other consequences of large-scale land transfers to the states does not account for how current users of these lands would fare. Indeed, to the extent that state ownership would result in higher grazing fees, recreational fees, or other user charges, particular user groups could well be worse off.

These same groups may also fear that the state will change management practices in other ways that could prove to be to their detriment. For example, many states now make state lands available for grazing by competitive bidding. If a state adopted this practice on newly acquired BLM lands, many ranchers who have grazed the same allotment for decades could be displaced from their traditional access to particular areas of federal rangelands. Indeed, environmental organizations in Idaho have submitted bids for grazing on state lands with the intent to curtail grazing. Although the state government refused to accept these bids from nonranching groups, this position may well not survive court challenge.

In the early 1980s, Utah proposed a large-scale exchange of state lands for federal lands. When public meetings were held to discuss this proposal, even ranchers who had previously advocated state ownership on further thought "opposed state takeover of the proposed BLM properties, voicing fears that the state, as new landlord, might not honor their present federal grazing permits" (*Salt Lake Tribune* 1981). In New Mexico, another place where state ownership was being discussed, one rancher complained that "the State Land Office has a philosophy of 'optimizing the dollar return.'. . . If we had to pay as much to lease the BLM portion of our ranch as we do for our two sections of state land (which are some of the least productive on the ranch) we would go out of business" (Hill 1979).

Hunters and fishermen fear that a state takeover of BLM lands could have adverse effects on them as well. First, the state might begin to charge for hunting and fishing access at places where BLM has always provided this service for free. Second, the state might decide to sell off lands in order to raise additional revenues. The private owners then might either impose their own hunting and fishing charges or cut off access altogether. The imposition of a fee could divide hunters into groups of winners and losers: those who can afford the fee and prefer the improvements in hunting conditions that may result, versus those who are less willing or able to pay, and might prefer more congested hunting at a lower cost. Out-of-state hunters, who already pay considerably more, may prefer the improved hunting conditions that might result from a higher fee on in-state hunters.

What is true of hunters and fishermen is true more broadly of the general class of recreationists. Hikers, bird-watchers, hunters, and other groups have long enjoyed free access to BLM lands. If the state were to take the lands, they fear that "the forest of No Trespassing signs would be as great as the one of remaining spruce, pine and fir" (Abrams 1979).

Miners fall in the same camp. Under the Mining Law of 1872 and subsequent amendments, they have long had access to explore for gold, copper, silver, and other hardrock minerals anywhere on public lands not explicitly closed to such exploration. When they make a discovery, they can obtain title to the land and minerals for a nominal charge. Some states, however, operate leasing systems and act more aggressively to collect revenue. Although the federal government has never collected a hardrock mining royalty, the states of Wyoming and Arizona in 1990 collected $7.6 million and $3.1 million, respectively, from such royalties. The mining industry thus shares the concerns of many grazers, hunters, hikers, and other user groups with respect to any proposal to transfer BLM lands to the states.

All these groups have established working relationships with the BLM. They have learned how to operate in the congressional circles where major public land decisions are typically made. They all benefit from the traditional financial arrangements by which the federal government pays most of the costs of public land administration, while typically complying with the wishes and meeting the needs of the user groups.

In short, any consideration of transferring BLM lands to western states could provoke considerable internal disagreement and political controversy within each state. State school systems and state taxpayers in general may benefit if BLM lands are added to existing trust land systems. The state as a whole may acquire much greater control over land use, infrastructure, and many other matters affecting its overall future. Ranchers, however, might lose, depending on the specific terms and conditions that they would be able to work out with the state.

Recreationists might also face an uncertain future. On the one hand, the state might choose to establish more state parks, thus adding to the availability of campsites and other forms of intensive recreation in the state. On the other hand, there might be fewer wild areas set aside. Downhill skiers might win, while cross-country skiers might lose—or it could be vice versa.

All this uncertainty would tend to inhibit any movement toward state assumption of ownership of BLM lands. As is often the case in political controversies, the potential losers may be more aware and better organized, relative to the potential winners. Thus, any plan for transferring BLM lands to states would need to take the concerns of the various affected user groups into careful consideration.

To mitigate the uncertainty, a western state might want to explicitly consider the following issues.

Fiscal Impact Planning

Each state could undertake a detailed analysis of the fiscal impacts of a state takeover of BLM lands. The analyses undertaken to date have been first cuts, necessarily based on a variety of very rough assumptions. New and better analyses would also clarify how alternative federal terms and conditions for a transfer might affect the state.

The states should make it clear that they will proceed only on the basis that federal mandates for land-use planning, environmental impact statements, and other expensive and ineffective decision-making procedures would no longer apply.

The Institutional Mechanisms for State
Land Management

Taking ownership of BLM lands would in most states greatly increase the total area of the lands under state management. Would the existing state land management agency continue to manage all the state lands? How might the organization of this agency be modified to reflect the major increase in its administrative responsibilities? Would all of the newly acquired BLM lands be put into a trust status, as most existing state lands in the West are at present? Or might lands be divided among existing state agencies—say, some lands going to the state park system, other lands going to the wildlife division, and still other lands going to the state trust lands system?

Sale of State Lands

Another key consideration would be the state policy with respect to potential sale of state land to private owners. Would such sales of former BLM lands be allowed? Might they be restricted to lands available in urban areas to facilitate development or for commercial purposes such as the building of a major resort area? Might there be quantitative restrictions on the annual magnitude of private sales—say, no more than 3 percent of the former BLM land in any one year or perhaps 10 percent cumulatively in any one decade? Would some special land areas received by the state be formally set aside for permanent retention in state ownership (as the state lands in Adirondack Park in New York are so designated in the state constitution)?

Future Open Access Guarantees

A major concern of many state residents is that they might lose their ability to hike, hunt, and otherwise participate in recreational activities that they now take for granted on existing BLM land. States might address this concern by providing guarantees of future access—although not necessarily at the same zero or low price of recreational access paid on federal lands. Open access easements could be attached to lands coming into state ownership that would carry over, even in the event that the land might be sold.

Grazing Status on State Lands

Despite the recent support given by many ranchers to the "county movement" and other efforts to reduce the federal role in the West, the majority of ranchers would probably oppose any transfer of lands to states that would expose them to sharply increased grazing fees, to the possible loss of their grazing permits, or to other major uncertainties. Given the substantial political influence of the ranching industry in most western states, a transfer of BLM lands to a state would probably not be possible if ranchers strongly opposed it.

Resolving rancher concerns would probably require detailed prior agreements between the state and current BLM permittees regarding their future status on newly acquired state land. Ranchers would want assurances that their tenure status on BLM lands would be maintained after a transfer. Complicating matters, ranchers currently operate under a system where many of the rules remain unwritten, based on an informal set of understandings that have evolved with prior public land managers over many decades. In order to provide similar assurances for the future, a state would probably have to define rancher tenure more precisely and formally. This might involve the explicit recognition of grazing rights on state land—potentially a marketable and tradable forage use permit (Nelson 1995, 282–84).

Hunting and Fishing Access

Although open access easements might be provided for hiking and other less obtrusive activities, this would not be appropriate for hunting and fishing. Indeed, the states already impose tight regulatory limitations on the time and place of hunting and fishing. Nevertheless, like other groups, hunters and fishermen would want a clarification of their potential future status under state land ownership before they would be willing to seriously consider a transfer of existing BLM lands. This might involve commitments to the designation of certain newly acquired state lands for wildlife management. Certain lands, for example, might be dedicated to use for the purpose of increasing fish and game populations—somewhat in the manner at the federal level of the national wildlife refuge system. It could also involve a formal statement by the state of its policy for determining future hunting and fishing access charges, with possible explicit limits set on any increases that could take place over, say, the next decade or longer.

Local Land Management

Many current BLM lands involve decisions that have more local than statewide impacts. Management decisions on these lands are analogous to zoning decisions elsewhere in the United States. Local mistrust of state government is a significant obstacle in some parts of the West to a transfer of BLM lands to the state. For many local people, the state is just another large bureaucracy, almost as far removed as Washington. These concerns might be alleviated in part by providing advance clarification of the expected role of local governments in managing any BLM lands transferred to the state from federal ownership.

It might be appropriate for a state to commit to transfer the management (and possibly ownership as well) of some former BLM lands directly to the local level. There could be a general transfer of most former BLM lands within a county for local management there. Or such a transfer could be limited to selected lands located near towns and cities, perhaps in part to create some local park and recreation areas.

Under the former and broader scenario, there would be important questions of the future relationship between the state government and local land managers and owners. Might the state prepare certain broad plans and goals, and then turn responsibilities over to local management, subject to the requirement that local actions must be consistent with the state goals? Or would the localities have the autonomy to manage newly acquired lands pretty much as they wished, much as local governments at present administer their own planning and zoning in most cases with little state oversight?

Commitment to a State Referendum

Before the various user groups and localities would be willing to enter into any such process of detailed planning for the possibility of a state takeover of BLM lands, they might want assurances that no transfer would occur until the planning was complete and a broad base of support was shown to exist in the state. One way to provide such assurance would be to commit in advance that any state decision to accept a transfer of BLM lands would have to be approved by the legislature and the governor and then submitted for approval by a statewide referendum of the voters.

Conclusion

The introduction of congressional legislation to transfer BLM lands to the states has served to stimulate further attention to the issue. Although there has been little movement toward enactment, this outcome partly reflects the complex issues raised. To date, however, the states in the West have done little to clarify the issues for their own citizens or to develop the analyses necessary for further informed discussion. This is an essential next step, if any forward movement is to occur.

Part of the problem is that the federal government has been vague about the possible terms and conditions of a transfer of BLM lands. The legislation introduced in 1995 in the Congress to offer the BLM lands to the states left a number of important issues to be resolved, leaving the states in the West to simply make their own guesses as to the eventual outcome. In subsequent discussions and analyses, the states tended to assume the worst, reflecting a risk averse approach perhaps appropriate to a matter of such great importance to a state.

Thus, a parallel process to state exploration of the issues of transferring BLM lands must take place at the federal level. The federal government should provide details such as federal plans for firefighting, toxic dump liability, payment in lieu of taxes, and a number of other matters that will have significant fiscal and other consequences for any states considering taking possession of BLM lands (Nelson 1996b).

It is likely to take some time before issues of these kinds can be resolved. Perhaps they should not be addressed and cannot be resolved on a comprehensive basis for the West as a whole. Because each state has its own special circumstances, the Congress might want to consider an approach of negotiating potential transfer arrangements on a state-by-state basis.

The Congress might consider enacting legislation under which an individual state could come forward to request formally the entering into transfer discussions with the federal government. If successful, these efforts would then lead to a detailed proposal for transferring BLM lands. Once this plan for transfer of BLM lands had been worked out, it would then have to be submitted to Congress for approval. The plan would also have to be formally approved by the state, perhaps as suggested above by statewide referendum.

If such a process were initiated, the chances are good, I believe, that an acceptable agreement could eventually be worked out. In the long run, properly structured, transfer of most BLM land to the states (and national forests as well, although they have not been addressed here) can be a winning proposition for the federal government, for the state, and for the affected user groups in the state. It would be consistent with the goal of a reduced role for the federal government in American life, a goal that more and more Americans are coming to share, however hesitant they are about making a large leap into the unknown that might initially be required.

Notes

1. These states are Arizona, California, Colorado, Idaho, Montana, New Mexico, Nevada, Oregon, Utah, Washington, and Wyoming. For land data, see BLM (1994).

2. It should be noted that Foreman also expressed reservations about the administrative capabilities and social tolerance of states and localities.

3. At its annual conference in Salt Lake City in October 1995, the Western Legislative Conference of the National Council of State Governments approved a resolution stating that the results of the existing public land system were "to usurp state control over its land and economy"; that the existing federal system "has failed, both economically and practically"; and that "there is a growing consensus that the solution to this failed policy is to transfer ownership of certain federal lands to the states" (Resolution Number 95-9).

4. It should be noted that there is considerable controversy over what is the correct fee because there are different costs to the permittees on state and federal lands.

5. "Public domain land" refers to all BLM lands except in Oregon where O&C lands are excluded.

6. It is interesting to note that the federal government has declined to provide similar compensation to private landowners who might press their own takings claims for owl-related financial losses.

7. If minerals are excluded, the picture for surface land management was much worse. In 1981, the federal government received only $41 million (again, excluding the O&C lands), while the surface management cost was $240 million.

8. This report was prepared by a team of consultants to the review committee assembled by the Natural Resources Law Center of the University of Colorado School of Law, principally Teresa A. Rice, Larry MacDonnell, Sally Fairfax, and Jon Souder.

9. The state of Arizona, for example, has been generating approximately $100 million per year from land sales, thereby increasing the size of the Arizona permanent fund by $600 million over the past decade or so.

10. See also Intertech Service Corporation (1996).

References

Abrams, Dan. 1979. The Rebellion Is Getting Hot. *Jackson Hole News*, December 5.

Biskupic, Joan. 1996. Justices Shift Federal–State Power. *Washington Post*, March 29.

Bureau of Land Management. 1994. *Public Land Statistics, 1993*. Washington, DC: U.S. Department of the Interior, September.

———. 1995a. BLM Report Cites Rewards from Public Lands. Press Release, Office of Public Affairs, July 31.

———. 1995b. *Public Rewards from Public Lands*. Washington, DC: U.S. Department of the Interior, August.

Calef, Wesley. 1960. *Private Grazing and Public Lands: Studies of the Land Management of the Taylor Grazing Act*. Chicago: University of Chicago Press.

Clarke, Jeanne Nienabler, and Daniel McCool. 1996. *Searching Out the Terrain: Power and Performance Among Natural Resource Agencies.* SUNY Press.

Commission on Fair Market Value Policy for Federal Coal Leasing. 1984. Report of the Commission on Fair Market Value Policy for Federal Coal Leasing. Washington, DC, February.

Foreman, Dave. 1996. Am I a Free Market Environmentalist? *PERC Reports.* Bozeman, MT: Political Economy Research Center, March.

Friar, Monica E., and Herman B. Leonard. 1995. The Federal Budget and the States, Fiscal Year 1994. Cambridge: Kennedy School of Government, Harvard University, July 28.

Gorte, Ross W. 1995. BLM Revenues and Expenditures. Library of Congress, Congressional Research Service, Washington, DC, July 28.

Hill, Janaloo. 1979. Rebellion Would Finish Ranchers. Letter to *Albuquerque Journal,* December 12.

Idaho, Office of the State Controller (J. D. Williams). 1995. *Taking Control of Federal Lands: A Good Deal for Idaho?* Report 95-2. Boise, September.

Independent Review Committee. 1995. Report to the Washington State Board of Natural Resources from the Independent Review Committee. Olympia, June 22.

Intertech Services Corporation. 1994. Identification of Public Land Transfer Issues and Preliminary Comparative Economic Analysis. Carson City, NV, November 22.

———. 1996. Alternatives for Management of an Expanded Land Base in Nevada. Carson City, February.

Leal, Donald R. 1994. Making Money on Timber Sales: A Federal and State Comparison. In *Multiple Conflicts over Multiple Uses,* ed. Terry L. Anderson. Bozeman, MT: Political Economy Research Center.

———. 1995a. State Would Benefit from BLM Land. *Great Falls Tribune,* December 6.

———. 1995b. Turning a Profit on Public Forests. *PERC Policy Series,* PS-4, Bozeman, MT: Political Economy Research Center.

Limerick, Patricia Nelson. 1995. A History of the Public Lands Debate. Paper presented at a conference on Challenging Federal Ownership and Management: Public Lands and Public Benefits. University of Colorado, Boulder, October 11–13.

Minard, Richard A., Jr. 1996. Comparative Risk and the States. *Resources* (Winter): 6–10.

Minerals Management Service. 1994. *Mineral Revenues, 1993.* Washington, DC: U.S. Department of the Interior.

Murkowski, Frank. 1996. Statement. In *Federal Forest Management,* Hearings before the Subcommittee on Forests and Public Land

Management of the Senate Committee on Energy and Natural Resources, November 2, 1995. Washington, DC: Government Printing Office, 355–57.

National Academy of Public Administration. 1995. *Setting Priorities, Getting Results: A New Direction for EPA*. Washington, DC.

Natural Resources Law Center. 1995. *Report to the Colorado Department of Natural Resources and the State Board of Land Commissioners*. Boulder: University of Colorado School of Law, October.

Nelson, Robert H. 1983. *The Making of Federal Coal Policy*. Durham: Duke University Press.

———. 1994. Government as Theatre: Toward a New Paradigm for the Public Lands. *University of Colorado Law Review* 65(2): 335–68.

———. 1995. *Public Lands and Private Rights: The Failure of Scientific Management*. Lanham, MD: Rowman and Littlefield.

——— 1996a. End of the Progressive Era: Towards Decentralization of the Public Lands. In *A Wolf in the Garden: The Land Rights Movement and the New Environmental Debate*, ed. Philip D. Brick and R. McGreggor Cawley. Lanham, MD: Rowman and Littlefield, 215–32.

———. 1996b. *How and Why to Transfer BLM Lands to the States*. Washington, DC: Competitive Enterprise Institute.

Nelson, Robert H., and Gabriel Joseph. 1982. An Analysis of Revenues and Costs of Public Land Management in 13 Western States—Update to 1981. Washington, DC: Office of Policy Analysis, U.S. Department of the Interior, September.

New York Times. 1996. Lurching Toward States' Rights (editorial). March 29.

Peffer, E. Louise. 1951. *The Closing of the Public Domain*. Stanford: Stanford University Press.

Rivlin, Alice. 1992. *Revising the American Dream: The Economy, the States and the Federal Government*. Washington, DC: Brookings Institution.

Salt Lake Tribune. 1981. Antagonists Swap Roles (editorial). October 16.

Souder, Jon A., and Sally K. Fairfax. 1996. *State Trust Lands: History, Management and Use*. Lawrence: University Press of Kansas.

Stegner, Wallace. 1987. *The American West as Living Space*. Ann Arbor: University of Michigan Press.

Tarlock, A. Dan. 1985. The Making of Federal Coal Policy: Lessons for Public Lands Management from a Failed Program. *Natural Resources Journal* 25(2): 349–71.

U.S. House of Representatives. 1993. Committee on Interior and Insular Affairs. *Multiple Use and Sustained Yield: Changing Philosophies of*

Federal Land Management. Committee Print No. 11. Washington, DC: U.S. Government Printing Office.

Waldo, Dwight. 1984. *The Administrative State: A Study of the Political Theory of American Public Administration.* Reprint. New York: Holmes and Meier.

Wiebe, Robert H. 1995. *Self-Rule: A Cultural History of American Democracy.* Chicago: University of Chicago Press.

Chapter 3

State Trust Lands: The Culture of Administrative Accountability

Sally K. Fairfax

Of the numerous forms of landownership in the United States, state trust lands are perhaps the most obscure. These public lands were granted, usually at the time of statehood, to provide support for common schools and kindred public institutions. They are now called trust lands because of the obligation of the managers, the state bureaucrats, to act as trustees for the schools. The trust mandate means that there is a measurable objective, namely to provide funds for the recipient school systems.

Recently state trust lands have been much more in the news. In at least three jurisdictions—Oregon, Idaho, and New Mexico—environmental groups have attempted to bid against ranchers to lease state lands traditionally leased for grazing. In a fourth state, Arizona, the trust land leasing program is being challenged by similarly motivated environmentalists, which raises similar issues about the state's leasing procedures.

These trust lands grazing debates are interesting for several reasons. First, those looking for examples of an unraveling of achievements in the environmental field in the face of the Republican victories of the early 1990s can find much fodder in the recent events in Oregon, Idaho, Arizona, and perhaps New Mexico. Second, at a time when market mechanisms are everywhere embraced by politicians seeking to save money, end subsidies, and put the government on firm business footing, many of the same politicians abandon first principles to protect subsidies to their constituents. Neither the state legislatures nor the land boards in the three states with contesting conservation bidders have responded positively to these attempts to use market mechanisms to resolve conflicts over the use of public lands.

This chapter will serve two purposes. The first, as always, is to tell interesting stories. The disputes in Idaho and Arizona are the primary focus of these stories. The conflict in Idaho is lengthy and complex. The press has put a not wholly accurate David and Goliath spin on the situation and I shall relate that tale in considerable detail. In Arizona, the dispute is less well formed and of more recent origin. I shall share what has happened in order to identify patterns. These two tales should underscore a point I apparently never tire of making: It is extremely unwise to generalize across state lines without careful grounding in the frequently slight but important differences in enabling acts, constitutions and other crucial trust documents, statutory law, and resource and regional and agency culture. The grazing stories unfold in very different ways because of important differences in some or all of those key variables.

My second purpose is to reflect on public resource policy reform. The grazing cases reviewed here leave one wondering whether the trust notion has as much to offer in the way of a model to emulate as some, myself included, have suggested. Colleagues as diverse as Wald and Hess conclude:

> All Americans should be free to acquire permits to federal grass and to use the lands to enhance wildlife, stabilize soils, protect endangered species, improve riparian areas or, if they prefer, raise red meat. This can be done if Congress eliminates base property requirements for permits, ends the "use it or lose it" rule for federal grass, and lifts restrictions on subleasing. (1995, 5)

Similarly, O'Toole (1995) has advocated a wholesale redefinition of federal lands as trusts.[1] Yet my stories are not, at first blush, encouraging regarding trusts as a model for reform. I shall discuss whether the stories herein ought to give us trust advocates serious pause.

Dilemmas of Bureaucratic Accountability

At bottom, the issue here is one of bureaucratic accountability. With bureaucrats having been delegated enormous power both "for reasons of efficiency and to take advantage of the[ir] professional competence, . . . how is their work to be controlled by ordinary people?" (Gruber 1987, 3). This question is fundamental to public administration. It is also as broad and durable as human relations. Indeed, it arises in every relationship in which "one individual depends on the action of another" (Pratt and Zeckhauser 1985, 2).

The trust concept is not a new entry in this field, but it is, as noted above, newly notorious, especially in the public resource policy arena. It is the core of the mandate under which all the lands discussed in this chapter are managed. The basic idea of the trust is to raise money for schools and other public institutions. This profit-oriented approach to public resource management is presently enjoying more than normal popularity as a possible answer to two ubiquitous questions in the context of government bureaucracies.

First, it addresses issues of self-subsidy by managers. It offers opportunities to insert "proper incentives" into an executive agency, most notably the possibility that management expenditures will be in some sense related to income generated by that management.[2] Our data suggest that this effect is observable across the board in trust land management programs—there is less overinvestment on trust lands, and what exists is relatively easily traced and described. However, we have found no reason to tie that outcome to any particular institutional arrangement—such as source of funding—other than the operating culture in the trust agencies (Souder and Fairfax 1996).

Second, the present stories deal directly with the other bugaboo of public resource management reformers—capture by clients.[3] The trust appears to offer opportunities to trump the political influence of client groups and lessees. There is ostensibly little room for shilly-shallying toward client groups' priorities under the mushy heading of achieving "the combination of uses that best meets the needs of the American people."[4]

Finally, the trust is enforceable: virtually all the advantages in reviewing the trustees' discretion run to the beneficiary (Fairfax, Souder, and Goldenmann 1992). I have gone so far as to argue in other settings that the trust notion is a promising starting point for institutional design when the goal is long-term sustainability (Souder, Fairfax, and Ruth 1994). Yet, under the close scrutiny that their fifteen minutes of fame have garnered for the state land trusts, the press stories suggest that the trust is as easily subverted as other forms of bureaucratic control. The ranchers, it appears, are as clearly in control on the state trust lands as they appear to be on the federal lands.

This chapter will sort out, in a preliminary way, the implications of trust mechanisms for bureaucratic accountability. It will proceed in four parts. The rest of the introductory section will provide a brief background on trust principles—clarity, accountability, enforceability, perpetuity and prudence—and their application to state trust land management programs. The goal is to understand why some reformers and commentators look to trust principles with envy and an eye to emulation.

The second part will tell two stories, both of which point in the same direction: the trust is less effective at preventing capture than earlier more optimistic reports have suggested. The third part will try to put the good news and the bad news together by focusing on "prudence," the trustee's equivalent of "administrative discretion." That section will identify patterns in issues that arise when nontraditional bidders enter into a well-established public resource management arena. Although it is focused on grazing, many of the same conflicts will likely be aired in the context of conservation bids in all resource areas.

Finally, we will use those patterns to reflect more generally upon the utility of the trust model as an arrow in our quiver of bureaucratic control mechanisms. Is the trust falling down on the job in these states and in these cases? If so, what does that suggest about related efforts at reform?

The School Lands and the Trust Mandate— A Brief Introduction

The basics of the school lands grants are familiar. Following a policy outlined under the Articles of Confederation in the General Land Ordinance of 1785, the Congress, at or near the time of statehood, granted sections of land in each township—first just section 16 and ultimately a total of four—to new states to support common schools. In 1803 Ohio became the first beneficiary of such a congressional grant (Mansfield 1878). The program evolved for over a century and a half and played an integral role in the westward expansion and state-making process until it ended, more or less, in 1912 when Arizona and New Mexico joined the Union, although the final allocation came when Alaska joined in 1959 (Souder and Fairfax 1996). Hence the grants are among our nation's oldest public policies and are certainly the core of our oldest public resource policy.

Of the almost 322 million acres originally granted to the states for school and related purposes, approximately 135 million acres of surface and 152 million acres of mineral rights continue to be held in state ownership.[5] The state school lands are not managed subject to the same multiple-use standard that currently directs federal resource management, which generally exhort federal land managers to achieve, on the public lands, "the combination of uses that best meets the needs of the American people."[6]

The school land and related grants are held "in trust" by the states. With the exception of Arizona and New Mexico, wherein the trust was clearly established by Congress in the states' enabling act, the trusts are established in state constitutions. Although the state legislatures are clearly authorized to make rules regarding the administration of the trust, the basic commitment to trust principles cannot be altered by legislative action.

Clarity. A trust is called by lawyers a fiduciary relationship—which means that the trustee holds and manages property for the benefit of beneficiaries identified by the trustor, or person who set up the trust (Fairfax, Souder, and Goldenmann 1992). The key characteristic of a trust mandate, and one that readily distinguishes state trust lands from federal lands, is clarity of the goal; the trustee must exercise skill and diligence in making the trust productive for the specified beneficiary.[7] Thus, the primary duty of the trustee is to act with *undivided loyalty* to the specified beneficiary. Some have argued that the principal goal is to secure the highest monetary return (Patric 1981, 7). Reality, as usual, is a bit more complex. Achieving maximum returns, short term or long term, is not the trustee's *only* responsibility.[8] Other trust duties are elaborated in ancient common-law principles, state statute, and case law. These additional principles can be summarized under headings of accountability, enforceability, perpetuity, and prudence.

Accountability. Clarity of goals facilitates accountability; the trustee is specifically and comprehensively accountable to the beneficiary. The trustee must keep property records and accounts of receipts and disbursements, and must furnish this information to the beneficiary.[9]

Enforceability. Trust doctrine allows the beneficiary[10] to sue to enforce the terms of the trust. Trust obligations are fully elaborated in common law, statutes, and many centuries of judicial experience in enforcing the trust doctrine. While a judge, a local banker, or even a citizen might be confused by the circumlocutions or technicalities of a modern resource management statute, they are far less likely to be thrown off course by trust principles.

Perpetuity. Preserving the corpus of the trust is one of any trustee's fundamental obligations. Ordinarily, beneficial trusts are not necessarily perpetual.[11] The school land trusts' peculiar emphasis on perpetuity derives from the existence of the permanent school fund. Constitutional language regarding the funds is frequently draconian, noting that the "principal can never be diminished" or the legislature "shall make good all losses." What this means is that undivided loyalty and financial productivity are forever balanced against the need to protect the productive capacity of the trust—in this case, in perpetuity.

Prudence. The trustee is supposed to manifest "prudence" in managing trust resources to balance undivided loyalty and perpetuity. The trustee makes many choices about the nature, intensity, timing, and location of development. The trustee is allowed to withhold resources from development while planning, to hold resources off the market awaiting higher prices, and to act to protect the trust's reputation in the community and the political climate necessary to profitable operations. An ordinary person serving at the request of friends of family as a trustee for a minor child will be held, by the courts, to a less onerous standard of care than a professional funds manager or forester who has made claims of expertise in areas relevant to the trust.

These five themes—clarity, accountability, enforceability, perpetuity, and prudence—form the core of the trust mandate. Supposedly these themes would facilitate the movement of resources to their highest valued use. In other words, if land that had traditionally been used for one purpose was now more valuable in another use, the trustee would respond to these market signals. In the present context, if land that had been leased for grazing has a higher value to society if it is producing environmental amenities, the trust relationship should constrain the land managers to recognize that fact. We now turn to the stories for evidence on that issue.

The Stories

Idaho

One Idaho case—there are several, actually—is the one getting all the out-of-region publicity. It is in many particulars precisely as presented; ranching industry frustrates highest bidder's quest to protect riparian areas. However, the issue of prudence in dealing with scattered parcels is equally interesting. Moreover, what really appears to be happening is a "disruption" of established culture and ways of doing business; for many decades a number of folks have been unchallenged in their approach to the land.[12]

In 1863 Congress reserved sections 16 and 36 in what is now Idaho "for the purpose of being applied to schools." It then took almost thirty more years for Idaho to join the nation and receive its grants. That occurred, and the same sections were granted in 1890 "for the support of common schools." The granted lands used for grazing in Idaho are concentrated in the southern portion of the state, while the more valuable lands in the north of the state are used primarily for timber production. For the most part, the state lands continue to be held in the scattered section pattern in which they were originally granted.[13]

The delay of thirty years between the land reservations and the actual statehood put Idaho into the period of accessions, started in Colorado in 1876, in which Congress began to put restrictions on management of the lands. In the Idaho enabling act, Congress provided that the granted lands may be "disposed of only at public sale," but "may be leased for not more than five years" (Thorpe 1909, 2:914). This language has been interpreted by the state in subsequent years to mean, among other things, that a lease is not a disposal and does not require a public auction.

The original Idaho Constitution is explicit about the existence of a trust. It directs that the lands shall be "judiciously located and carefully preserved and held in trust, subject to disposal at public auction for the use and benefit of the respective objects for which said grants of land were made" (Thorpe 1909, 2:937). The constitution also established a State Board of Land Commissioners,[14] consisting of the governor, the superintendent of public instruction, the attorney general, and the secretary of state. It is the board's duty to "provide for the location, protection, sale, or rental of the lands . . . granted to the State . . . under such regulations as may be prescribed by law and in such manner as will secure the maximum possible amount therefor" (Thorpe 1909, 2:937). An amended Idaho constitution modifies the original language to provide that the board must secure "the maximum long term financial return. . . ."[15]

In Idaho, timber is the primary revenue producer. Grazing is extremely small potatoes; grazing accounted for $1.07 million in receipts and fourteen staff members in 1990, and timber produced $19.5 million in receipts utilizing fifty-nine staff members in the same year. However, when the land is considered, the data are approximately reversed; grazing leasing occurs on just over 2 million acres of endowment land and timber is managed on 881,000 acres (Souder and Fairfax 1996).

It is also important to keep in mind the pattern of landholding; as noted above, most of the state lands leased for grazing, and virtually all of the ones that have been involved in the cases discussed herein continue to be held in scattered sections 16 and 36, located in the townships as originally granted. The state lands typically appear as orderly, rectangular measles across Bureau of Land Management (BLM) and/or Forest Service holdings. The standard practice is for the state to enter into cooperative management plans with the BLM and/or the Forest Service for managing allotments that typically include federal, much less private and a smattering of state lands.

The State Land Board (SLB) accordingly leases most of its lands for grazing. Other uses on the leased lands are tolerated, even encouraged, and to the degree possible, integrated with a grazing lease. For example, if the SLB receives an application for a lease to develop a backcountry guide camp, a put-and-shoot hunting operation, or a cow camp on land that is already leased for grazing, the agency will explore the possibility of blending the two uses. The grazing lessee holds the state land lease subject to both general public hunting and recreation access and the possibility that subsequent lessees will manage the parcel for nongrazing uses.[16] The Idaho Code provides the relevant guidance for cases when two or more applicants apply for a grazing lease on the same piece of land; the SLB is directed to "auction off and lease the land to the applicant who will pay the highest premium bid therefor."[17] The price of the animal unit months (AUMs) is fixed by appraisal, and the bidders offer a premium for the lease.

Several recent challenges to SLB timber management are relevant to the grazing disputes at issue in this case. In a recent dispute, the Selkirk-Priest Basin Association (SPBA), an environmental group, challenged SLB timber management practices, alleging that clear-cutting and liquidating old growth assets, among other things, violated the trustee's duty to protect the corpus of the trust and the constitutional duty to "carefully preserve" the granted lands. The supreme court of Idaho was unambiguous in concluding that the SPBA, and the schoolchildren and parents of schoolchildren who had joined the case as named plaintiffs, lacked standing to raise issues of the board's timber management practices. It concluded that only beneficiaries of the trust have the legally protected interest necessary to sustain its cause of action.[18]

Chronology of Key Events

State leases in the Herd Creek Allotment were scheduled to expire in December 1993. In September 1993, as is required, the existing lessee, William Ingram, submitted an application to renew his lease. Several days later, Jon Marvel, president of the Idaho Watershed Project (IWP), an environmental group established "to protect important watershed and riparian areas on the school lands of the State of Idaho," submitted an application on the same parcel, one of four state parcels in the allotment.[19] At the 21 December SLB meeting, it was announced that Marvel had, as required by law, "submitted an affidavit stating that he has received a copy of the [BLM] management plan [for the allotment] and will comply with the plan. The BLM has been notified of Mr. Marvel's intent and has indicated that as long as fencing is restricted to the south side of Herd Creek Road, there should be no substantial impact of [sic] the overall management of the allotment. This section is classified for exchange with the BLM."[20]

On 11 January the Department of State Lands sent notice of the auction to Ingram and Marvel. The auction was held on 28 January 1994. Marvel made an opening premium bid of $30. Ingram did not bid, stating, "$30 is too much—we are not bidding."[21] On 4 February Ingram filed an administrative appeal, seeking board review of the conflict auction. At its regular meeting on 8 February 1994, the board considered the Ingram appeal, and by a vote of four to one, awarded the lease to Ingram.[22] IWP sued.

The district court, in a Blaine County decision, dated 25 October

1994, supported the SLB's decision. It held that the SLB has considerable discretion to "determine what the maximum long range financial return will be. In making such determination, factors other than the highest bid are involved." The decision lists a number of factors that support the board's exercise of its discretion: the allotment is managed predominantly by the BLM, the state section is "strategically located and provides critical access for the trailing of Ingram's cows into and out of the [BLM] allotment," and because the state section "provides the first dependable water available to the cows as they trail into the Herd Creek Allotment, the state section is of extreme importance to Ingram's total annual livestock operation and to the overall management of the Herd Creek Allotment."[23]

The court also addressed a number of procedural issues raised by the plaintiff. IWP complained that the board did not operate under normal Idaho Administrative Procedures Act rules and regulations; that is, that it proceeded under [until recently unpublished[24]] guidelines centering on *Robert's Rules of Order* and did not adequately inform participants of the ground rules, expectations, and their rights. However, the court concluded that Marvel had participated fully in the 8 February hearings. He was specifically asked during the hearings whether he believed the fact that they were proceeding under a protest from Ingram "was adverse to you in any way or prejudicial . . . have you been able to prepare everything you need to make your presentation to the board." Marvel replied, "No, I don't consider that to be a problem."[25] He was therefore considered to have waived any rights to complain about the process that he might have had otherwise.

In September 1994, one month before the decision in the Herd Creek issue was published, IWP bid on four more leases involving contests with four other existing lessees. IWP was the high bidder on all three of the parcels offered. Nevertheless, following appeals by the losing bidders, the SLB awarded the leases to the existing lessees. Interestingly, the SLB did not charge either the high bid or the lessees' first and only bid—the leases were awarded without premium to the low bidder in all three cases.[26] IWP's request to the board for a formal hearing on the leases was turned down,[27] and IWP filed lawsuits protesting the outcome in the Swan, Simplot, and Faulkner leases. Those cases were subsequently dropped when Marvel switched attorneys.

On the fourth auction, which was delayed because of the suggestion of collusion between ranchers bidding on the lease,[28] the existing lessee won a later auction with a premium bid of $13,550. The successful bidder then "requested that the SLB set aside the results and issue a new lease to Sheridan for the original, prepaid, fair market value of the 320 acres."[29] After the appeal was heard, and before the SLB rendered an opinion, the successful bidder decided to drop the issue and paid his premium.[30]

Meanwhile, another environmental group, Committee for Idaho's High Desert (CIHD), had entered the fray. It too followed the normal process for bidding on expiring leases. It also failed to obtain leases, but the problems it encountered were significantly different. CIHD originally applied for leases on three parcels. The Department of State Lands (DSL) subsequently informed CIHD that two of the three parcels did not separately constitute a "manageable unit" and that they would be auctioned together. CIHD accordingly submitted an application for the two parcels, located in Cottonwood Draw, and its application was accepted by the DSL.

At the time the deadline for applying to bid on a lease passed, CIHD was the only valid applicant. The existing lessee for the parcels was Owens Ranches, which had been purchased by Simplot in August 1994. Neither Owens nor Simplot filed for a renewal before the September 30 deadline. On 5 October, the DSL reminded Simplot regarding the missed deadline, and about the conflict application, but did not solicit an application from any other potential bidder. Simplot's "failure to file a timely application," the DSL concluded, did not mean that CIHD would be awarded the lease at the appraised price, without premium. Rather, it meant that the lands could be leased as "unleased" lands. That established a new deadline for applications.[31] Simplot applied and the application was accepted.

At the auction, the two plots upon which CIHD was planning to bid were combined into one lease. Simplot was the successful bidder. The state subsequently declared that the two units had been combined because separately they did not constitute manageable units. CIHD appealed at a land board hearing in April 1995.[32] When the SLB awarded the lease to Simplot, CIHD sued. Combining the units was, according to CIHD's complaint, contrary to law and procedurally irregular, and reduced the financial returns to the school fund.[33]

The state responded that CIHD had no standing to sue. It had not demonstrated that it had suffered any injury. The state argued that CIHD was unable to demonstrate that combining the parcels had harmed its ability to prevail in the auction, and pointed out that even if CIHD had been high bidder, it would not necessarily have been awarded the lease. It noted that CIHD's complaints that the combination of parcels reduced the income to the school fund was irrelevant as, following the SPBA cases, the environmental group had no standing to raise the issue. Finally, it argued that it is "within the Department's discretion to configure the auctions to best fit its requirements in the management and administration of state endowment lands."[34]

The court's decision, which the state did not appeal, gave CIHD victory on one narrow part of its argument. The court was "not persuaded that the error [in failing to give adequate notice of the combining of the parcels] was harmless."[35] All other issues raised by CIHD were rejected by the court. It did not find favoritism for the ranching industry in the SLB's efforts to "prompt" a tenant of need to apply to renew the lease; "just because the statutes and regulations do not specifically authorize it does not mean that common courtesies are somehow prohibited."[36]

Meanwhile, IWP had entered the 1995 grazing leasing season by filing four separate lease applications for parcels where the applications were expiring in December 1995.[37] One might think that IWP and CIHD were getting the hang of it by this time, and might actually win a lease. However, the legislature acted in the fall of 1995 to redefine the qualifications for bidders on a state grazing lease. Known in some circles as the "anti-Marvel bill" because it appears to have been adopted to prevent the kind of contested lease auctions as precipitated by IWP, the stated purpose of the bill is to support the endowment lands and the state "by encouraging a healthy Idaho livestock industry so as to generate related business and employment opportunities on a state and local level, thus supporting additional sales, income and property taxes."[38] The bill establishes criteria to be considered by the board in deciding who shall be a qualified applicant:

> whether the current lessee owns or controls sufficient real property to adequately feed the livestock in the lessee's agricultural operation when the lessee is not utilizing the state lands for grazing purposes; the importance of the state grazing lands to be leased upon the current lessee's total annual livestock operation, and the ability of the lessee to remain economically viable without the lease; the impact of each proposed leasehold operation will have on any adjacent public grazing lands and related grazing management units; whether the current lessee has managed the conflicted parcels in accordance with a written cooperative grazing management plan which meets department standards; or, whether the current lessee has applied in writing to the director for the development and implementation of a written cooperative grazing management plan which meets department standards.[39]

In December 1995, the board used the criteria of the new statute to find Jon Marvel and IWP not qualified as applicants for the expiring 1995 leases. Again, IWP sued.

Claims, Counterclaims, and Key Issues

The litigation is shaped by Idaho's narrow view of who has standing to inquire about the trustee's compliance with his fiduciary obligations. Beyond that, these disputes boil down to three fundamental issues: (1) landholding patterns—and the relationship with the BLM and Forest Service—as a factor in defining SLB discretion; (2) the predictability of the rules of procedure under which the SLB operates; (3) the tension between the board's discretion and the appearance of a captured agency in determining what constitutes prudence and long-term benefit.

Arizona

In Arizona there are no disappointed or rejected bidders—just the Center for Law in the Public Interest suing to raise fundamental questions about the state's conduct of grazing leasing. This is the same group that successfully sued to force the trustee to pursue the beneficiaries' interests more aggressively in the context of minerals management.[40]

Arizona had a rocky road to admissions, and finally joined the Union under the same enabling act as New Mexico, passed in 1910. By that time, Congress had turned to granting four sections of land per township and imposing intense restrictions on the sale and management of the granted lands. Arizona and New Mexico thus provide the two unequivocal examples of a trust and a full panoply of public auction, advertising, and similar procedural requirements imposed by the Congress in the enabling act. Therefore, one might predict that if ever the strict obligations of the trust and the specific procedural requirements for leasing and/ or disposing of trust assets at public auction were going to be in evidence, it would be in these two states. Because the issues are not as fully developed as in Idaho, it may be premature to draw conclusions, but preliminary indications are not precisely what one might anticipate.

The granted lands are treated in six lengthy sections of the Arizona–New Mexico enabling act. Section 10 of the act specifically declares that the lands granted to the state were to be held in trust, and declares that it is the duty of the attorney general of the United States to enforce in court the provisions relation to the lands. As in Idaho, the previously reserved lands are granted and sections 16 and 36 are granted, and sections 2 and 32 are added. Mineral lands are excluded from the grants. By the time of the Arizona–New Mexico accession, federal land reservations were recognized as extensive and permanent: Arizona was therefore granted the appropriate portion of the receipts from the state sections within forest reservations until in lieu lands could be selected.

Thus, while there are many scattered sections throughout portions of the state, many of Arizona's holdings were blocked during the in lieu selection process.

Arizona presently holds and manages 88 percent of the total lands granted at statehood, a higher percentage than any other state, including Alaska. Alaska holds considerably more land, 86 million acres as opposed to Arizona's 9.47 million acres, but only 82 percent of the original grant. By far the most important use of Arizona's trust lands is grazing, with more than 8.4 million acres of the state's holdings leased for that purpose. However, the grazing program is not a big moneymaker for Arizona, which gains most of its revenues from its commercial lands leasing program.[41]

Unlike in many other states, including New Mexico, Congress has amended Arizona's enabling act frequently and extensively. Because one of those amendments plays a key part in the dispute, I shall address it below the context of discussing the litigation. Also unlike New Mexico, Arizona's state constitution contains many specific requirements regarding management of the trust lands. The state courts have been quite specific that the enabling act and the Arizona Constitution are separate sets of guidance regarding the management of the trust.[42] Compliance with the enabling act is not necessarily compliance with the state constitution.

Among the state's constitutional provisions was the establishment of an administrative structure for managing the grants. Arizona has a land commissioner appointed by the governor. Arizona also has a land board but it meets only to hear appeals of land office decisions and does not have any other powers.

The Arizona State Land Office is funded not from revenues but from a direct annual appropriation approved by the legislature. Although that is unique (most states rely on a percentage of receipts as either a floor or a ceiling for expenditures and only a few require legislative approval of expenditure of those receipts), disbursement of Arizona's receipts to beneficiaries is fairly straightforward; renewable resource receipts, such as grazing, are distributed directly to the beneficiary, while royalties for nonrenewable resource disposition are placed in the permanent fund. Interestingly, in Arizona timber is treated as a nonrenewable resource for these purposes, as is water.

Chronology of Events

Arizona's case is peculiar in the context of the other states discussed here; it does not center on an effort by environmentalists to bid on leases presently held by ranchers, at least not directly at the present time. Mercifully, after the complex web of litigation and administrative and legislative actions that characterize the Idaho situation, the Arizona dispute is confined to one rather straightforward lawsuit.

In April 1995, the Arizona Center for Law in the Public Interest filed a complaint about the way the state's grazing lands are leased. The center argued that leasing policies violate both the state constitution and the trust obligation to achieve a high return for the resources. Contrary to what one might expect based on Idaho's narrow definition of standing, the center had no trouble gaining standing to bring the case. Acting as attorney for two individuals who are both taxpayers and parents of children attending public schools in Arizona, the plaintiffs were granted standing because they are taxpayers. Oral argument on the Defendant's Motion to Dismiss was heard in July, and in September 1995, Judge Michael Dann granted only part of that motion.

Claims, Counterclaims, and Key Issues

The plaintiff's arguments are, again mercifully, simple and uncomplicated by tedious integration with fine points of state administrative procedures law. The court had no difficulty in resolving the plaintiff's constitutional claims. The center argued that granting grazing leases without advertising and public auction violates section 28 of the Arizona Enabling Act of 1910.[43] A careful reading of the enabling act reveals that grazing leases of less than five years were exempted from the statute's stringent public auction requirements. But Arizona's grazing leases are typically for ten years.

However, in 1936, Arizona's constitution was amended. The amendment increased the term of permitted leases from five to ten years and directed that lease sales take place "in a manner as the State Legislature may direct"[44] for the previous advertising requirements. The pleadings are filled with fine-grained readings of reports, letters, and the usual grist for such mills. The plaintiff's pleadings are not without weighty words to support their interpretation, but the court was clear, at least in the opening barrage: the constitution does not require advertising and public auction of grazing leases of less than five years in duration.

The more interesting issue is the second one raised by plaintiffs. After a review of the Idaho conflict, the core of the matter ought to be familiar; the plaintiffs alleged that numerous leasing practices clearly violate the obligations of the trustee, even if they do not violate the detailed rules of the enabling act and constitution. Trust law is violated, plaintiffs assert, when the department's rules confer a preferred right of renewal on existing lessees of trust lands because it precludes competitive bidding to achieve fair market value, and because it effectively awards a lease for longer than ten years; the department's rule/policy of offering "open" or unleased land within an established ranch unit first to the owner or person controlling the ranch also constitutes a breach of the trust. Finally, offering a lease first to people owning land contiguous to the state trust parcel is a violation of the trust. All these policies limit the market for state leases and therefore are likely to reduce the amount of return to the trust.

In support of the alleged violations of the trust obligations, the center introduced an array of data designed to demonstrate that Arizona is not meeting its obligation to make the trust productive. "Arizona has the distinction of having the lowest grazing lease rates in the Western United States," charged the plaintiffs. "Grazing fees in Arizona are 72 percent lower than average lease rates on comparable private land."[45]

The court grouped the plaintiffs' complaints about the overall practices of the State Land Office into a slightly different bundle than they actually presented. It summarized their position as follows:

plaintiffs allege and argue that a combination of local practices result in a system of grazing leases on trust land that fails to maximize return for Arizona's schools. Namely plaintiffs point to the following practices, among others:

1.   The granting and administering of a number of "preferred rights" . . . to those holding or seeking grazing leases.
2.   The failure of the trust to benefit from a practice of lucrative subleasing of public lands.
3.   The absence of advertised public auctions.

According to plaintiffs, these practices artificially depress trust income to the point that:

1.   Arizona's grazing lease rates are the lowest in the United States . . . [and] are 72 percent lower than rates on comparable private land; . . .
2.   The 9 million acres of trust land leased for grazing generates less than 25 cents per acre for schools; . . .[46]

"These allegations," the court concluded, "if proven, may entitle plaintiffs to relief. That is enough to require a denial of the Motion to Dismiss."[47] Presently pending in Arizona is a trial to determine the effect of leasing practices on the income to the trust.

The Consistent Issues

One of the interesting things about these cases is the extent to which, in the name of environmental protection, environmental advocates have embraced maximum economic return as the sine qua non of trust land management. If there is a higher bidder than the traditional, existing grazing lessee, the environmental groups are arguing, the trust mandate obliges the trustee to embrace top short-term dollar. However, the trustee is not concerned only about short-term financial returns. The trustee must also act to protect the long-term productive capacity of the trust. And the trustee cannot embrace a 30¢ or a $30 advantage in an auction when doing so will, or will likely, increase management costs. Thus it is important to underscore the myriad conflicts that result when a trustee is called upon to evince prudence.

Landholding Patterns and Prudence

Persistent problems for the trustee arise from the arrangement of the landscape and the parcels, and the patterns of ownership that exist between and among Forest Service, BLM, state, private, and lessee holdings. In Idaho, for example, the originally contested parcel is one of three state sections in a huge pasture of more than 20,000 acres. The land is part of a grazing allotment plan developed by the BLM in cooperation with the state and the BLM permittee who is also the state lessee. Part of the process of bidding on a lease in Idaho is for the potential lessee to present a notarized statement certifying that the lessee will comply with the established BLM grazing plans operative on the parcel. This arrangement clearly limits the market to those interested in grazing. It does not allow the state to act as independently regarding trust resources as one might wish. However, it reflects long-standing realities in the market for such land, and arguably reduces management costs on parcels that are not likely to generate much income for the trust under any circumstances. In areas where the BLM is the dominant owner/manager, the BLM will likely define the use of interspersed state parcels.

Landholding patterns produce even greater problems for the trustee when the owner of the land surrounding the state parcel is the state lessee. Landlocked parcels complicate state efforts to locate a rival bidder and raise important questions of how someone other than the holder of the surrounding rights would protect, monitor, and access a landlocked parcel. These complications do not necessarily resolve the issue in favor of the rancher, especially when rival bidders have presented themselves. However, when bidders do not fit into the established pattern, it is not clear how much investment in administration and monitoring is prudent.

The scattered parcel issue is a subset of what I have come to call the "logical leasing unit" issue. Accustomed to leasing the lands for grazing, trustees are now obliged to define defensible parcels or collections of sections that make sense to lease as grazing units. Trustees have tended to try to define logical *grazing* units. They and/or the ranchers frequently assert that to remove a parcel, or part of one, from a unit would make the whole unit less attractive as a grazing unit and therefore lower overall gains to the trust. However, there is no reason to presume that the leasing will be for grazing. There may be parcels of such importance for conservation or recreation purposes that it is prudent to let all the grazing-based income go and develop some other aspect of the resource. The implication of this argument is that the trustee ought to design logical *leasing* units.

Prudence does appear to eliminate one permutation of this argument. Ranchers have been somewhat successful in securing statutes that state that one factor to consider in defining either leasing units or qualified bidders is the impact that removing some or all of a parcel would have on a rancher's operation. If so doing would endanger the rancher's operation and risk destabilizing the long-term stewardship required for protecting the trust sections, there may be some prudential argument in favoring a known steward. However, there is a simple answer to the essential parcel issue. When confronted in Idaho with the argument that a particular isolated parcel was absolutely essential to the rancher's operation, both for water and for access, the plaintiff's attorney suggested that perhaps the defendant ought to have bid on it.[48]

The courts have been fairly clear, in numerous jurisdictions over many decades, that prudence does not include subsidizing ranching or farming communities, nor does it extend to forgoing a short-term advantage in order to maintain a stable economic environment for trust land leasing.[49] Whether those clear general rules apply to scattered sections, or what kind of guidance they give in the trust grant landscape, is less clear.

Lease Terms, Sale Design, and Prudence

Important sale terms include the bidder qualifications, the nature of the sale itself (all the normal issues of sealed versus oral bids operate here), the right of the existing lessee to match the high bid, and the policy regarding disposition of improvements. It is normal and appropriate for the lessor to establish minimum criteria for bidders, simply to assure that the bidder can make the payments promised and proceed without harming the resource. Traditional bidder qualifications have focused on proven capacity to ranch or farm. These qualifications may limit the market when bidders do not want to ranch. A similar issue arises with improvements. Bidders who do not intend to raise cattle may not want to buy improvements installed on the assumption that the land will be used for cattle.

Administrative Law

Our generation of resource analysts has grown up with the notion—much of it attributable to the 1970 National Environmental Policy Act—that changes in outcome can be achieved through changes in process. Much of the material associated with the cases discussed above is relatively uninteresting, bordering on impenetrable, because it turns on a very fine-grained reading of state administrative law. Advocates trying to pry open the door in an established culture put great stock in changing the process, or more specifically, in imposing standard Administrative Procedures Act rules on land boards. Despite the numbing effect of their specific claims, there are two issues that deserve some attention.

First, there is a fairly consistent complaint, and some evidence, particularly in Idaho, that the rules followed by the trustees are informal, difficult to locate, different from the rules of other state administrative agencies, and, therefore, easily bent to the advantage of one traditional category of participant. It is, as was noted by the district court in Idaho, polite and arguably prudent to remind existing lessees to bid. However, at some point "simple courtesies" for the ranchers translate into an atmosphere of favoritism that imprudently limits the market for trust resources and skews the decision-making process in the direction of traditional users.

Second, is the awkwardness of the land office's two hats. The courts treat the land managers as an administrative agency, and apply principles of administrative law to its adjudication of issues, or they treat the same agency, in other contexts, as a trustee, and use trust principles in resolving very similar issues. In almost all of the issues discussed above, the issue has been framed in terms of the agency's discretion—discretion to decide what is a logical unit to lease, discretion to select the best way of marketing a lease, discretion to deny the high bidder, and so on. When the issue of discretion is on the table, judges use normal standards for review of administrative decision making. This has meant, and means increasingly, that the courts defer to agency decisions in at least two ways. First, they give the agency wide latitude to interpret law and facts. Second, they allow agency decisions to stand unless they appear arbitrary and capricious. The field varies to be sure, but it clearly favors the administrator.

Trust law puts an entirely different spin on issues of discretion. The cases look very different when a disappointed beneficiary challenges the trustee as opposed to a disappointed bidder challenging the administrator. One of the striking things in these cases is that the beneficiaries are absent, hence, the administrator rather than the trustee is on the carpet. Elsewhere we have discussed a pattern that courts generally use a different standard of review when a trustee's administrative discretion is challenged than when the beneficiary challenges the trustee citing undivided loyalty (Souder and Fairfax 1996, 33B34).

Perhaps the best way to explore this issue is in the context of the initial holding in the Arizona case; if achieving returns for the beneficiary is a trust goal, is the trustee required to demonstrate that he or she has approached or achieved that goal? Or does the absence of a specific public auction requirement allow the trustee discretion to choose programs and policies that lose money?

Implications for Accountability

The stories above directly bear on converging issues of agency accountability and capture. But they suggest, contrary to our aspirations for the trust mechanism, that grazing programs on state trust lands are as clearly dominated by the lessees as they are on federal lands. Thus, they raise important questions about grazing reform. Is the emerging consensus regarding a market in grazing access doomed to failure? It may be so; as noted at the outset, even the most ardent advocates of markets, efficiency, an end to subsidies, and a smaller role for federal government weaken when those principles threaten their own constituents and privileges. This is not news. But what of trust principles—do they have a role on the road to accountability? Can trust principles find a place in altering the direction of the capture game in grazing? These stories suggest four points about the trust concept and how it operates in the present context.

The first major point has to do with the incremental nature of reform in general and in the context of the trusts in particular. For much of the history of trust lands management, the state trusts were managed pretty much like the federal lands, that is, without regard to their trust status, and characterized by a close and mutually supportive relationship between the lessees and the managers. Following *Lassen*,[50] *Ebke*,[51] and similar cases emphasizing the trust mandate and the trustee's obligations to the beneficiary, trust principles have become the central guiding principle of trust land management. O'Toole (1995, 2) has asserted that "state reform is no faster than the slackwater behind a Bureau of Reclamation dam." I disagree, pointing to those and similar cases, and argue that in the state trust lands field, the opposite appears to be true; a few well-placed beneficiary originated law suits have radically and quite rapidly altered the priorities and the outcomes in state trust land offices.

So what happened here? Are we, in these four grazing cases, looking at a slackwater? In part, I believe the answer is yes—although I would

be more inclined to call it "incrementalism." This chapter looks at four
deviant cases, each in a different state of pendency and issue development. It is important to underscore that these cases are not the norm in
trust land management. Not all grazing programs are run to the total satisfaction of economists, beneficiaries, lessees, or environmentalists in all
jurisdictions, but other trust land managers have been able to establish
appraisal and leasing systems that do not flounder on the no-brainer issue of permitting rival bidders to participate in competitive auctions. The
trust principles and associated enforcement mechanisms work in many
jurisdictions and in many resource areas, including grazing.

These cases suggest that enforcement takes time. It may be necessary
to establish trust principles as controlling in each resource area in each
state. Arizona will not believe an Oklahoma court; parties must hear the
trust principles defined as applicable in Arizona by an Arizona court.
Given the diversity of founding documents and current statutory language—both regarding the trust and state administrative law, this makes
excellent sense. It also appears necessary to establish trust principles in
each resource culture within each state; ranchers in Arizona will not believe that principles adumbrated by an Arizona court regarding minerals
development are applicable to grazing.

One way to interpret these grazing disputes is in terms of the place
of each state's grazing program on some trajectory toward trust-oriented
reform. The characteristic response to a beneficiary challenge—as, for
example experienced in Nebraska or Oklahoma—is an almost literally
overnight turnaround in the policies, fee structure, and conduct of the
leasing program.[52] In Arizona, the same litigants who earlier brought trust
principles to state minerals management[53] are now seeking reform in
grazing, a tougher culture to be sure. In Idaho, there has still not been a
major trust land case that writes the trust notion indelibly on the mast-
head. Perhaps the present grazing dispute will ripen into such a suit.

Moreover, the issues have not come close to the appropriate forum as
of this writing. A statewide elected public official has made a preliminary decision, but it has been challenged by environmentalists; thus no
final decision has been made. In Idaho, the trust-ness of the grazing program again contrasts with the way the more valuable timber resources
are managed. And, because of its rather draconian rules regarding standing, the trust in Idaho has always been problematic. One could argue that
the trust is weakest in Idaho where the enforcement mechanisms of the
trust have been severely impoverished by the narrow definition of standing. Because of the incremental nature of reform and the diversity of the
states, it would be wrong, at the very least premature, to conclude from
these cases that trust accountability mechanisms are not effective against

capture. A more accurate observation would be that trust principles are at work and the outcome is not yet clear.

This suggests a second point, that trust principles will be most effective if there is some money on the table. The trust enforcement opportunity is not without cost. The trust mandate is enforceable in a particular context and forum. And enforcing it can be tedious process. Land commissioners are not free to impose their view of trust law on a legislature headed in a different direction. They must wait for litigants to sue and for the courts to vindicate trust principles. It is notable that the beneficiaries are not up in arms about rancher subsidies in the present situation.

Perhaps they are less concerned than the facial issues might suggest because the programs in question are not a big moneymaker for the trust—indeed two of the four states lose money on the grazing program. Beneficiaries frequently exist in the same political climate as legislators and, occasionally, trustees. We cannot, therefore, count on beneficiaries to vindicate trust principles if there is little for them to gain therefrom. One might conclude that Idaho, with its tight restrictions on standing to sue to protect the trust, risks underenforcement of trust principles. A better inference might be the contrary; if there is very little money at stake, it is not worth having the dispute in the first place.

Third, it is important to consider whether grazing is not the extreme hard case of any proposal for reform—again, both in general and in the specific context of the trust. Grazing appears, looking back over a century of public lands policy, as an unusually fractious and emotional arena. Ranching frequently appears at the tip of Sagebrush Rebellion–type icebergs. This is only in part because other commodity interests are quite happy to exploit the positive public image of the cowboy to press their advantage for less attractive exploitations, such as mining and clearcutting. Ranching seems more deeply tied to owner operators than other commodity industries, more deeply tied therefore to communities and families, connections that are heightened by the admixed landholding patterns and title arrangements that characterize the leasing. The culture of the range livestock community is, therefore, rather difficult to regulate. Ranchers have a long and successful history of "legalizing the illegal,"[54] and very little in their experience with government landlords teaches that there is any kind of advantage to them in complying promptly with many rules and regulations. To the contrary, much experience suggests that flouting authoritative orders is likely to result in the order being reversed or ignored.

These rancher expectations are mirrored in the expectations of federal range managers. They have long recognized that there is little in it for them to assert federal priorities on public lands. Where the expectations evolved in federal grazing programs—among both ranchers and managers—dominate, it is difficult for state managers to make a big dent very fast. It is no coincidence that the examples of rapid turnarounds in state grazing programs are in Nebraska, Oklahoma, and less federally dominated states. And it is not unexpected that the best predictor of a rancher-oriented state grazing program is the degree of ownership of federal land in the state.[55]

The state trustee is better positioned than federal managers to deal with these contentious matters. These four stories suggest, at the very least, that there are norms and forums to which those seeking redress can turn. However, grazing is the hard case for the trust manager as well as for the federal land manager. The lynchpin of trust land enforcement is the beneficiary; sensing that their interests are not being served, their assets diluted, beneficiaries are fully empowered and demonstrably capable of turning the tables. However, there is almost no incentive for a beneficiary to get involved. In these cases, we see environmental groups standing in for beneficiary groups. The political costs and expense of pursuing the subsidies to ranchers are not likely to be recouped by beneficiaries, many of whom are part of the same political culture as the ranchers. Evidence from around the West suggests that if there is significant money on the table, beneficiaries will take risks and fight for adequate returns to the trust.

Finally, it is important to reiterate that the trusts are, in general, established in state constitutions. It is very important not to confuse the effects of trust principles with the impacts of constitutional status. And, therefore, it is important not to advocate trust mechanisms when what is desired is something that is more or less immune from legislative manipulation. The trusts are not legislature-proof, at least in the first instance as we have seen, but they are more so than pronouncements that come in the form of normal legislative action. No trust principles that were imposed by legislative action would enjoy that status. I have been disappointed in our previous work by our inability to draw clear lines between particular institutional arrangements and observed policy outcomes. Economists are likely to embrace, in theory, the importance of tying expenditures to agency earnings. I, as a political scientist, am perhaps more inclined to argue for the importance of elected as opposed to appointed land commissioners. No data that we have analyzed clearly support either set of connections. In lieu of those absent connections, I point merely to the fact that for many understandings of the term, basic state trust land policy is durable and less amenable to self-subsidy by managers and agency capture by lessees because it is beyond the reach of the legislature.

These cases indicate that the trust notion is not a silver bullet. They demonstrate beyond debate that the trust exists in the same political climate that surrounds federal land management. However, it is also striking that the culture of the trust is coming incrementally to the state trust lands. It is well established in many jurisdictions and in many resource fields. It is less well established in other areas, and least of all in grazing programs in states dominated by federal grazing programs. It is not clear how the disputes described above will turn out. Can trust principles turn around grazing programs? It is probably more fruitful to ask how much, where, under what circumstances, and in what ways, than to look for yes or no answers. From observing the process we can learn much about reform in the particularly resistant field of grazing.

Notes

1. Note also that Baden (1995) has recently suggested that national parks in general could benefit from a trust management and Hess (1993) concludes a book on Rocky Mountain National Park with a call for a trust to manage the area.

2. To suggest the nature of the problem, in the Pacific Northwest, counties and state governments in Washington and Oregon *combined* employ 541 professionals in their timber programs; the Bureau of Land Management employs 222; and the Forest Service employs 2,330 (GAO 1996).

3. Best described in the public lands field by Culhane (1981, 27–29).

4. *Multiple Use and Sustained Yield Act of 1960*, 16 U.S.C. § 531.

5. See Gates (1968, 805–6). Additional data compiled from Western States Land Commissioners 1988–89 annual volume is on file with the author. Recall that the National Park Service is responsible for about 85 million acres, the U.S. Fish and Wildlife Service for about 100 million acres, and the U.S. Forest Service for about 180 million acres.

6. *Multiple Use and Sustained Yield Act of 1960*, 16 U.S.C. §§ 528–31; National Forest Management Act, 16 U.S.C. §§ 1600–47; Federal Land Policy and Management Act of 1976, 43 U.S.C. §§ 1701–84.

7. *Restatement (Second) of Trusts*, §§ 170–83 (1959).

8. In fact, the trustee can tolerate uncompensated use if it does not impose costs on the beneficiary. Private trusts routinely make charitable donations when they have reason to believe that the status of the trust will be enhanced by the good community relations that putatively accrue to such donations.

9. *Restatement (Second) of Trusts*, §§ 172, 173, 179.1–.2 (1959).

10. Or others with an identifiable interest (*Restatement (Second) Trusts,* § 172). One of the major distinctions observable in the stories below is the rigid definition of "identifiable interest" adopted in Idaho as compared with the other states. Compare with the situation in Arizona. Most recently, see Plaintiffs' Brief in Opposition to Motion for Summary Judgment at 26–47, *Selkirk-Priest Basin*

Association, Inc. v. Idaho, 1st Dist., Idaho, Bonner Co., No. CV-92-0037, 9 October 1992.

11. The trust purposes can also be changed or the trust terminated if the purpose for which the trust was established is no longer reasonable. Change in trust purposes can be sought under the cy pres doctrine of charitable trusts. See Fairfax, Souder, and Goldenmann (1992, 875–77) and references therein.

12. Stan Hamilton, director, Idaho State Board of Land Commissioners, interview by author, 18 March 1996, Boise.

13. A considerable portion of the original granted lands chiefly valuable for agriculture were sold during the early 1970s.

14. At the time of its creation it was called the State Board of Land Commissioners. It has since come to be known as the State Land Board (SLB) in many public documents.

15. Idaho Constitution, art. 9, sec. 8, discussed in Souder and Fairfax (1996, n78). Since the permanent school fund that constitutes the corpus of the trust has always been perpetual, it is not clear that this language change has much meaning other than to underscore long-standing obligations of the trustee to protect the long-term productivity of the trust. In an interview by the author on 18 March 1996 in Boise, Stephanie Balzarini, attorney for the state in the Idaho case, stated she believes nonetheless that Idaho constitution's emphasis on long-term returns is both unique and a grant of special discretion to choose against short-term or maximum profits.

16. Stan Hamilton, Jay Bilideau (deputy director, State Land Board), and Stephanie Balzarini, interviewed by author, 18 March 1996, Boise.

17. Idaho Code § 58-310.

18. *Selkirk-Priest Basin Association, Inc. v. State of Idaho*, 95.11 ISCR 431 (1995) (rehearing requested) (Lower Green Bonnet case) discussed in *IWP v. State Board of Land Commissioners*, No. 21774 (Idaho Supreme Court, 16 August 1995), Respondent State of Idaho's Brief at 22–23.

19. IWP's purpose in leasing these lands is the protection and restoration of the watersheds and riparian areas for their intrinsic educational values as well as for the benefit of Idaho's wildlife," Appellant's Opening Brief, *IWP v. State Board of Land Commissioners*, No. 21774 (Idaho Supreme Court, July 1995) at 2.

20. State Board of Land Commissioners Minutes of 21 December 1993 meeting at 4.

21. Plaintiff/Appellant's Opening Brief, *IWP v. State Board of Land Commissioners*, No. CV-94-1171, District Court, 5th District, County of Blaine, 19 May 1994, at 5, citing Document 13.a, p. 173.

22. See State Land Board Minutes of 8 February 1994 meeting at 2ff.

23. Memorandum, Decision at 3–4, *IWP v. State Board of Land Commissioners*, CV-94-1171, 25 October 1994.

24. Debra Kronenberg, attorney for plaintiff IWP, interview by the author, 19 March 1996.

25. State Land Board Minutes of 8 February 1994 meeting at 6. Cited in State Board of Land Commissioners Opening Brief, *IWP v. State Board of Land Commissioners*, CV-94-1171, at 9.

26. In all three cases, IWP opened, the existing lessees bid once, IWP responded, and the auction was over (per author's interview of Debra Kronenberg, attorney for IWP, 19 March 1996, in Boise). See also State Land Board Minutes of meetings on 31 March and 4 April 1995.

27. State Land Board Minutes of 14 February 1995 meeting at 6.

28. State Land Board Minutes of 26 January 1995 meeting at 9.

29. State Land Board Minutes of 11 April 1995 meeting at 6.

30. State Land Board Minutes of 13 June 1995 meeting at 9.

31. Opening Brief in Support of Petition for Judicial Review, *Committee for Idaho's High Desert v. State Board of Land Commissioners*, No. CV-OC-9502027D, District Court of Fourth Judicial District of the State of Idaho, County of Ada, 14 August 1995, at 2–13.

32. Opening Brief in Support of Petition for Judicial Review at 2–13; see also Memorandum Decision at 1–2, *Committee for Idaho's High Desert v. State Board of Land Commissioners*, No. CV-OC-9502027D, 14 December 1995.

33. Opening Brief in Support of Petition for Judicial Review at 16ff, *Committee for Idaho's High Desert v. State Board of Land Commissioners*, No. CV-OC-9502027D, 14 December 1995.

34. State of Idaho's Reply at 16–20, *Committee for Idaho's High Desert v. State Board of Land Commissioners*, No. CV-OC-9502027D, 21 September 1995.

35. Memorandum of Decision at 7–9, *Committee for Idaho's High Desert v. State Board of Land Commissioners*, No. CV-OC-9502027D, 14 December 1995.

36. Memorandum of Decision at 7–9, *Committee for Idaho's High Desert v. State Board of Land Commissioners*, No. CV-OC-9502027D, 14 December 1995.

37. Complaint at 3, *Idaho Watersheds Project v. State Board of Land Commissioners*, (IWP II) No. CV-9600088D, 8 January 1996.

38. Idaho Code § 58-310b (2) a, b.

39. Idaho Code § 58-310b (6). It is not even necessary according to the new qualifications to be in compliance with a written plan, merely to have "applied in writing" for the development of one.

40. *ASARCO v. Kadish*, 490 U.S. 650 (1989).

41. The Central Arizona Project land exchanges put the State Land Office in possession of enormous acreage of developable urban lands in and around Phoenix and, accordingly, the largest state trust land commercial real estate development program.

42. *Deer Valley Unified School District v. Superior Court*, 760 P.2d 537 (Arizona 1988) at 538–39.

43. Decision at 1, *Jeffries v. Hassell*, CV-95-06303 (Maricopa County Superior Court, 1 September 1995). See also Complaint at 2–3.

44. *Act of June 5, 1936*, Ch. 517, 49 Stat. 1477.

45. Plaintiff's Response to Motion to Dismiss and Plaintiff's Motion for Partial Summary Judgment (Oral Argument Requested) at 2, *Jeffries v. Hassell*, CV-95-06303, 30 May 1995.

46. Decision at 10, *Jeffries v. Hassell*, CV-95-06303, 1 September 1995.

47. Decision at 10, *Jeffries v. Hassell*, CV-95-06303, 1 September 1995.

48. Debra Kronenberg, interview by author, 19 March 1996, Boise. All these

arguments about the essential nature of a particular parcel appear to have this same hole in the middle.

49. The issue was squarely raised in Ebke (Nebraska), Skamania (Washington), and Nigh (Oklahoma), and longtime cozy relationships between state legislatures and trust lessees were disallowed. What complicates the issue here is the explicit invocation of the landholding patterns.

50. *Lassen v. Arizona Highway Department*, 385 U.S. 458 (1966).

51. *Ebke v. Board of Education Lands and Funds*, 47 N.W. 2d 520 (Neb. 1951).

52. Discussed extensively in Souder and Fairfax (1996, 279 ff).

53. *ASARCO v. Kadish*, 490 U.S. 650 (1989).

54. This pattern, a mainstay of many classes over the years, refers to the ability of many interest groups from squatters to the present, to successfully reverse previously stated federal policy toward the public domain.

55. See Souder and Fairfax (1996, ch. 5).

References

Baden, John. 1995. Endowment Boards for the Parks. *Different Drummer* (Summer): 43.

Culhane, Paul. 1981. *Public Lands Politics*. Baltimore: Resources for the Future and Johns Hopkins University Press.

Fairfax, Sally, J. Souder, and G. Goldenmann. 1992. The School Trust Lands: A Fresh Look at Conventional Wisdom. *Environmental Law* 22(797): 847–50.

GAO. 1996. *Public Timber: Federal and State Programs Differ Significantly in Pacific Northwest*. Report to the chairman, Committee on Resources, House of Representatives. GAO/RCED-96-108.

Gates, Paul. 1968. *History of Public Land Law Development*. Washington, DC: U.S. Government Printing Office.

Gruber, Judith E. 1987. *Controlling Bureaucracies: Dilemmas in Democratic Governance*. Berkeley: University of California Press.

Hess, Karl. 1993. *Rocky Times in Rocky Mountain National Park: An Unnatural History*. Boulder: University Press of Colorado.

Mansfield, M. 1878. Educational Land Policy of the United States: Land Grants for Educational Purposes within the State of Ohio. *Barnard American Journal of Education* 28(59).

O'Toole, Randal. 1995. Why State Lands? *Different Drummer* (Summer): 2.

Patric, William C. 1981. *Trust Land Administration in the Western States*. Denver: Public Lands Institute.

Pratt, John W., and Richard J. Zeckhauser, eds. 1985. *Principals and Agents: The Structure of Business*. Cambridge: Harvard Business School.

Souder, Jon A., and Sally K. Fairfax. 1996. *State Trust Lands: History, Management, and Use.* Lawrence: University Press of Kansas.

Souder, Jon A., Sally K. Fairfax, and L. Ruth. 1994. Sustainable Resources Management and State School Lands: The Quest for Guiding Principles. *Natural Resources Journal* 34(271): 272–304.

Thorpe, F. W. 1909. *The Federal and State Constitutions, Colonial Charters, and Other Organic Laws of the States, Territories, and Colonies Now or Heretofore Forming the United States of America.* 7 vols. Compiled and edited under the Act of Congress, 30 June 1906. Washington, DC: U.S. Government Printing Office.

Wald, Johanna, and Karl Hess. 1995. Grazing Reform: Here's the Answer. *High Country News*, October 2.

Chapter 4

Federalism and Wildlife Conservation in the West

Dean Lueck and Jonathan Yoder

Recent changes in American politics have brought into question the desirability of federal government involvement in programs ranging from education to welfare. The role of the federal government in environmental protection has also come into question because problems of environmental quality are often perceived as local or regional issues best handled by states or other smaller, nonfederal units of government. This general political philosophy—decentralizing government authority as much as possible—has come to be known as "federalism." In this chapter we study wildlife conservation policy to determine the extent to which federalism is a guide to understanding the organization of government. Wildlife policy is a useful topic for an empirical study because most of the important institutions governing wildlife have been in place for nearly a century. As a result, we can be comfortable with the assumption that we are studying equilibrium policies (Alchian 1950; Stigler 1992). For other environmental policies such as air and water pollution regulations, this assumption is less tenable because there have been major institutional changes in recent years.

The critical questions underlying wildlife policy are *who* owns the wild populations and the habitat that sustains them, and *to what degree* is ownership complete. Consider a situation in which wildlife habitat is the only valuable use of a parcel of land. The value of the land in this case would be maximized where landownership coincides with the population's territory, and the landowner would have de facto ownership of the resident wildlife stock so long as property rights to the land and its attributes are complete. In reality, of course, wildlife habitat is rarely the only valued land use, wildlife stocks often inhabit numerous landhold-ings, and rights to wildlife are poorly defined unless formal or informal contractual agreements are reached with all involved parties. If such a contract does not develop or is not maintained, open access ensues and the value of the wildlife stock is dissipated. This provides an incentive to contract over the property rights to the wildlife in order to maximize its value. On the other hand, specifying and maintaining such a contract is costly, and these costs increase as the number of involved individuals increases; mutual agreement over the specification of rights among those involved becomes more difficult.

An alternative to landowner contracting is to place the rights to a wide-ranging wildlife stock into the hands of a third party such as a reg-ulatory agency, which does not require unanimous consent to impose its policies, thereby reducing the cost of contracting. For wildlife with larger territories spanning many small government jurisdictions, the prob-lem of mutual agreement arises again, and yet a higher level of jurisdic-tion may be appropriate. But there are several problems associated with public agencies. They are composed of numerous individuals whose per-sonal well-being does not necessarily coincide with those objectives specified for the agency. This leads to the potential for principal–agent problems that may increase with the size of the agency. Also, an agency with jurisdiction over wildlife in many cases does not control the habitat on which it resides, creating a new contracting problem that does not exist without third-party involvement. And finally, with higher levels of jurisdiction comes a weaker social, political, and economic connection between the agency and the private sector it purports to represent.

To the extent that government ownership or regulation is a relevant alternative, optimal wildlife policy can be viewed as a question of federalism. Our approach parallels that of Shapiro (1996), who pro-vides a theoretical model of optimal jurisdiction over air quality based on a trade-off between welfare losses from transboundary pollution externalities under small jurisdictions and welfare losses from uniform policy prescriptions over heterogeneous populations under more central-ized jurisdiction.[1] As we shall illustrate throughout this chap-ter, the level of organization and jurisdiction over wildlife has varied widely across species, between political jurisdictions, and over time, in response to the diversity in land characteristics and ownership patterns.

Interestingly, the problem of wildlife conservation is analogous to the problem of petroleum conservation. Wildlife populations, like an oil and gas reservoir, occupy territory that usually does not coincide with sur-face land tenure boundaries. As a result, both wildlife and oil can be overexploited unless the landowners—with or without the involvement of a third party such as a government agency—can successfully contract for the ownership of the wildlife or oil stocks. As a result of the oil rushes in the early part of this century and the huge waste of reserves that accompanied them, oil conservation institutions have matured much further than the institutions associated with wildlife today. The similarity between these two otherwise very different natural assets will be examined occasionally through the course of this chapter, in hope that it will provide some insight into the future of wildlife ownership and conservation (Craft 1995; Lueck and Schenewerk 1996).

To examine the structure of wildlife ownership within a federal system, we will begin by developing a model to examine the costs of contracting for wildlife ownership among a group of landowners who jointly provide habitat for a game population. The model shows that a separate wildlife agency can often reduce contracting costs, but that inefficiencies inherent in bureaucratic institutions will limit the effectiveness of the agency. We will also apply the model to such issues as the existence of public landowners and the problem of protecting endangered species. We then apply our model to evidence from the United States, with a focus on the seventeen western states.

Economics and Wildlife Ownership

The mix of institutions—laws, private rights, contracts, and customs—that govern wildlife differs among regions, across species, and over time. In this section we develop a contracting model to illuminate the ownership and regulatory issues involved in wildlife management.

Private Landowner Contracting
for Ownership

To examine landowner incentives for wildlife use and conservation, we extend a model developed by Lueck (1991, 1995a). First, assume that a homogeneous tract of land has two potentially valuable uses, ranching and wildlife. Also assume that the stock of wildlife is composed of homogeneous units (individual animals) and, for now, there is no public good characteristic to wildlife. For ranching, the optimal size of the land tract in acres is S_R. If ranching is the only valuable use of the land (i.e., there is no indigenous wildlife population or the wildlife stock is neither valuable nor costly), then the pattern of landownership and livestock production depends on the relative value, net of property rights enforcement costs, of the various types of ranching. Thus, where there is no wildlife population, the optimal plot size (S^*) depends only on the value of land in ranching and equals S_R.

Adding a valuable wildlife stock to the land, such as an elk herd, creates a different situation. Assume that the wildlife stock's optimal territory size (S_w) is not influenced by ranching, but the wildlife coexists with the livestock. In general, S_w can be greater or less than S_R. If elk require 10,000 acres and the optimal plot size for ranching is at least 10,000 acres, then the ranch owner would de facto own the elk population if the ranch and the territory of the herd exactly coincide. If the optimal ranch size is only 1,000 acres, then the landowner's (or another agent's) ability to own the "elk management rights" will depend on the cost of transacting and enforcing an agreement among ten 1,000-acre ranchers. These contracting costs among landowners may eliminate the potential gains they could acquire from jointly specifying their rights to the wildlife.

Given a discrepancy between the wildlife's territory size and the optimal size of landholdings for ranching, the willingness of landowners to establish rights to wildlife on their property depends on the costs and benefits of doing so. On a per-acre basis, assume that ranching is a more highly valued use of land (V_R) than is elk (V_w). These values consist of two elements: the value *per unit* of livestock or elk, and the total net productivity of a plot of land, which would likely be different for livestock and elk. A landowner's net value of a wildlife stock is $W^P = V_w - C^P(S_R, S_w)$ where C^P is a simple landowner contracting cost function that depends on wildlife territory and optimal ranch size. We assume that C^P decreases as the optimal size of a livestock ranch (S_R) increases and as the optimal wildlife territory (S_w) decreases. This is because, for a given wildlife territory size, as S_R increases there are fewer ranchers with whom to contract and for a given optimal ranch size, as the wildlife territory decreases there are fewer ranchers with whom to contract.

So far there are two possible outcomes: one in which a contract for joint ownership of the wildlife stock is agreed upon, and one in which no contract is agreed upon. When the gains from owning wildlife are overwhelmed by the costs of contracting among landowners, no wildlife is actively produced, implying that W^P approaches zero.[2] When the total value of the wildlife stock outweighs the contracting costs, however, landowners will seek ways to establish rights to the wildlife, implying $W^P > 0$.

From this model four predictions can be derived (Lueck 1991, 1995a). First, as the relative per unit value of wildlife increases, the greater will be the gains from transacting an agreement among landowners and the more likely it is that private rights to wildlife management will be established. Second, the more productive land is for wildlife, the greater will be the gains from an agreement among landowners and the more likely it is that private rights to wildlife management will be established. Third, as the size of landholdings increases, the resulting decrease in the costs of contracting among landowners will increase the gains from transacting an agreement among landowners and the more likely it is that rights to the wildlife stock will be established. Fourth, as the territory of the wildlife stock increases in size, the resulting increase in the contracting costs among landowners will decrease the gains from transacting an agreement and it will be less likely that rights to the wildlife stock will be established.

In oil and gas production, a group of individuals owning land overlying any single reservoir (analogous to S_w) faced the same problem under the rule of capture during the late nineteenth and early twentieth centuries. The value (V_w) of the existing reserves in most cases could be increased dramatically if the individuals were able to agree on a share-contract over joint production output, which would remove the incentive for each to race for the oil, a costly and wasteful process. The barrier to these "unitization" agreements comes in the form of contracting costs, which in the most cases in the first half of the century were apparently higher than the potential gains, leading to rampant overproduction and a low resource value, V_w (Libecap and Wiggins 1984).

Wildlife Agencies as Contractual Solutions

As the model shows, wildlife ownership will depend on wildlife value, wildlife productivity, landownership patterns, and wildlife territorial requirements. When $W^P < 0$, then private landowners will not contract with each other to establish ownership of the wild stock. This might result even when V_w is high if the costs of contracting are large enough. An alternative organization, however, might be able to enforce rights to the stock at lower costs so that some of the potential wealth can be realized. Let $C^G < C^P(S_w, S_R)$ be the total costs of a third-party "game manager" establishing and enforcing rights to the stock. Since these costs do not depend directly on the relationship between wildlife territories and optimal plot size as they do with private landowners, it is possible that an outside party (a nonlandowner) may be the most efficient owner of the rights to the stock of game.[3] In particular, a political organization such as a game department may have lower costs of enforcing rights to game stocks because it does not require total agreement among all landowners to take action. As a result, total contracting costs can be lower than with a private contract, and the net value of the wildlife stock can be greater than it would be under a completely private contractual arrangement.

The analogy with oil and gas continues (see Craft 1995; Lueck 1995b). Reservoirwide units are formed when a group of landowners or leasing producers overlying a common oil or gas reservoir form an agreement to manage the reservoir as a single entity. Similarly, landowner contracting for control of game can be viewed as unitization of a wildlife population. Moreover, all oil- and gas-producing states except Texas have compulsory unitization laws that require the formation of a reservoir unit, provided that a super-majority sign the agreement. The existence of this regulatory framework reduces the cost of unitization significantly and therefore increases the chances of unitization. Management and control of game populations by state agencies are similar to compulsory unitization in that state agencies intervene in private contracting. With oil unitization, however, private parties still retain ownership of the natural resource and face few restrictions on the market transfer of their production.

Although a game department in principle can capture the value of wildlife when private contracting costs are prohibitive, it has two imperfections. First, because the land is the habitat for the wildlife, a non-landowning game manager will be unable to control land uses to maximize the value of the wildlife. Agriculture and other uses of land will affect the ability of the land to support game. For instance, drainage of sloughs increases wheat production but lowers waterfowl production. The farmer owns the net agricultural benefit from drainage, but does not face the costs of the reduction in wildlife output if a third party owns the waterfowl. Thus, without an explicit agreement to compensate landowners for habitat improvement, the game department will find that landowners can impose costs on game populations, reducing their value. Recognition of this fact led the famous conservationist Aldo Leopold (1933) to suggest the landowner as the logical owner of game.[4]

The second imperfection inherent in a game department exists because the game manager as a government bureaucracy is constrained from optimal behavior by collective action and interest group forces. Because the ownership rights within a typical agency are not explicitly allocated to individual agency personnel, agency activity will not achieve a first-best solution. Further, interest groups may be able to influence agency behavior in ways that reduce the net gains from ownership of the game (Stigler 1971; Laffont and Tirole 1991). For example, it is possible that state game agencies might price hunting licenses below what a competitive market would generate in order to build constituency support, but in doing so also create excess demand and potential overexploitation of game (Davis 1995; Wenders 1995). An agency might also be particularly responsive to local landowner complaints of property damage due to wildlife while neglecting the value of wildlife to nonlandowners. In sum, the gains from a game department are in overcoming prohibitive costs of private contracting for ownership of wildlife populations that inhabit many different landholdings. At the same time, a game department will be unable to effectively control land use that affects wildlife, and it will be driven by various inefficiencies common to government bureaucracies. In terms of the model, the separation of ownership from control will reduce V_w and the bureaucratic incentives will increase C^G, especially as the government grows. As long as it is costly to enforce property rights to wildlife, this trade-off between private contracting costs and government bureaucratic incentives cannot be avoided.

There are additional costs associated specifically with agency activity that have not been addressed. When land is publicly owned and managed—as it is for much of the West—it is usually not as clear who holds the rights to the residual benefits and losses of agency activity as it is when the activity occurs within a private firm (in this case a ranch). In other words, there is not a distinct set of owners who have a clear incentive to maximize V_w. One might also expect that the strength of the contractual arrangements among agencies and landowners depends in part on the extent to which the agency is a local entity. For federal agencies, such as the Fish and Wildlife Service with staff that move around the country, the benefits (in terms of contracting cost reduction) of developing long-term contractual relationships rather than short-term relationships are lost. Similarly, agency representatives who are responsible for large geographic regions or are responsible for managing a wide spectrum of species will not be able to acquire as much place- or species-specific knowledge as would be the case with representatives from agencies with smaller jurisdictions. The fixed costs associated with setting up agencies might in fact lead to a small number of agencies with otherwise suboptimally large jurisdictions (Haddock 1997).

Wildlife Values Dominate

Consider further the case in which wildlife is the dominant value of the land, as was arguably true for territorial rights defended by many aboriginal hunting, fishing, and gathering societies (Demsetz 1967). In such societies, property rights were designed to protect valuable wild populations that required greater territories than did agriculture. In fact, for these situations, agriculture may have had no value ($V_R = 0$). This also describes many modern wildlife refuges, both private and public, where agricultural uses are nil. Another alternative is the modern case of a wildlife refuge where the owner leases out subsections of the land for agricultural purposes, a common practice on both federal wildlife refuges and private refuges. In this case the incentives for wildlife management are properly aligned but there are contracting (or leasing) costs for nonwildlife land uses (Lueck 1995a). Importantly, in this setting the contracting problem disappears because the wildlife stock and the land it inhabits are under control of a single economic unit, be it a private individual, firm, or a public agency.

In this section we extend on the basic model by considering other issues that can alter both contracting costs and wildlife value. We initially assumed that the rancher was the landowner, rather than a wildlife manager. This is likely to be the case when ranching provides the dominant value of the land and a ranching specialist has a comparative advantage relative to a wildlife manager in the joint production of livestock and wildlife. Although this case seems to be the most important contemporary situation, it is possible that wildlife values, $(V_W,)$ could dominate ranching values, (V_R) and lead to a different ownership pattern of land. For example, land devoted to a wildlife refuge on an Indian reservation[5] describes the case where the wildlife attribute of the land is dominant and the land is owned and managed by a wildlife specialist $(S^* = S^W)$, though subparcels of wildlife land can be leased for livestock use. This possibility raises the fundamental question of wildlife ownership: What is the optimal pattern of landownership when the land has numerous valued attributes that require property rights to be defined over different margins?[6]

In general, if wildlife (livestock) is the most valued attribute of the land the game manager (rancher) would be the most efficient landowner.[7] When the game manager owns the land he has the incentive to generate the maximum value of the wildlife (V_W), while the rancher generally will not be able to reach the potential value from ranching (V_R) because of the costs of leasing parcels from the landowning wildlife manager. The converse is true if the land is owned by the rancher. Alternative property rights schemes can only shift the incentives for distortionary behavior, they cannot remove them completely (Barzel 1997; Grossman and Hart 1986).

Our model applies to a setting with small agricultural plots underlying large wildlife territories, a set of ranchers and a game manager. Either the ranchers or the game manager will ultimately own the land. If the ranchers own the land, they can contract over the wildlife among themselves, or with a game manager, or not at all. If the game manager owns the land, he chooses whether or not to lease land to ranchers.

Additional Contracting Problems

In practice, the landowner contracting cost function (C^P) depends on other factors besides wildlife territory and optimal farm or ranch size.

These factors include landowner heterogeneity, the extent to which land tenure boundaries coincide with wildlife territory boundaries, the public good aspect of wildlife, herd interaction, and legal constraints including those introduced by regulatory agencies themselves.

Libecap and Wiggins (1984) suggest that contracting costs would increase with landowner heterogeneity. For example, if elk require 10,000 acres owned by only ten homogeneous ranchers, the wildlife contract is expected to be a simple equal-share agreement and the costs of contracting would be relatively low. On the other hand, if the ranches are of various sizes with many different land characteristics across landholdings, bargaining problems are more likely to prevent contract formation. In general, we expect landowner contracting costs to increase as landowner heterogeneity increases.

Another characteristic of landownership that will affect contracting costs is the extent to which property boundaries coincide with wildlife population or herd territory boundaries. Consider a herd of elk whose summer range lies in the higher forested elevations (often owned and managed by a federal agency such as the U.S. Forest Service) but whose winter habitat lies in the lower and warmer mountain valleys where private ranchers commonly raise domestic livestock and crops. A contracting problem can arise even if the landholdings of both groups are each large enough to hold the entire elk herd. If landholdings are 10,000 acres each but the herd's territory is seasonally divided so that 5,000 acres lies on public land (the summer habitat) and 5,000 lies on private land (the winter habitat), a contracting problem exists. In general, as land tenure boundaries become less coincident with wildlife territory boundaries, we expect contracting costs to increase.

Contracting costs also rise if we allow for the possibility of nonconsumptive use (e.g., wildlife viewing) or existence value of a wildlife stock. In such a case, contracting becomes costly because landowners will find it hard to collect from those who benefit from these public good characteristics (i.e., landowners will find it hard to collect that element of V^w arising from these characteristics of wildlife). In general, we expect that as the public good aspect of wildlife increases, private landowner contracting costs will increase.[8]

Additional costs can arise because of biological forces. To this point we have assumed that wildlife populations or herds are completely distinct. This may not be the case in reality; in fact it is generally maintained by wildlife biologists that population interaction is common and important in maintaining the genetic integrity of a wildlife population (Lidicker and Caldwell 1982). Such herd interaction may either increase or decrease the economic value of a particular wildlife herd, depending on the characteristics of the herd with which it is mixing. Furthermore, the greater the herd interaction, the more reasonable it is to suggest that the true boundary of a herd is in fact defined by the entire (contiguous) range of a species. Continuing with our elk example, consider two herds and twenty landowners. We would expect a contract to emerge for each of the two sets of landowners for the management of the individual herds and another contract between the two groups to specify the ownership rights to the animals flowing in either direction from one herd to another. In general we have two effects of greater interaction. Contracting costs (C^P) will increase, and the value of the stock on the land of any particular set of landowners (V^W) may increase or decrease with herd interaction depending on the relative value of the characteristics of each herd. Because both V^W and C^P can be changing in different directions and at different rates, we cannot be sure whether private contracting will be more or less likely.

Although game agencies may be able to reduce contracting costs unilaterally by setting regulations that limit private activity over wildlife, these same regulations can generate contracting problems that would not otherwise exist. For example, there is an increasing trend to form private cooperative game management units in order to jointly sell access rights to hunter groups. Such units presumably increase the value of resident wildlife by allowing hunters easier access to larger contiguous landholdings and by internalizing the effects of one landowner's management and access decisions on all other landowners in the group. However, many state game agencies pursue policies that limit this type of private management activity, thereby reducing the potential value of game on these landholdings.

The Economics of Western Wildlife Policy

The contracting model of wildlife ownership implies that the relationship between private landownership and the territorial requirements of wildlife stocks will largely determine the institutions that govern wildlife. To this point, we have directly discussed nine predictions that arise from the model:

1. As the per-unit value of wildlife increases, contractual agreements among landowners (or with an agency) over wildlife ownership become more likely.

2. As land becomes more productive for wildlife relative to other agricultural uses, contractual agreements among landowners become more likely.

3. As the size of landholdings increase, contractual agreements among landowners become more likely.

4. As the wildlife's territory increases, contractual agreements among landowners become less likely.

5. As landowner heterogeneity increases, contractual agreements among landowners become less likely.

6. As the coincidence of agricultural land boundaries with wildlife territory boundaries increases, contractual agreements among landowners become more likely.

7. As the public goods characteristic of wildlife becomes more dominant, contractual agreements among landowners become less likely.

8. As wildlife herds tend to be more geographically distinct from each other, contractual agreements among landowners become more likely.

9. Landownership is likely to be held by the party who has comparative advantage in the production of the most valued attribute.

The remainder of this chapter will extend Lueck (1989, 1991) and show that wildlife institutions within the United States reflect a structure consistent with the contracting model developed above. We focus on wildlife policy in the seventeen western states and certain aspects of wildlife contracting that are either unique to or currently changing in the West.[9]

Geographic Jurisdictions in the United States

In the United States, government agencies with large geographical jurisdictions tend to control wildlife with large territories, while private parties or local governments tend to control those with small territories. Control of migratory waterfowl such as ducks and geese lies with the federal government in cooperation with the governments of Canada (represented by the United Kingdom) and Mexico via a 1916 treaty. The federal government also has responsibility for whales and other marine mammals; many of these species are controlled by international treaty, many are migratory, and all inhabit territory that is not expressly controlled by states.

The regulation of migratory waterfowl hunting is guided by several Flyway Councils composed of agencies from the appropriate states and provinces. In their biannual migrations, North American waterfowl populations use flyways that support distinct populations, and their control roughly corresponds with this distinction. Many animals do not range across more than one state, but still require territory larger than most private landholdings. States uniformly control upland game birds such as quail and partridge, which have relatively small territories and do not migrate. Big game mammals, which include ungulates such as deer and elk as well as large predators such as bear and cougar, are ordinarily controlled by state governments. Mammals with even smaller territories, such as fox and bobcat, are usually controlled by states, but in some cases, such as with gophers, they are unprotected and thus effectively controlled by landowners.

We have not yet discussed the possibility that smaller government units, such as county agencies rather than more centralized state agencies, might provide the appropriate level of jurisdiction. Another twist to the jurisdiction question is that for each of its major game species, all state agencies break their state into various substate management units, which are sometimes smaller in acreage than are the state's counties.[10] Yet game animals in the United States are rarely managed at the county level. *Why not?* The answer may have to do in part with the prediction that as landowner or jurisdiction boundaries coincide less with wildlife territory boundaries, contracting will become more costly. With few exceptions, substate game management units have been delineated by state game departments to correspond with habitat transitions or barriers such as rivers, mountain divides, and major transportation thoroughfares, so their borders coincide closely with herd territories. County boundaries, on the other hand, not drawn for wildlife management purposes, do not emulate natural borders, and therefore do not tend to coincide with herd territories. If county governments managed wildlife whose territories often overlay one or more county lines, a vast array of (costly) interaction among counties would be necessary to manage most wildlife populations.

Furthermore, there may be economies of scale in wildlife management. To the extent that general knowledge regarding wildlife management is applicable to relatively large geographic regions, centralization may reduce the costs of research efforts and information dissemination regarding management techniques. For example, through its Animal Damage Control Program, the U.S. Department of Agriculture is actively involved in abatement of property damage caused by wildlife, an activity that often employs the use of complicated information and technology.

The Organization and Regulatory Policies of State Game Agencies

As American wildlife law developed it initially borrowed from English common law. The earliest state controls simply restricted the time of year during which it was legal to kill game (Tober 1981), and the regulations were enforced by the county or local police. Numerous court decisions bolstered the states' authority to regulate the taking and trading of wildlife when these restrictions were contested. State authority came to be known as the state ownership doctrine. The game laws developed rapidly during the late 1800s and early 1900s. Arguably because of the increasing complexity and restrictiveness of the laws, traditional enforcement mechanisms became unsatisfactory, forcing states to hire special police (game wardens) to enforce game laws. States also began to create agencies devoted to wildlife management during this period (Palmer 1912).

Today, states have the dominant regulatory authority over wildlife control and use, typically vested in a state "fish and game" or "wildlife" agency. Each of these agencies is overseen by a commission or a commissioner appointed by the state's governor, and statutory requirements often stipulate the composition of the commission. In particular, six of the seventeen western states require some minimum number of ranchers or farmers on the commission. This organizational feature supports the thesis that a game agency is a substitute for landowner contracting (Wildlife Management Institute 1987).[11]

The key components of modern game laws and regulations, administered and enforced by game departments, are prohibition or severe restrictions on game trade, restrictions on the methods by which animals can be taken, and licensing requirements for legal taking of game. The rights associated with these licenses are restricted by season closures, bag limits, and weapon requirements. Our model implies that state regulations will depend on the ability of landowners to establish rights to wildlife and on the relative value of wildlife as an attribute of the land. Because larger landholdings tend to lead to lower contracting cost, ceteris paribus, states with larger landholdings are more likely to have longer hunting seasons and less restrictive rules on bag limits and weapons since landowner control substitutes for state regulations. Also, given that states maintain regulatory authority over wildlife, states and highly valued wildlife stocks are more likely to have shorter seasons and more restrictive rules.

Returning to the oil and gas analogy, wildlife hunting regulations compare to those dealing with the spacing of wells. In order to reduce the inefficiently high levels of production that was occurring in the early 1900s under the rule of capture convention, one of the first sets of regulations to evolve was a set of limits to the number of wells that could legally be drilled for a given surface land acreage. Although well-spacing regulations do not specify on whose land the wells should be drilled, they do limit the overall rate of oil extraction, as do limits on hunting season length and the number of permits issued.

Restrictions on Hunters

Hunters can cause third-party effects by shooting other hunters, shoot-ing livestock or protected wildlife, and damaging roads or other prop-erty. To increase the value of wildlife, state hunting regulations must reduce the losses from these externalities. They do so by prohibiting hunters from using fire, explosives, or bait, destroying nests or dens, shooting from vehicles or from roads, hunting while intoxicated, and using certain weapons. The use of shotgun requirements for big game hunters and Sunday hunting prohibitions can be applied to the model as well (Lueck 1991). If the number of hunters or the local human popula-tion is large or landholdings are small (S^* is small), requiring the use of shotguns is consistent with maximizing the net value of the wildlife be-cause, compared to rifle ammunition, shotgun slugs travel considerably less distance and have less energy beyond the immediate range, thus re-ducing the chance of damage from errant shots. Also, because the value of the land can be increased by setting aside a day for uses other than hunting, prohibiting hunting on Sundays is consistent with attempts to maximize the value of land with alternative uses. There are no Sunday hunting bans in the West, but there are in some eastern states where the human population density is larger.

Intrastate Variation in Hunting Regulations

Not only do laws vary across states as predicted by the model, they also vary within states. Regulatory control is too centralized when loss-es in wildlife values (V_w) from a regulatory framework not well suited to localized contingencies outweighs the additional contracting costs (C^G) associated with further decentralization. In all states, at least some as-pects of wildlife regulation and management are disaggregated to small-er working units. This is especially true of larger western states that have considerable variation in wildlife habitat and land uses within their bor-ders. Table 4.1 provides a small sample of the wide variation in regula-tions within states.

Geographical management units are the most conspicuous examples of such variation. State regulations for season lengths and bag limits typ-ically are divided into relatively homogeneous geographic units or units delineated by physical borders such as rivers, mountain ridges, and even roads. For example, typical of Rocky Mountain and Pacific Coast states, Wyoming has 124 distinct elk hunting units and 168 deer units, across which seasons, bag limits, and other rules may vary. In contrast, the rel-atively homogeneous Great Plains states of Kansas and Nebraska have been divided into just eighteen and seventeen deer and elk management units respectively, and Texas is the only western state whose deer man-agement units coincide with county boundaries. Although we are focus-

Table 4.1
Examples of Intrastate Variation in Western Wildlife Regulation

State	Wildlife Regulation
Colorado	Private land only seasons are found for antelope, deer, and elk. Beaver trapping is more restricted on public land than on private land.
Montana	Portions of several drainages in six counties are closed to beaver/otter trapping.
New Mexico	Special regulations for hunting antelope, Barbary sheep, and elk on private land.
North Dakota	Only shotguns can be used in several small wooded valleys where population is relatively dense.
Oregon	Regulations distinguish Cascade elk population from Rocky Mountain elk population.
South Dakota	Beaver is regulated differently in eastern versus western areas of the state.
Texas	Exotic species introduced by private landowners with very large holdings are not regulated by the state wildlife department. The exception to this rule is the aoudad (Barbary sheep) inhabiting the Palo Duro Canyon. The state introduced the sheep there in 1957 and continues to regulate the population.
Washington	Regulations differ for upland birds and furbearers on either side of the Cascades.

Sources: Various state wildlife agencies; see also Musgrave and Stein (1993).

ing on elk and deer here, many states have developed distinct management units for each of the major game animals of the state. For example, management units for pheasant, turkey, and other game birds tend to be larger than do those for elk and deer. The apparent value of these management units is that they provide a basis from which to vary management and hunting regulations to suit location-specific management goals. They allow states to vary hunting season, bag limits, and specify regions for permit hunts according to the borders of the management units. In addition to the aspects of hunting regulations that vary on an annual basis such as those listed above, there are many examples of region-specific regulations applied on a more permanent basis.

The Sunday hunting and shotgun regulations also provide evidence of intrastate variation. For instance, while New York and New Jersey generally ban Sunday hunting, they allow it in areas where landowner control is greater and where alternative uses of the land are lower. Similarly, several states—Michigan, Minnesota, and North Dakota—require shotguns for hunting big game in certain regions where landholdings are smaller and the likelihood of hunting accidents and property damage is higher. There are no Sunday hunting bans in the western states, and until recently as population density has increased, there have been few shotgun requirements in the West either. This makes sense because of the relatively large landholdings and low rural density (see table 4.5). Finally, perhaps the most obvious example of intrastate variation in regulation is the ubiquitous bans on hunting in urban areas.

Legal Classification of Wildlife

State laws classify species into such categories as big game and small game, migratory and upland game birds, furbearers, predators, nongame animals, and endangered species. For most of these categories killing is restricted, but for nongame animals and predators, restrictions are few or nonexistent. Classification by state agencies is part of the process of delineating property rights among private individuals and public agencies. The model predicts that classification will depend on the net value of the wildlife and landowner contracting costs. If landholding patterns make it less costly for landowners to own rights to wildlife stocks, it is less likely the state will impose restrictions. In addition, it is more likely that a wildlife stock will be protected when its net value is high.

Coyotes, for example, are valued for their winter pelts, but they also impose costs by killing domestic sheep. The net value of the coyote population is reduced when the animals are killed during summer months when fur values are low, so the value of these stocks can be enhanced by restricting harvest to those months when fur values are highest. At the same time, damage to sheep flocks can be reduced by allowing coyotes to be killed year-round. As predicted, Lueck (1991) finds that high pelt prices increase the likelihood of state protection, but that states with valuable sheep stocks and large private landholdings are less likely to protect coyotes.

Wildlife Damage Institutions

Damage by wildlife to landowner property such as crops, livestock, and buildings creates incentives and contracting problems as well. When a wildlife stock is not confined to a single landholding, an individual landowner does not face the full costs of property loss associated with the stock, and hence will not have the incentive to undertake an optimal level of damage abatement unless he can contract with neighboring landowners. Consider again the case where land sustains both ranching and wildlife but the wildlife have no value of their own and compete with livestock for forage. If the territory required for ranching is coincident with the territory of the population causing the damage, the rancher will have the optimal incentive structure for damage abatement. On the other hand, if the offending wildlife population inhabits the territory of many ranchers, then each will tend to free-ride on the others' damage control unless they can form a contract to coordinate the activity and share associated costs and benefits.

The implications parallel those derived for the case when wildlife are considered to be a valued asset. Private damage control efforts are most likely to be present for relatively large landowners. Indeed, large private landowners have a long history of hiring hunters and trappers to reduce the stocks of undesired animals (Lueck 1989). For example, owners of large forest tracts in Washington have routinely hunted and trapped bears that damage tree seedlings. Furthermore, private cooperatives often form to deal with damage problems. The Montana Stock Growers Association, formed in 1884, coordinated efforts to control wolves and coyotes (Fischer 1995). As expected, however, the same private contracting difficulties present for valued wildlife are common for undesirable wildlife. Since private landholdings are often small and scattered compared to the large territorial requirements of damaging wild populations, government agencies are predicted to emerge to coordinate efforts to reduce wildlife damage. Indeed, animal damage control programs have been a part of game departments since their inception (Lund 1980; Musgrave and Stein 1993). These programs have included bounties for undesired animals, hired hunters, and compensation of individuals for documented losses from wildlife damage. This public involvement occurs despite the fact that neither the federal government nor the states have been found liable by the courts for property damage by wildlife over which they hold jurisdiction, unless specific statutes impose liability (Favre 1983).

Regulating the Game Trade

Important and common components of wildlife institutions are restrictions and prohibitions on market activity. Prohibitions on market hunting and game trade emerged around the turn-of-the-century in state wildlife law and persist to this day (Lund 1980; Musgrave and Stein 1993). Since that time, it often has been illegal to sell animal parts even if they are legally taken. The Lacey Act of 1900 added federal enforcement authority by prohibiting interstate and international sale of wildlife and wildlife products obtained in violation of state and federal laws. More recently, both the Endangered Species Act (ESA) and the Convention on International Trade in Endangered Species (CITES) restrict trade in endangered species and their products.

Unlike most conservationists,[12] economists tend to view restrictions on trade as limits on the creation of wealth. If property rights were perfectly delineated, such restrictions could not enhance net wealth. A recognition of the often substantial costs of enforcing property rights to wild populations suggests that the traditional economic view must be made conditional on the property rights system governing a particular population (Goldstein 1991, Lueck 1989). For wildlife populations subjected to open access, trade restrictions reduce the potential gains from theft (poaching) and may thus increase the net value of the stocks. With these restrictions in place, poachers have no smoothly functioning game market in which to sell, and ownership of the wildlife stocks is strengthened. Two implications follow. First, as rights to wildlife stocks become more secure, it is more likely that transfers will be allowed. Second, as the value of the game stocks increases, greater effort to enhance rights will be exerted and the more likely it becomes that transfers will be allowed.[13] A number of observations are consistent with this thesis, including the variation in rules between Great Britain and the United States and variation within the United States itself.

Analysis of game trade law in the United States shows a basic structure consistent with the thesis that trade will tend to be restricted when property rights to the wild populations are insecure. For instance, there was a rapid and pervasive prohibition on trade at the turn of the century, when open access was the dominant property rights regime. Today, even though prohibitions on game trade are customary, when ownership of wildlife stocks is relatively secure the transfer of live or killed game is relatively unrestricted. This is most apparent for domestic game such as livestock and pets, but it is also the case for exotic or imported wildlife on private ranches, shooting preserves, game farms, and private ponds, and for animals owned by zoos (Musgrave and Stein 1993).[14] For these cases, property rights to the live stocks are quite secure relative to wilder populations inhabiting parcels of land held by many different owners.[15] Also, when the gains from wildlife trade are extremely high, as they are for commercial fisheries and certain furbearers, the state allows transfers. In doing so, however, the state typically administers a system of policing to ensure that animals are taken in accordance with state game laws and regulations.[16] For example, furs must be tagged and sold only to licensed dealers (Musgrave and Stein 1993).

Extending Control Beyond State Boundaries

Because state boundaries are not perfectly correlated with the wildlife territories, there can be incentives to move away from simple state level jurisdiction and management. Since the late 1800s there have been changes in two directions, driven by discrepancies between the territorial requirements of wildlife and the geographical size of states. First, when states are too small to cover the entire territory of a species, federal or international control has evolved. Today, the federal government regulates migratory waterfowl whose territories reach across and beyond North America and endangered species whose existence could arguably be valued by individuals across the country and even the world. The federal government also enforces international treaties and environmental legislation affecting wildlife, regulates wildlife commerce, operates wildlife research programs, controls wildlife on federal land, and conducts animal damage programs. Second, where state control is too extensive, ownership has shifted to the private sector or smaller existing government units such as the intrastate management units discussed earlier. For example, states routinely allow private fish ponds, shooting preserves, and game farms when private control is expected to be effective because contracting costs are quite small.

When a stock of wildlife inhabits an area controlled by two or more governments, agreement for unified control can increase wealth. In general, the nature of the arrangement will depend on the interest each government agency has in the particular stock. International control of wildlife is likely when a valuable population—such as migratory geese, halibut, salmon, northern fur seal, polar bear, and some whale species—does not live completely within one national boundary. The first international game treaty was signed in 1911 for the northern fur seal by the United States, Great Britain, Russia, and Japan. Others have followed, including the Migratory Bird Treaty Act of 1916 between the United States and Great Britain (acting on behalf of Canada), as well as treaties for Pacific halibut and salmon, polar bear, and caribou, all of which range into each of the countries involved. Like a private contract, international wildlife treaties jointly specify the rights and responsibilities of each party—in this case, national governments—with respect to management of and actions affecting wildlife. By strengthening property rights, these treaties reduce wealth dissipation associated with these assets otherwise subject to nonexclusive use.

The Migratory Bird Treaty Act of 1916 and its subsequent amendments provide the federal government with ultimate legal jurisdiction over migratory bird populations within the fifty states.[17] In 1947 the U.S. Fish and Wildlife Service (FWS) delineated four flyways for the purpose of setting geographically distinct hunting regulations. In the early 1950s the states within each of these flyways developed Flyway Councils for the explicit purpose of coordinating migratory bird management. The Flyway Councils act as the avenues through which states interact with the FWS and provide an illustration of an attempt to minimize the sum of contracting costs and bureaucracy costs. Because migratory bird populations span huge geographic areas, it would be very costly for the state agencies to repeatedly contract among themselves in an attempt to maximize the net value of the bird stocks ($V_W - C^G$), where C^G in this context would be the total costs of contracting among all involved government agencies. As a result, states have in effect given up ultimate jurisdiction of the stocks to the federal government. For each flyway, the FWS sets broad outer limits on waterfowl hunting regulations including opening and closing dates, season lengths, and bag limits, and each state then sets its own regulations within these bounds. This arrangement arguably reduces C^G while still allowing flexibility for state agencies to respond to unique local situations.

Formal Agreements between States

There are other examples of interstate contracting similar to Flyway Councils. Interstate wildlife agreements are most often undertaken for freshwater fishery resources. The Snake River compact between Idaho and Washington and the Colorado River fishery compact between Arizona and Colorado are two western examples (Lueck 1989). Because the costs of contracting are larger for control of a species that is not tied closely to a plot of land, such as fish and other aquatic species, this discrepancy between fishery resources and other wildlife is not surprising. Even for highly valued migratory bird populations, federal control was required to coordinate states' activities. A summary of the formal agreements already discussed, informal agreements discussed in the next section, and additional agreements not discussed are presented in table 4.2.

One example of a large-scale formal interstate agreement over mammals is the Blue Mountain Elk Initiative being developed to manage elk herds and habitat spanning approximately one million acres in the Blue Mountains of eastern Oregon and Washington. The primary actors in this cooperative are the game departments of the two states, but twenty-one other organizations are apparently participating, including hunter and landowner organizations from both states, three Indian tribes, and three federal land management agencies. More than 55,000 elk inhabit the Blue Mountains, and about 72,000 hunters spend almost $15 million annually in the Blue Mountain Region (Washington Department of Fish and Wildlife 1995).

Another example of an interstate elk management agreement exists between the Nebraska Game and Parks Commission and the South Dakota Department of Game, Fish and Parks. A domesticated herd that

Table 4. 2
Examples of Interstate Wildlife Management Agreements

Formal Agreements	Species Involved	States Involved
Pacific Flyway Council	migratory birds	Arizona, California, Colorado, Idaho, Montana, Nevada, New Mexico, Oregon, Utah, Washington, Wyoming
Central Flyway Council	migratory birds	Colorado, Kansas, Montana, Nebraska, New Mexico, North Dakota, Oklahoma, South Dakota, Texas, Wyoming
Blue Mountain Elk Initiative	elk	Oregon and Washington*
Joint elk hunting season	elk	Nebraska and South Dakota
Joint deer hunting season	deer	Arizona and Utah
Bear Lake Fishery	fish	Idaho and Utah
Colorado River Fishery	fish	Arizona and Colorado
Snake River	fish	Idaho and Washington
Lake Powell	fish	Arizona and Utah
Missouri River Boundary Waters Cooperative	fish	Iowa, Montana, Nebraska, South Dakota
Informal Agreements		
Lolo Elk Herd	elk	Idaho and Montana
Coordinated seasons	elk	Idaho and Wyoming; Montana and Wyoming; Idaho and Montana; Nevada and Utah
Coordinated seasons	mule deer, antelope	Nebraska and Wyoming
Joint herd management	deer	California and Oregon; California and Nevada

* Co-operators also include various Indian tribes, federal agencies, and private associations.
Sources: Telephone interviews and letters from wildlife agency personnel for the various states and Lueck (1989).

recently escaped from its enclosure on a South Dakota Indian reservation and whose adopted territory straddles the South Dakota–Nebraska border has grown to the point where crop predation has become a point of contention with local farmers. Although the Nebraska Game and Parks Commission prefers to eliminate the herd, the South Dakota Department of Game, Fish and Parks wants to maintain it. The two departments have compromised with a joint elk hunting season to reduce the size of the herd. The herd is currently about thirty-five head, and there are twelve permits issued this year, six for each state. The joint season will likely continue into the future with one or two permits issued each year.[18]

The Arizona Game and Fish Department and the Utah Division of Wildlife also have a formal agreement for deer management. In early-snowfall years, a deer herd in a Utah trophy deer hunting zone migrates to lower elevations across the border into Arizona. In the past Arizona's deer hunts have reduced Utah's trophy deer populations. As a result, the two game departments are developing joint management and hunting regulations for this deer population.

Informal Interstate Agreements

State wildlife agencies also use informal agreements for dealing with wildlife populations that cross state boundaries. For example, the elk of the Lolo Pass area of western Montana and central Idaho migrate seasonally across the border of the two states. Much of the elk's territory in Idaho is on uncultivated public land, whereas significantly more of the elk's Montana territory is private cropland. Following years of high crop predation in Montana, through informal agreements between the two state game departments, Idaho issues supplementary hunt permits to reduce the elk population. In this case, the Montana Department of Fish, Wildlife, and Parks is entering into these agreements in response to pressure (the engagement of an existing implicit contract) by agricultural landowners.

Arguably, these informal agreements are utilized in many cases where the costs of formalizing an agreement outweigh the additional benefits from formal joint regulation. One cost of a formal agreement stems from the U.S. Constitution, which requires an act of Congress for states to enter into compacts of any kind, including those for managing wildlife stocks common to more than one state.[19] This requirement arguably increases the costs of contracting and, accordingly, reduces the number of formal interstate agreements. Furthermore, it makes it more likely that informal agreements between state agencies will be used to manage common populations.

Public Preservation of Wildlife

Recall that wildlife can potentially have public good characteristics that may rationalize government involvement. Live animals are valuable not only because they have harvest value, but also because they can produce aesthetic value from activities like viewing or photographing, or simply from their existence. Public responses for the preservation of wildlife stocks can be placed into two categories: the purchase or lease of habitat as illustrated by public wildlife refuges, and placement of uncompensated legal or regulatory constraints on landowner actions potentially injurious to a species or its habitat, an approach embodied by the federal Endangered Species Act.

In 1903 President Theodore Roosevelt created by proclamation what is generally considered to be the first national wildlife refuge, the Pelican Island National Wildlife Refuge off the east coast of Florida. As a follow-up to the Migratory Bird Treaty Act of 1916, Congress passed the Migratory Bird Conservation Act of 1929, the first federal statute authorizing habitat acquisition and the basis upon which many of the first refuges were created (Fink 1994). As of 1995, the U.S. Fish and Wildlife Service administered 508 separate refuges encompassing 92.3 million acres of land, including 76 million acres in Alaska and approximately 7.5 million acres in the seventeen western states (table 4.5).[20] Of that total acreage, 82 million acres were already held by the federal government and 4 million acres were purchased from the private sector.[21]

In the context of our model, the FWS appears to have the comparative advantage in wildlife management because it is able to reduce contracting costs over a large set of interested parties, maintaining higher wildlife values than would be the case without a contractual solution. That refuge land is highly valuable as wildlife habitat does not imply that it is of *no* value for other uses. To the contrary, Fink (1994) finds that farming or grazing leases apply on over one-third of the refuges, and oil and gas leases on nearly one-fourth of them. In addition to federally owned refuge land, 3 million acres are protected as refuges under easement, lease, or other agreements with the private sector. This land can be categorized for our purposes as land for which the primary land values stem from nonwildlife uses, but for which its value as wildlife habitat justifies a contractual arrangement for wildlife uses.

Just as the FWS acquires land primarily for waterfowl and migratory bird habitat, state game agencies also hold land primarily reserved for wildlife habitat. As with federal landholdings, to the extent that state game agency demand for landholdings is an indication of the value of land as wildlife habitat, our model predicts that land will be purchased or leased and managed by a game agency when its most valued attribute is wildlife. State game agencies also hold cooperative agreements with various other sets of landowners, including individuals, business firms, other state agencies, and various federal agencies. As the model suggests, this would be expected where the primary value of land draws from a characteristic other than wildlife, and where the potential increase in wildlife values outweighs the costs of forming and maintaining an agreement with outside parties.

The federal government utilizes another tool, the Endangered Species Act, that may be rationalized in the public good context. Although the ESA provides supplemental land acquisition authority to the federal government for endangered species protection, its major innovation is that it prohibits taking any endangered species within the United States on either private or public land, and limits projects and land uses on both federal and private land that would jeopardize the continued existence of endangered species.[22] Two features of the ESA make it distinct from typical restrictions on taking game. First, it puts endangered species under federal jurisdiction even though the protected populations rarely overlap state boundaries, let alone encompass the territory of many states.[23] In fact, in many cases the small populations required for a species being listed as endangered coincide with small territorial requirements, suggesting that state control would be sufficient. The most extreme illustration of this would come in the form of endangered plants or the various species of snails listed as endangered, whose territories are quite small indeed. Second, the ESA restricts the use of land (public and private) where endangered species reside. Traditional game protection laws do not restrict land use that might have adverse effects on a wild population.

The rationale for federal control over endangered species must lie outside the simple version of the landowner contracting model because of the commonly small territorial requirements for protection. A demand for biodiversity or species preservation offers a possible explanation for protection of endangered species, either by adding acreage to the federal refuge system or by restricting land use under the ESA. If this value is spread across individuals outside the species' actual territory, the rationale exists for control by a party that represents those holding this value.[24]

Compared to federal purchase or lease of private land to protect endangered species, the ESA can create landowner incentives that act counter to the ESA's intent (Mann and Plummer 1995). Dolan (1992) notes numerous cases in which private landowners have destroyed habitat (and killed animals) in fear of being shackled by ESA restrictions. For example, in Riverside County, California some farmers have changed crop rotations so that an endangered kangaroo rat does not take up residence on their land. In other cases southern forest owners have logged old growth pine in order to prevent nesting of the red-cockaded woodpecker. These incentives to destroy habitat seem to be a growing force behind criticism of the ESA (Mann and Plummer 1995). These are strong examples of the types of costs wildlife managers can impose through the ESA when they do not own the land upon which wildlife resides and do not have to compensate landowners.

Many states also maintain state-specific endangered species listings. In fact, most western states, including Kansas, Montana, and Oregon, for example, explicitly protect federally listed species, and additionally include locally endangered species not listed federally (King and Schrock 1985). State endangered species acts, like the federal ESA, prohibit the killing of listed species. It is notable, however, that *no state acts* impose land-use restrictions pertaining to endangered species habitat such as those found in the federal ESA. This distinction could be explained by the fact that state game agencies are more accountable to private landowners within their states, who are the constituents most likely to bear the costs associated with land-use restrictions.

Wildlife in the Private Sector

Although federal and state agencies tend to dominate wildlife institutions, the role of the private sector is important and growing. The property rights model showed that contracting costs among landowners can eliminate the gains from ownership of wildlife populations and thus create a demand for a government agency as a game broker. At the same time, the performance of such an agency will be limited both by its inability to directly control habitat and by the incentives within bureaucracies. This inefficiency inherent in third-party control over wildlife means that limits on game department authority and concessions to landowners can increase the value of land used for wildlife. To illustrate how private wildlife regulation conforms to the property rights model, we consider the market for private hunting rights, private hunting units, and the private preservation of biodiversity and endangered species.

In England, both under the common law and under the Game Laws of the late Middle Ages, private landowners were accorded special treatment with respect to wildlife and have been consistently granted greater control over game than nonlandowners. The distinct treatment of landowners has continued in the United States, although in slightly different form. Distinctive consideration of landowners is consistent with the property rights model that notes the importance of the landowner in providing habitat for wildlife by controlling other uses of land that can influence the extent and quality of habitat. Institutions that divest all rights to game from the landowner create the incentive for the landowner to ignore the provision of wildlife habitat. As it stands, by distinguishing landowners, the laws and regulations implicitly reflect the important connection between the landowner and wildlife habitat provision, as well as the costs of private contracting among landowners. Table 4.3 shows some special privileges held by western landowners.

Under current state laws, landowners typically control a well-specified set of rights to wildlife. One of the longest standing landowner rights is the legal authority to kill animals that damage crops and livestock (Lund 1980; Musgrave and Stein 1993). For many species, landowners are not required to purchase a license for hunting on their own land and often they have a greater bag limit than other licensed hunters.

Indeed, landowners are gaining more control. Large landowners often hold substantial power in state game commissions that oversee the activities of the state game agencies. As discussed previously, some department guidelines require a minimum number of ranchers or farmers to be appointed to the commission. Their presence in the game bureaucracy supports our view of the game department as a contractual institution. The distinction between large and small landowners is also consistent with the model. Owners of large holdings are more likely to completely control a population's territory and thus be an optimal owner. On a less formal level, state departments often rely on landowners for information. Texas, for example, often bases harvest guidelines solely on direct recommendations of landowners and landowner groups.

Private Provision of Habitat for Hunting

Landowners can establish partial ownership and control of wildlife (and thus gain from habitat provision and enhancement) by enforcing rights to their land for hunting, fishing, or trapping.[25] Given the ability of landowners to define rights to certain aspects of wildlife, even when government control dominates, the model still has important implications. In particular, as the size of a landholding increases, it is more likely that access rights will be sold for hunting because larger landowners face lower costs of establishing rights to wildlife stocks. This implies that owners of larger holdings will control access to more species and, therefore, will lease access rights more frequently than small landholders will. Lueck (1991), for example, finds that landowners in Texas and Montana selling access fees to their land for hunting held larger than average landholdings. Furthermore, because the size of agricultural holdings has increased, especially in the past fifty years, the amount of fee hunting on private lands should be increasing. Indeed, outdoor writers and wildlife biologists have presented abundant evidence that fee hunting has increased dramatically in recent years (Davis 1995). Texas has a particu-

Table 4.3

Special Landowner Hunting Regulations

State	Regulation
Idaho	Landowner preference permits are issued if there is no general hunt in the unit where the property (of 640 acres or more) is located.
Kansas	Owners, lessees, and managers (of 80 acres or more) are guaranteed permits to hunt own land and are eligible for drawings to hunt anywhere in management area of residence.
Montana	Owners (of at least 160 agricultural acres) receive preference in license drawings. One preference designation is allowed per landowner, per hunting unit, but landowner may transfer the designation to a relative or ranch employee.
Nebraska	During firearm deer season, animals other than deer may be hunted only with a shotgun or a .22 caliber weapon; ranchers and farmers hunting on their own land are exempt from this restriction. Farmers and ranchers can apply for a special permit to hunt on land they own or manage; legal description of landholding must be presented with application ($10 cost to landowner).
New Mexico	The director may allot up to 6,625 elk licenses for use on those ranches whose owners or lessees sign a hunting agreement with the department.
Oregon	The Access and Habitat Board organizes deer and elk raffle hunts to help pay for habitat improvements on private land and damage relief projects for private landowners.
South Dakota	Licenses are not required for hunting and trapping of small game on own land.
Utah	A limited number of private landowner permits are available for limited entry buck deer and bull elk units.
Wyoming	Landowner and manager licenses are available where hunting is otherwise under a limited quota. Two licenses per landholding; other restrictions apply.

Sources: 1995 and 1996 hunting regulations for various states.

larly strong tradition of landowners charging hunting fees and cooperatively managing wildlife for hunting purposes, dating back to at least the 1940s.[26]

When individual landowners do not act to establish rights to game, brokers may use contracts to bind separate landholdings together, placing hunting rights to a large area under unified ownership. These third parties might be for-profit businesses (such as guides or hunting companies), hunting clubs, state agencies, or local farm cooperatives. Although data on these organizations are too scarce to allow tests of specific propositions, it is clear that wildlife values exceed the costs of landowner contracting in many cases. Tober (1981) describes a rich history of hunter clubs and organizations in the eastern United States dating back at least to the 1840s, and Barclay and Bednarik (1968) report that over 5,000 waterfowl hunting clubs leased 2.5 million acres of privately owned habitat in the Mississippi River basin. The Sportsman–Landowner Club owns hunting rights for big game animals on over 100,000 acres of private land in southeastern Washington. The United Sportsman Hunting Club in Utah has hunting rights to nearly 500,000 acres. These are examples of groups of consumers, rather than producers, consolidating rights to hunting territory.

In recent years, many state game departments have begun relaxing game regulations by formally allowing landowners more power over game management and hunting on private land, and by allowing formal cooperative agreements among landowners. Like the oil and gas units discussed earlier, these cooperatives generate efficiency gains from jointly determining production (harvest) and management decisions that tend to outweigh the costs of contracting among themselves.[27] This trend toward more private authority over game management would be expected as the average size of rural landholdings increases (see table 4.5) and as western population growth leads to an increase in the demand for game. Table 4.4 summarizes some western programs. Note that all of these programs allow extended seasons and supplemental harvest for participating landowners, and maintain minimum acreage requirements for program participation, though the acreage varies significantly.

The Utah Division of Wildlife Resources has a program through which a private group whose combined contiguous landholdings are 320 acres or more can apply to register a Posted Hunting Unit.[28] Once registered, landowner associations may petition for extended seasons; they are eligible to receive state support for habitat improvement and may enter exclusive drawings for hunt permits. There are also supplemental license allocations and protection against libel lawsuits for landowners. Primar-

Table 4.4
Programs for Wildlife Management on Private Lands in Western States

State	Program (date established)	Minimum Unit Acreage Requirement	Supplemental License Allowances	Extended Seasons Allowed
California	Wildlife Habitat Enhancement and Management Area Program (1983)	NA	614	yes
Colorado	Ranching For Wildlife (1985)	12,000	1,710	yes
New Mexico	Private Land Allocation System (NA)	10,000	7,600	yes
Oklahoma	Deer Management Assistance Program (NA)	1,000	yes	yes
Utah	Posted Hunting Unit Program (1993)	320	440	yes
Washington	Private Land Wildlife Management Area Pilot Program (1992)	5,000	NA	yes

Sources: Arha (1996); state game agency documentation and communication.

ily, however, the structure provided by this program appears to be an attempt to facilitate contracting among landowners in joint habitat management and sale of hunting rights to large tracts of land. As of 1989, there were fifteen landowners participating, with a total of one million acres of land (Arha 1996).[29]

California's Private Lands Management and Enhancement Program initiated in the mid-1980s allows special hunting permits and extended seasons for landowners who draft a satisfactory management plan and satisfy additional requirements, including sufficient evidence of habitat improvement. As of 1992, forty-six landowners representing 544,139 acres were participating (Arha 1996).

Oklahoma's Deer Management Assistance is designed to facilitate and provide incentives for the provision of hunting habitat. These units must have a minimum of 1,000 acres, and if the requirements are satisfied, higher harvest levels are allowed. Most landowners in this program satisfy the 1,000-acre minimum alone, but some have combined their acreage to meet the minimum.[30]

The Colorado Division of Wildlife instituted the Ranching for Wildlife program in 1986, and by 1993 there were twenty-two participating ranching units totaling 13 million acres, each with one or more landholdings totaling at least 12,000 acres. These units benefit from extended seasons for private hunts in some cases twice as long as the states' normal rifle seasons for deer and elk and six times as long as the antelope rifle season, as well as supplemental license allocations (Arha 1996; Davis 1995).

In South Dakota, a group of four landowners cooperatively manage several thousand acres as Dakota Safari east of the Black Hills. Their land comprises about 20 percent of the state management unit within which the landholdings reside. At present, the South Dakota Department of Game, Fish, and Parks does not systematically incorporate landowner preferences in the license allocation process, but the owners of Dakota Safari and other owners of large landholdings in the state have instigated the development of a departmental task force to look at the license allocation system.[31]

States' support of this apparent trend toward wildlife unitization is evident, but it is not always rapidly forthcoming. New Mexico, for example, allows landowners with 10,000 acres or more to submit management plans and request a specific number of permits from which they retain revenues, but the state game department does not yet allow unitization to meet these requirements, though there is some indication it is moving in that direction.[32] And although the Montana Department of Fish, Wildlife, and Parks has implemented a program[33] for improving public access and relieving costs to landowners imposed by hunters, the department has not been open to extending more authority over hunting rights and regulations to landowners.

Private Preservation of Wildlife

Private rights for fishing, hunting, and trapping are mechanisms by which private landowners are able to capture a portion of the value from wild populations that inhabit their land. For wildlife values characterized as public goods, private action would seem to be limited because of potential free-riding. Yet the provision of nonconsumptive wildlife values by private action is substantial and growing (Goldstein 1991; PERC 1994). Groups like the Nature Conservancy (TNC), Ducks Unlimited, and the National Audubon Society own and manage millions of acres of wildlife habitat. For example, in 1990 TNC bought the 500-square-mile Gray Ranch (roughly 320,000 acres) in the Animas Mountains of New Mexico, and later sold the acreage while maintaining conservation easements on the land (Nature Conservancy 1997). These easements will allow TNC to set and maintain conservation benchmarks for the biota on the ranch and prevent the ranch from being subdivided in the future. Another example is the Lillian Annette Rowe Sanctuary in Nebraska. Owned by the Audubon Society, it is a 2,200-acre stretch of the Platte River providing wetland habitat for various species of migratory birds, including whooping cranes and sandhill cranes. A study by PERC (1994) also finds numerous smaller, local groups that own private preserves, and reports a total of over 12 million acres of habitat protected by private organizations.

One of the most innovative approaches to private wildlife preservation is the Greater Yellowstone wolf program of Defenders of Wildlife (Fischer 1995). The reintroduction of the gray wolf into Yellowstone Park by the U.S. Fish and Wildlife Service generated strong opposition from landowners and stockmen neighboring the park who fear stock depredation by wolves that stray out of the park. Defenders of Wildlife has tried to soothe these fears by using market payments to encourage private landowners to protect wolf populations and to compensate stockmen who can prove depredation from wolves. For example, from 1987 when the wolf compensation fund was established until September 1994, Defenders of Wildlife had paid $16,347 to twenty-one ranchers for the losses of thirty-six cattle and ten sheep. The wolf reward program was established in 1992, and is designed to pay ranchers who can show that a viable wolf den exists on their property. Defenders of Wildlife made its first payment to a Montana rancher in early 1994 (Defenders of Wildlife 1994). Both the landownership approach and the market payment approach recognize the connection between wildlife habitat and landowner control.

Distinctly Western Issues

Although we have been focusing on the western states throughout this chapter, the contracting issues we have discussed generally apply in the eastern states as well. Other aspects of wildlife management, however, are uniquely western. In this section we examine a few of these, including the influence of large public landholdings; geographical distinctions among the Pacific Coast, Rocky Mountain and Great Plains regions; railroad checkerboarding; Native American jurisdiction over wildlife; trends in urban–rural demographics; and the distinct nature of western wildlife.

A number of landownership characteristics provide a setting for wildlife management and ownership that is quite distinct from the eastern United States. First, note in table 4.5 that a vast majority of federal lands are located west of the Great Plains. More importantly for our purposes, the percentage of total state land in this region that is federally managed is generally high compared to the rest of the United States. Seven states have at least 40 percent of total state land under federal ownership, and all of them are in the Rocky Mountain and Pacific Coast regions. Most federal lands are national forest, national parks, and BLM lands; wildlife refuges represent less than 5 percent of total state land area for all seventeen western states. In relation to our model, with federal lands come large tract sizes, which suggests that contracting over wildlife management will become less costly. At the same time, however, the participation of federal government agencies introduces larger bureaucratic incentive problems that make contractual agreements less efficient.

The Great Plains states, on the other hand, contain only very small proportions of federal land, and average rural landholdings tend to be smaller than those in the Pacific Coast and Rocky Mountain regions. This would suggest that for a given species territory size, the contracting problem would be more difficult. At the same time, however, land uses tend to be more homogeneous in the Plains states, leading to reduced contracting costs as adjacent landowners face quite similar wildlife-related costs and benefits. For example, in mountainous regions, game animals tend to spend summer months in higher elevations on publicly owned land but move into lower elevations in the fall and winter, both imposing costs on private landowners in terms of crop and livestock losses and affecting a larger, more diverse set of landowners. This particular complication does not occur on the Great Plains.

Another interesting and quite complicated aspect of western wildlife management stems from the fact that federal Indian law gives jurisdiction over wildlife residing within their borders to all recognized tribal reservations regardless of their size (Getches and Wilkinson 1986). Reservations in the West show great variation in size. Of the more than 150 western reservations, twenty-three of them are more than 500,000 acres in size, and at least sixteen are less than 50 acres.[34] Some of the big reservations, such as the Ute in Utah and the Navajo and Apache of Arizona, have become actively involved in wildlife management and enforcement. Many reservations throughout the West, however, have some form of management mechanism in place but enforcement is lax or nonexistent, and in some cases near open-access prevails and game populations are decimated (Anderson 1996). In addition, few if any of the small and medium-sized reservations in the West have any wildlife management programs at all, effectively resulting in open access. This lack of an effective wildlife management structure and enforcement mechanism likely stems in some cases from weaknesses in the broader tribal government institutions as a whole (Cornell and Kalt 1992).

The nature of wildlife management on Indian reservations is of interest to states within which they lie if the territories of the wildlife on reservations extend beyond reservation boundaries, which is more likely as reservation size decreases. Although the human populations of the smallest tribes may not have a significant impact on local wildlife stocks whose territories are significantly larger than the reservation itself (especially state and federal game trade restrictions), reservations with larger populations of hunters will tend to have a greater impact on wildlife stocks. Presumably, where tribal hunting significantly impacts these stocks, state agencies will have an incentive to enter into agreements with tribal authorities and possibly even provide support for management and enforcement. Indeed, some states have entered into such agreements. The Montana Department of Fish, Wildlife, and Parks currently has a management agreement with the Flathead Tribe, but they are now developing a commission with members from all tribes in Montana except the Northern Cheyenne in an attempt to better coordinate wildlife management decisions.[35] In Nebraska, all tribes have wildlife management programs of some form and periodically attend meetings with agents of the Nebraska Game and Parks Commission to coordinate management efforts.[36]

Certain parts of the West still feel the effects of federal land grants made to railroads in the late 1800s. Railroads were given 640-acre

Dean Lueck and Jonathan Yoder

Table 4.5
Land Ownership in the Western States

Region/State	Total Land (thousands of acres)	Federal Land (%)	Farm/Ranch Land (%)	Average Farm Acreage	Federal Refuges (% of total land area)
Great Plains					
Kansas	52,511	0.8	88.9	738	0.08
Nebraska	49,032	1.4	90.5	839	0.28
North Dakota	44,452	4.2	88.7	1,267	0.64
Oklahoma	44,088	1.6	72.9	480	0.32
South Dakota	48,882	5.7	91.7	1,316	0.11
Texas	168,218	1.3	77.8	725	0.18
Regional mean	67,864	2.5	85.1	894	0.23
Rocky Mountains					
Arizona	72,688	47.2	48.2	5,173	2.19
Colorado	66,486	36.3	51.1	1,252	0.08
Idaho	52,933	61.6	25.4	609	0.13
Montana	93,271	28.0	63.9	2,613	1.12
Nevada	70,264	82.9	13.2	3,205	3.21
New Mexico	77,766	32.4	60.2	3,281	0.49
Utah	52,697	63.9	18.3	712	0.18
Wyoming	62,343	48.9	52.7	3,772	0.09
Regional mean	68,556	50.2	41.6	2,577	1.01

–continued–

Table 4.5
(continued)

Region/State	Total Land (thousands of acres)	Federal Land (%)	Farm/Ranch Land (%)	Average Farm Acreage	Federal Refuges (% of total land area)
Pacific Coast					
California	100,207	44.6	28.9	373	0.28
Oregon	61,599	52.4	28.6	552	0.89
Washington	42,694	28.3	36.8	520	0.36
Regional mean	76,787	41.8	31.4	482	0.43
U.S. Mean	45,427	28.6	42.9	492	0.71*

* Does not include 76,787 thousand acres in Alaska.

Sources: Total land and federal land data are compiled or calculated from Bureau of the Census (1994, 225), table 354; farm and ranch land percentages and average farm acreages from USDA (1992), items 0A00003 and 0100003; U.S. mean calculated from Bureau of the Census (1994, 225); federal refuges land area percentage compiled from Zaslowski and Watkins (1994).

alternating tracts of land along their proposed lines. For example, the Northern Pacific Railroad received a tract extending from Minneapolis to Seattle. The pattern of checkerboarding that resulted as homesteaders claimed the nonrailroad parcels is characterized by discontiguous ownership and plot boundaries that do not conform to local geographic characteristics. To the extent that checkerboarding has reduced consolidation of landholdings, it is likely to have increased contracting costs over wildlife populations because landholdings are smaller and are likely not closely coincident with wildlife habitat boundaries. In many places, such as along the Idaho–Montana border, checkerboarding remains a dominant feature of landownership patterns.

Two human demographic trends in the West with important implications for wildlife are suburban expansion and rural consolidation. Metropolitan areas like Albuquerque, Boise, Denver, and Salt Lake City continue to grow rapidly, chopping farm and ranch land into tiny plots in the process. At the same time, rural landholdings in the West are being consolidated into increasingly large units, and more landowners are capitalizing on land as wildlife habitat. Media magnate Ted Turner, for example, owns a half-million-acre ranch in New Mexico and another slightly smaller one in Montana, both of which are extensively used for fee hunting and wildlife production, particularly bison and elk. Our model suggests that wildlife agencies are likely to lose influence in many rural areas as the owners of increasingly large landholdings push for stronger rights over wildlife but will continue to gain influence on the edge of urban development as landholdings diminish in size, making private contracting more costly.

Western wildlife is also different from wildlife in the East. The West has many highly valued and wide-ranging species not found in the East, such as grizzly bear, elk, and salmon. Further, for some species common to both regions (e.g., white-tail deer), territorial requirements are often larger in the West due to its arid climate and less abundant vegetation, relative to the East. All else equal, the larger territory requirements will tend to lead to larger contracting costs because of the increased likelihood that a particular stock will range over numerous landholdings. As mentioned previously, the prevalence of seasonal migration, often drawing wildlife populations to move regularly between high-elevation federal land and lower-elevation private land as well as across state boundaries, is a problem of particular relevance in the Rocky Mountain and Pacific Coast states. On the other hand, elk, grizzly bear, and some other western species are highly valued as game animals and can be the source of significant income for private landowners through the sale of hunting rights. Private elk hunting, in particular, is often a driving force behind the development of the types of hunting units discussed previously.

Conclusions

The structure of wildlife institutions generally complements the modern political philosophy of federalism. Where involvement of more centralized tiers of government is of little use, their influence seems to be weak. For prevalent species with small and intermediate ranges, the federal government is involved only minimally, even though it controls a great deal of wildlife habitat in the form of the federal lands. Federal involvement is only strong for species with vast territories (migratory waterfowl are the prime example) or where the public good aspect of a species weighs heavily (such as with endangered species).[37] In these cases the benefits of federal jurisdiction appear to outweigh the costs, and even international cooperation is pursued. At the same time, in areas with large private landholdings, landowners hold significant power over wildlife management. The relative absence of the involvement of local or county governments possibly suggests that these jurisdictions are so small that they provide little savings in contracting costs over private contracting arrangements, yet they still hold the trappings of a government bureaucracy.

To the extent that wildlife institutions conform to the federalism paradigm, the more mature oil and gas conservation institutions in effect today provide a glimpse of the direction in which wildlife institutions are heading. It can be argued that oil and gas institutions evolved more rapidly because of the potential for huge losses in wealth. As the value of wildlife and wildlife habitat increases over time, we expect that the analogous institutions corresponding to wildlife will become more well defined over time. As rural landholdings become more consolidated and wildlife institutions continue to mature, we might expect to see more private management units, such as those in Utah and elsewhere, with government regulations assigned only to those aspects of private contracting that are most contentious.

Notes

1. Shapiro (1996) focuses on optimal jurisdiction over air quality management in the face of heterogeneity of preferences within and across states in a federation and incomplete government information regarding citizens' preferences.

2. Wildlife stocks will not necessarily be extinguished because full open access is unlikely.

3. For example, $W^G = V_W - C^G > 0$ and $W^P = V_W - C^P \leq 0$.

4. Leopold's idea suggests that wildlife and land are "complementary" assets best owned by the same party (Hart and Moore 1990).

5. See Anderson (1996) for a discussion of wildlife management on the Fort Apache Reservation in Arizona.

6. Lueck (1995a) examines many alternatives.

7. The analysis here parallels that of Grossman and Hart (1986).

8. One possibility in this situation is for a group of consumers to own the land, as illustrated by private conservation groups such as the Nature Conservancy.

9. We collected data from published sources and by contacting the appropriate agency in each of the states. We do not discuss Alaska and Hawaii.

10. These management units will be discussed in more detail later.

11. In addition, three states require some minimum number of sportsmen and representatives from environmental organizations, and all states have statutes that limit the number of commission members from the same political party.

12. For example, see Geist (1988).

13. In his seminal article on property rights, Demsetz (1967) shows that game trade (beaver fur) leads to a more precise system of property rights in a wildlife population (beaver). Demsetz ignores, however, the possibility that open access harvest might proceed at a rate that exceeds the ability of people to establish the property rights to game protection.

14. Trade restrictions are often the result of concern over the spread of diseases carried by animals (live or dead). Indeed, the bacteria or viruses that cause these diseases can be viewed as "wildlife" for which property rights are extremely costly to establish.

15. Only state game departments can legally sell wild animals, often to game departments from other states and from certain private parties. Many interagency trades do not involve money but are purely animal swaps (Musgrave and Stein 1993; King and Schrock 1985).

16. Even so, elk thieves in Colorado have been known to capture one hundred or more live elk for sale on the elk market.

17. Unless otherwise noted, we rely on A. S. Hawkins (1984) and FWS (1988).

18. Kevin Church, Wildlife Research Supervisor, Nebraska Game and Parks Commission, telephone interview, 6 February 1996.

19. U.S. Constitution, art. I, sec. 10: "No state shall, without the consent of Congress, lay any duty of tonnage, keep troops, or ships of war in time of peace, enter into any agreement or compact with another state, or with a foreign power, or engage in war, unless actually invaded, or in such imminent danger as will not admit of delay."

20. As of July 1996, acquisitions of ten more refuges totaling 10,502 acres have been approved (FWS 1995).

21. Another 2.5 million are managed by federal agencies other than the FWS. Although the FWS has the power of eminent domain, less than 1 percent of land has been acquired this way (FWS 1997).

22. Endangered Species Act of 1973, 16 U.S.C. §§ 1531–43 (1988).

23. Note that the dominant role of federal authority—migratory waterfowl is the leading example—is usefully viewed as the result of the inadequacy of state jurisdiction.

24. Again, we refer to the Nature Conservancy as an illustration of a private group of "public goods consumers" that own wildlife habitat.

25. Indeed, hunting rights severable from the land have medieval origins (Blackstone 1971; Christian 1817).

26. Jerry Cooke, director of Upland Ecology, Texas Parks and Wildlife Department, telephone interview, 20 May 1996.

27. The legal institutions with respect to wildlife "unitization" have not developed to the extent they have in the oil and gas industry, where state laws often require unit formation over an entire reservoir with less than 100 percent agreement among interested parties.

28. Landowner participation is strictly voluntary.

29. For additional information, see Utah Department of Natural Resources (1995).

30. Michael Shaw, wildlife research supervisor, Oklahoma Department of Wildlife Conservation, telephone interview, 20 May 1996.

31. Ron Fowler, game staff specialist, South Dakota Department of Game, Fish and Parks, telephone interview, 28 May 1996.

32. Dale Hall, landowner/sportsman coordinator, New Mexico Department of Game and Fish, telephone interview, 2 October 1996. In 1992, there were 1,250 participants in this program (Arha 1996).

33. The program has 443 participants with over 4 million acres (Arha 1996).

34. For example, the Navajo Reservation, primarily in Arizona, includes almost 14 million acres, whereas the Celillo Reservation in Oregon is 17 acres (Confederation of American Indians 1986).

35. Wayne Phillips, legal council, Montana Department of Fish, Wildlife, and Parks, telephone interview, 2 October 1996.

36. Kevin Church, wildlife research supervisor, Nebraska Game and Parks Commission, letter to the authors, 6 February 1996.

37. The issue of whether to approach the endangered species problem by public land acquisition or by imposing land-use restrictions continues to be a contentious debate.

References

Alchian, Armen A. 1950. Uncertainty, Evolution, and Economic Theory. *Journal of Political Economy* 58(3): 211–21.

Anderson, Terry L. 1996. Conservation—Native American Style. *PERC Policy Series*, PS-6. Bozeman, MT: Political Economy Research Center.

Arha, Kaush. 1996. Sustaining Wildlife Values on Private Lands: A Survey of State Programs for Wildlife Management on Private Lands in California, Colorado, Montana, New Mexico, Oregon, Utah, and Washington. In *Transactions of the North American Wildlife and Natural Resources Conferences*, vol. 61. Washington, DC: Wildlife Management Institute, 267–73.

Barclay, John, and Karl E. Bednarik. 1968. Private Waterfowl Shooting Clubs in the Mississippi Flyway. In *Transactions of the North American Wildlife and Natural Resources Conference*, vol. 33. Washington, DC: Wildlife Management Institute, 133–42.

Barzel, Yoram. 1997. *Economic Analysis of Property Rights,* 2nd ed. Cambridge: Cambridge University Press.

Blackstone, William. 1971. *Commentaries on the Laws of England.* Facsimile of the first of edition of 1765–1769. Chicago: University of Chicago Press.

Bureau of the Census, U.S. Department of Commerce. 1994. *Statistical Abstracts of the United States.* Washington, DC.

Christian, Edward. 1817. *A Treatise on the Game Laws.* London: Clarke.

Confederation of American Indians. 1986. *Indian Reservations: A State and Federal Handbook.* Jefferson, NC: McFarland.

Cornell, Stephen, and Joseph Kalt. 1992. Cultural and Institutions as Public Goods: American Indian Economic Development as a Problem of Collective Action. In *Property Rights and Indian Economies*, ed. Terry L. Anderson. Lanham, MD: Rowman and Littlefield, 215–49.

Craft, Rance. 1995. Of Reservoir Hogs and Pelt Fiction: Defending the *Farae Naturae* Analogy between Petroleum and Wildlife. *Emory Law Journal* 44: 697–733.

Davis, Robert K. 1995. A New Paradigm in Wildlife Conservation: Using Markets to Produce Big Game Hunting. In *Wildlife in the Marketplace*, eds. Terry L. Anderson and Peter J. Hill. Lanham, MD: Rowman and Littlefield, 109–25.

Defenders of Wildlife. 1994. *Defenders of Wildlife's Wolf Compensation Program: Using Economic Incentives to Encourage Recovery.* Fact Sheet. Washington, DC.

Demsetz, Harold. 1967. Toward a Theory of Property Rights. *American Economic Review* 57(2): 347–59.

Dolan, Maura. 1992. Nature at Risk in a Quiet War. *Los Angeles Times*, December 20.

Favre, David S. 1983. *Wildlife: Cases, Laws, and Policy*. Tarrytown, NY: Associate Faculty Press.

Fink, Richard J. 1994. The National Wildlife Refuges: Theory, Practice, and Prospect. *Harvard Environmental Law Review* 18: 64–66.

Fischer, Hank. 1995. *Wolf Wars*. Helena, MT: Falcon Press.

Fish and Wildlife Service, U.S. Department of the Interior. 1988. *Final Supplemental Environmental Impact Statement: Issuance of Annual Regulations Permitting the Sport Hunting of Migratory Birds*. Washington, DC: U.S. Government Printing Office.

———. 1995. Land Protection Policy [Online], September. Available: http://www.fws.gov/~r9realty/lpp.html.

——— 1997. Landowner's Guide [Online], February. Available: http://www.fws.gov/~r9realty/guide.html.

Getches, David H., and Charles F. Wilkinson. 1986. *Cases and Materials on Federal Indian Law*. American Casebook Series. St. Paul, MN: West.

Geist, Valerius. 1988. How Markets in Wildlife Meat and Parts, and the Sale of Hunting Privileges, Jeopardize Wildlife Conservation. *Conservation Biology* 2(1): 15–26.

Goldstein, Jon H. 1991. The Prospects for Using Market Incentives to Conserve Biological Diversity. *Environmental Law* 21(3): 985–1014.

Grossman, Sanford, and Oliver Hart. 1986. The Cost and Benefits of Ownership: A Theory of Vertical and Lateral Integration. *Journal of Political Economy* 94(4): 691–719.

Haddock, David D. 1997. Sizing Up Sovereigns: Federal Systems, Their Origin, Their Decline, Their Prospects. This volume: chapter 1.

Hart, Oliver, and John Moore. 1990. Property Rights and the Nature of the Firm. *Journal of Political Economy* 98(6): 1119–58.

Hawkins, A. S. 1984. *Flyways: Pioneering Waterfowl Management in the North*. Washington, DC: U.S. Department of the Interior, Fish and Wildlife Service. Available from Superintendent of Documents, U.S. Government Printing Office.

King, Steven T., and J. R. Schrock. 1985. *Controlled Wildlife*. Vol. 3 of *State Wildlife Regulations*. Lawrence, KS: Association of Systematics Collections.

Laffont, Jean-Jacques, and Jean Tirole. 1991. The Politics of Government Decision Making: A Theory of Regulatory Capture. *Quarterly Journal of Economics* 106(4): 1089–127.

Leopold, Aldo. 1933. *Game Management*. New York: Scribner's.

Libecap, Gary D., and Steven N. Wiggins. 1984. Contractual Responses to the Common Pool: Prorationing of Crude Oil Production. *American Economic Review* 74(1): 87–98.

Lidicker, William, and Roy Caldwell, eds. 1982. *Dispersal and Migration*. Stroudsburg, PA: Hutchinson Ross.

Lueck, Dean. 1989. The Economic Nature of Wildlife Law. *Journal of Legal Studies* 18(2): 291–324.

———. 1991. Ownership and Regulation of Wildlife. *Economic Inquiry* 29(2): 249–60.

———. 1995a. Property Rights and the Economic Logic of Wildlife Institutions. *Natural Resources Journal* 35(3): 1–47.

———. 1995b. The Rule of First Possession and the Design of the Law. *Journal of Law and Economics* 38(2): 393–436.

Lueck, Dean, and Philip Schenewerk. 1996. An Economic Analysis of Unitized and Non-Unitized Reservoirs. In *Proceedings of the 1996 Society of Petroleum Engineers Annual *Technical Conference*. Dallas: Society of Petroleum Engineers, *International, 67–76.

Lund, Thomas A. 1980. *American Wildlife Law*. Berkeley: University of California Press.

Mann, Charles, and Mark Plummer. 1995. *Noah's Choice*. New York: Knopf.

Musgrave, Ruth S., and Mary Anne Stein. 1993. *State Wildlife Laws Handbook*. Rockville, MD: Government Institutes, Inc.

Nature Conservancy, New Mexico Branch. 1997. Other Leading Conservancy Projects [Online], February. Available: http://www.tnc.org/infield/State/NewMex/foo.htm.

Palmer, T. S. 1912. *Chronology and Index of the More Important Events in American Game Protection, 1776–1911*. Biological Survey Bulletin 41. Washington, DC: U.S. Department of Agriculture.

PERC. 1994. Private Environmental Protection: Conservation Examples. *PERC Briefing*. Bozeman, MT: Political Economy Research Center.

Shapiro, Perry. 1996. Which Level of Government Should be Responsible for Environmental Regulation? The Federalists Versus Calhoun. In *Environmental Policy With Political and Economic Integration*, eds. John B. Braden, Henk Folmer, and Thomas S. Ulen. Cheltenham, UK, Brookfield, VT: Edward Elgar, 132–44.

Stigler, George J. 1971. The Theory of Economic Regulation. *Bell Journal of Economics* 2(1): 3–21.

———. 1992. Law or Economics? *Journal of Law and Economics* 35(2): 455–68.

Tober, James. 1981. *Who Owns the Wildlife?* Westport, CT: Greenwood Press.

U.S. Department of Agriculture. 1992. *Census of Agriculture*. Washington, DC.

Utah Department of Natural Resources, Division of Wildlife Resources. 1995. *Big Game Proclamation: Hunting Rules Summary*. Lebanon, OR: Blackford.

Washington Department of Fish and Wildlife. 1995. *Blue Mountain Elk Initiative: Charter for 1996–2000*. Proposed final draft. Olympia, WA.

Wenders, John. 1995. The Economics of Elk Management. In *Wildlife in the Marketplace*, eds. Terry L. Anderson and Peter J. Hill. Lanham, MD: Rowman and Littlefield, 89–108.

Wildlife Management Institute. 1987. *Organization, Authority, and Programs of State Fish and Wildlife Agencies*. Washington, DC.

Zaslowski, Dyan, and T. H. Watkins. 1994. *These American Lands*. Washington, DC: Island Press.

Chapter 5

Pesticides and Environmental Federalism: An Empirical and Qualitative Analysis of § 24(c) Registrations

Andrew P. Morriss

> The authority to permit the use of a pesticide is an awesome power.
>
> — Senator Philip Hart (U.S. Senate 1970, 1)

> The whole concept of state regulation of pesticides resembles closing the barn door after the horse is long gone.
>
> — Martha McCabe, Assistant Attorney General, New York (McCabe 1989, 37)

Pesticide regulation in the United States is the product of cooperation between state and federal governments. The federal government establishes minimum safety standards for products sold nationally, determines acceptable residue levels for food crops, and sets national restrictions on use, while states act as agents of the federal government and exercise significant authority to vary pesticide regulation at the state level. In addition, state liability laws exert an important influence over manufacturers and distributors because of the potentially huge liability if a pesticide in widespread use damages crops.[1] This chapter examines one area where state–federal cooperation is required by the basic regulatory statute: states' registration of pesticides to meet special local needs.[2] Under section 24(c) of the Federal Insecticide, Fungicide, and Rodenticide Act (FIFRA), states have the authority to permit within their borders, subject to approval by the Environmental Protection Agency (EPA), uses of a pesticide that EPA has not approved for the country as a whole.

This attempt at shared authority raises three important questions concerning environmental federalism: (1) Will the central government share authority or will the incentives for centralization prevent states from exercising significant authority? (2) Can shared authority with the states improve national regulatory programs? and (3) Will states subvert the national environmental protection goals of the central government in a "race to the bottom"?

With respect to the first question, the experience of Special Local Needs (SLN) registrations suggests that shared authority has been successful. States have retained the ability to vary national norms significantly by registering products locally. Shared regulatory authority is thus possible despite resistance by federal authorities when local conditions create a significant need to vary these norms.

With respect to the second question the record is less clear. SLN registrations have mitigated the problems caused by the national model of regulation by allowing states to register uses for minor crops. Despite their considerable authority, however, significant constraints on states remain because of the overall structure of national regulation; thus they have been unable to develop new, potentially more effective forms of handling the environmental problems pesticide use creates. Because SLN registrations are part of a national regulatory scheme they have not produced the type of policy innovation usually associated with successful examples of federalism.

With respect to the third question, there is some evidence that the delegation of national authority to states has produced a few inappropriate exercises of that authority. Overall, however, the results presented here suggest that states have not abused their authority in most cases and that there are not widespread circumventions of national health and environmental standards.

In the following sections I set out a brief description of the properties of pesticides that influence regulation, describe the nationalization of pesticide registration, and discuss the development of Special Local Needs registration as a response. I then examine the pattern of SLN registrations empirically.

A Brief Overview of Pesticides

Before World War II, pesticides were few, costly, and extremely toxic. Acute poisoning of users and product effectiveness were regulators' primary concerns. The chance discovery of DDT's insecticidal properties during World War II led to the development of powerful, broad-spectrum organic pesticides. These new products' pest control properties were seen as close to miraculous and "DDT was given a hero's welcome" after the war[3] (Wharton 1974, 249). They were also seen as the solution to the residue problems that had plagued the inorganics (Wharton 1974, 212). The lower acute toxicity of the new products reduced that concern but many presented new, more complicated long-term impacts. The postwar years also brought the development of new types of pesticides beyond insecticides and fungicides. Nematicides, defoliants, desiccants, plant growth regulators, and others came into widespread use (U.S. Senate 1972a, 7). These new developments produced dramatically increased usage, including a fivefold increase between 1950 and 1978 (Rogers 1994, 399).

Product innovations solved some problems even as they created new ones.[4] Advances in pest control have produced products that are capable of narrower focus and fewer side effects. Fleas on dogs, for example, can be effectively controlled through administration of a hormone to the dog that prevents maturation of the fleas without harm to the dog. These design changes affect manufacturers' incentives since selectivity reduces both undesirable externalities and a pesticide's potential sales. Product innovation has also led to types of environmental harm that are more difficult to measure than acute toxicity to nontarget species. For example, introducing genetic pest resistance into plants is more narrowly targeted[5] at specific pests than spraying a broad-spectrum insecticide, but the environmental impact of introducing genetic changes is more difficult to quantify than the acute toxicity of a broad-spectrum pesticide like DDT on birds. Pest control technology, of which pesticides are but one part, is radically different today from the heavy reliance on broad-spectrum pesticides developed in the 1940s and earlier.

Pesticides are different from other environmental risks in several important ways. First, and most important, using pesticides involves the deliberate introduction to the environment of substances that are toxic to some part of the environment rather than the use of the environment as a disposal mechanism for unwanted wastes. William Rogers (1994, 394) characterizes pesticide use as "excused pollution." Not only are pesticides deliberately introduced into the environment, their toxicity to the target is critical to their usefulness. In the conventional picture of a factory chimney or outfall emitting waste products, the environmental impacts are solvable in principle by ending the discharge. (In the classic statement of this view of pollution control the Clean Water Act mandates an end to all discharges.[6]) Successful pesticide use, in contrast, requires altering the environment by the introduction of a substance toxic to at least some part of the environment. Indeed, the original emphasis of national regulation was to ensure that pesticides were strong enough to have an impact.

Pesticides also present a different set of environmental externalities than other environmental pollutants. While their negative externalities are similar to those caused by the use of any toxic substance, unlike other pollutants there are positive externalities associated with pesticide use. The use of a pesticide in my field, for example, may reduce the chances of pest infestation in my neighbor's field. Early regulatory efforts were sometimes aimed at overcoming the collective action problem in encouraging additional use. In addition, there are negative economic externalities: not only does use of a pesticide enhance pest resistance to the pesticide, increasing costs for other users in the future, but the manner of use (timing, dose, formulation, and other characteristics) may alter the impact on resistance (Georghiou and Taylor 1986, 165–66). Similarly, use may cause a secondary pest outbreak if the pesticide eliminates a predator of a nontargeted species. The negative externalities are often enhanced by the use of application methods in which the vast majority of the pesticide does not reach the target pest (Rogers 1994, 397).

Many of the consequences of pesticide use are local. Aerial spraying of a pesticide when there is too much wind can lead to drift onto a neighbor's field or house, and failure to control a pest early in an infestation can lead to the spread of the pest to a neighbor's farm or home. At the same time, pesticide use poses significant national and international issues such as acceptable levels of pesticide residues on food, groundwater contamination, the presence of DDT in Antarctica where it has never been used, and the health effects of use on workers in developing countries. Pesticides' environmental impacts are complex. Even if a pesticide's direct impact is well understood scientifically, differences in byproducts and impurities in the active ingredients between manufacturers and even among different batches produced by the same manufacturer (U.S. HEW 1969, 249) and the effects of "inert" ingredients with which the active ingredients are mixed are not (Hogan 1990). Characteristics of the location in which a pesticide is also used affect both the environmental impact (Gustafson 1993, 82–101) and the efficacy of the pesticide (U.S. House 1977a, 7). Even something as apparently simple as drift of a pesticide onto a neighbor's crops turns out to be complex in many respects.

As this brief overview suggests, pesticide use presents a highly complex regulatory problem. There are two major rationales for national regulation: (1) interstate externalities that would not be taken into account by state regulations and (2) the reduced transaction costs for pesticide manufacturers from having a single, uniform national regulatory scheme rather than diverse and conflicting state rules.

However, there are also strong reasons to have state rather than national regulation. The information requirements for effective regulation are very time and place specific, and states are much better suited than a national regulatory body to respond to these local conditions. Regulation can also be tremendously inefficient, and competition between states can reduce some of that inefficiency. As states experiment with different levels and types of regulation, both consumers and producers have the opportunity to vote with their feet, and in the process produce incentives to search for efficient rules. The history of pesticide regulation in the United States shows at least partial recognition of the desirability of both national and state efforts.

The Evolution of Regulation in the United States

The complexity of pesticides' impact on the environment and the mix of positive and negative externalities associated with their use have produced a long regulatory history in the United States. This history spans the range from purely local to federal regulation and back to increasing state involvement. Since 1947 the federal regulatory program has been built around the requirement of national registration of pesticides. Through the requirement that manufacturers of pesticides seek permission to sell pesticides in the marketplace, the federal government assumed the role of a gatekeeper. First with respect to efficacy, and later with respect to a variety of safety and environmental concerns, federal regulators attempted to impose uniform national standards on pesticide regulation.

The Nationalization of Regulation

Much of the regulatory history of pesticides in the United States reflects a steadily increasing nationalization of authority. By treating pesticide use as regulation of a national market for products rather than as the outcome of a series of individual decisions about a range of pest control strategies, regulatory authority flowed inexorably to Washington, D.C. Even state regulators, like New York Assistant Attorney General Martha McCabe quoted above, continue to view state authority as "by definition, incomplete responses to a national problem" (McCabe 1989, 37). However, the national, uniform solutions also created significant pressures for variations to meet local conditions, and so when nationalization began to significantly constrain users, limited authority was returned to the states. As nationalization proved unworkable in practice in the 1970s and 1980s, the states have again obtained considerable authority to vary the terms of pesticide regulation within their borders.

Creating a National Framework

Regulation of pesticides in the United States began in the early 1900s, growing out of concern over the impact of the early inorganic pesticides on fruit in the Pacific Northwest. Indeed, some early efforts at regulation were aimed at solving the positive externalities of pest control by *requiring* farmers to either spray or pay for the state to spray their crops (Wharton 1974, 72). A few states undertook some regulatory action before the federal government; national regulation began with the federal Insecticide Act of 1910.[7] The 1910 act was primarily concerned with efficacy and its controls were post-market; once a product was discovered to fall short of the sellers' claims, it could be removed from the market. Proper labeling of products was the primary means of control (Rogers 1994, 412–13). Health concerns over the nonorganics were centered on concern about poisoning people, not about broad environmental impacts (Wharton 1974, ix).

While most state regulation centered on commercial applicator licensing and consumer protection–oriented product market controls to protect consumers from incompetent individuals and ineffective products, states required manufacturers to register products and meet state labeling requirements. Some states did impose use controls aimed at protecting neighboring agricultural users from pesticide drift. States played little role in the primary area of pre-FIFRA regulatory activity, residue control. Wharton's comprehensive history of pre-*Silent Spring* regulatory activity notes that "the states essentially merely understudied, and often without much enthusiasm, the federal role in residue control" (1974, 122).

By the mid-1940s, the pesticide industry was ready for an enhanced federal role. State regulations were becoming increasingly burdensome, primarily because state laws differed in details rather than because they imposed particularly onerous requirements. Testifying in favor of the proposed increase in federal regulation, one industry representative claimed the industry was subject to 270 state laws (U.S. House 1946, 41). Another noted that more than thirty states regulated pesticides and predicted that within a year or two, forty-five would be doing so (U.S. House 1946, 56).

Congress responded in 1947 with a new federal regulatory scheme. The Federal Insecticide, Fungicide, and Rodenticide Act[8] had two stated goals: "to protect the users of economic poisons by requiring that full and accurate information be provided as to the contents and directions for use and, in the case of poisons toxic to man, a statement of antidote for the poisons contained therein" and "to protect the reputable manufacturer or distributor from those few opportunists who would discredit the industry by attempting to capitalize on situations by false claims for useless or dangerous products" (U.S. House 1946, 56). The statute was a compromise that required manufacturers and distributors to federally register products and to provide the U.S. Department of Agriculture (USDA) with some minimal efficacy data but denied USDA the authority to reject a requested registration. Although more ambitious than the 1910 act, the 1947 FIFRA continued the earlier act's consumer protection focus.

As weak as the 1947 FIFRA was, the new federal regulators were confident their abilities exceeded those of their state counterparts. For example, USDA proposed limiting industry to references to materials from USDA, the Department of the Interior, the Public Health Service, and state experiment stations to support statements on labels. Congress proved more trusting, however, and FIFRA allowed reliance on state experiment stations, agricultural colleges, and other "similar . . . institutions or agencies authorized by law to conduct research in the field."[9] Similarly, USDA was suspicious of even other federal agencies, like the Fish and Wildlife Service, where the staff was not as committed to agriculture (Graham 1970, 28–29).

While state authority over pesticide regulation was extensive, little attention was paid to the state role in the increasingly sharp policy debate over pesticide use and regulation sparked by Rachel Carson's *Silent Spring* in 1962. The Mrak Commission, appointed in response to the furor raised by Carson, spent only one brief paragraph in its massive report on the state role, concluding "[i]n all probability most State regulation will follow Federal guidelines and will likely be less demanding" (U.S. HEW 1969, 80). Similarly, Frank Graham Jr.'s comprehensive analysis of pesticide policy in the 1960s rarely mentions state regulation at all (Graham 1970).[10]

A substantial part of the explanation was that state regulators were usually state agriculture departments and suffered from conflicts of interest and capture problems similar to those of USDA. These problems were arguably more severe at the state level because state agriculture departments were closer to their constituencies and often lacked the USDA's professional staff. Advocates of increased regulation to prevent environmental problems saw little hope in state agriculture departments, whose views of pesticides were likely to be close to those of their farm constituents. Further, the critics described the environmental impacts of pesticides in broad terms that demanded a national solution.

Registration

The most significant step in nationalizing pesticide regulation was the requirement of premarket, national registration of products. Although this was not a novel regulatory method, some manufacturers resisted national registration on the grounds that it would require "getting a federal license in order to do business" (U.S. House 1946, 12 and 46). USDA, on the other hand, argued that only bad actors had reason to fear the agency; reputable manufacturers "would welcome" the opportunity "to check their products" with the agency (U.S. House 1946, 4).

National registration was introduced in the 1947 FIFRA for two purposes: "to facilitate administration and to aid in the prevention of violation of the act and to prevent injury to the user by providing a means for review of the labeling, together with the claims made for the material before it is offered for sale" (U.S. House 1946, 3). Registration would bring new products to the attention of USDA and save on agency manpower by eliminating the need for a force of field inspectors to be collecting samples of pesticides throughout the country.[11] The initial requirements for registration were minimal: the registrant's name and address, the name of the pesticide, a complete copy of the label, a statement of all claims made for the product, a copy of the directions for its use, and, if requested by the Secretary of Agriculture, a description of the tests and results upon which the claims of effectiveness were based.

Registration's benefits for consumers, the nominal beneficiaries of the entire program, were limited. Consumers could not tell if a product was registered because the 1947 FIFRA prohibited manufacturers from making mention of the registration in their sales materials or labels or even including the registration number on a label. This was done "because it may otherwise be misunderstood as an endorsement of the article by the Department of Agriculture"[12] (U.S. House 1946, 3).

Most importantly, the 1947 FIFRA registration provision did not provide USDA with the power to refuse to register a pesticide. If a registrant refused a "correction" suggested by USDA, the pesticide would be registered under protest. (Similar provisions were included in many state laws and in the Council of State Governments' 1948 suggested act.) USDA could challenge these pesticides as "misbranded" but the government bore the burden of proof. Registration under protest seriously limited USDA's ability to regulate. This did not escape notice in Congress and when asked, USDA conceded "it might be more effective to make the thing even tighter than it is at the present time in the bill" (U.S. House 1946, 14). It was not "tight," however, because FIFRA was a compromise worked out with the industry and because recognition of the significant environmental problems pesticides could cause was still years away.[13]

Closing the Loopholes

Protest registration appears illogical today because allowing registration despite USDA's objections undermines the safety function of national registration. Viewed in context, however, it was not as self-defeating as it now seems. Organic pesticides were relatively new products and the primary regulatory concern was efficacy. Of all the potential problems presented by pesticides, efficacy concerns are the most likely to be responsive to market pressures. A bad product might enter the market but it would not long survive if it did not work. Most importantly, protest registration did not undercut the uniformity function of national registration.

Relatively few registrants took advantage of the procedure "because of the stigma which would attach to their product" (U.S. House 1963, 26–27). Between 1947 and 1963, 76,000 products were registered as pesticides with the USDA. Only twenty-seven of these were registered under protest, only seven of which were still on the market in 1963 (U.S. House 1963, 12). Of these seven, four were lindane vaporizer tablets that did not specify that they were not intended for home use, two were swimming pool chemicals that included mercury, and one was an alfalfa crown treatment that had previously had its registration canceled for lack of efficacy (U.S. House 1963, 16).

USDA was willing to accept protest registrations in 1946 both because FIFRA was the result of compromise with the industry and because USDA, the pesticide industry, and pesticide users all shared a common goal of maximizing U.S. agricultural production through modern agricultural practices. After the pesticide scares in the late 1950s and *Silent Spring* produced pressure on USDA to act against efficacious pesticides on environmental grounds, however, the focus of registration shifted to being a method of controlling which efficacious products would be allowed on the market. This new role for registration, far from the helpful, expert advice envisioned by the 1947 FIFRA, left protest registration with few friends by 1963. Even the Chemical Specialties Manufacturers Association, a trade group of household products makers, endorsed its elimination since the new provisions provided for administrative and judicial review of denial of registrations (U.S. House 1963, 63). Indeed, Senator Abraham Ribicoff claimed "the unanimous support of everybody in this field" for measures to eliminate it (U.S. House 1963, 8).

Advocates of increased regulation argued that the elimination of protest registrations was a "first essential" in achieving "greater control." Given the low numbers of protest registrations, however, they needed a rationale other than the threat of actual, dangerous products registered under protest. They first argued that manufacturers *could* register large numbers of products under protest if they chose, noting that 4,022 labels had been rejected in fiscal 1963 alone (U.S. House 1963, 13).

The main argument for eliminating protest registrations was not because manufacturers would knowingly register harmful products, however, but because USDA was better positioned to monitor safety. Ribicoff argued that

> We must remember that no manufacturer of a pesticide wants to put a harmful product on the market. He wouldn't be in business long. My concern is with the responsible manufacturer of such a product who has absolute faith in his product and whose research has turned up no dangerous side effect whatever. This man is a businessman—convinced he is right—and having good reason to believe so on the basis of what is known about the product at the time. He is confronted with a doubting Federal employee who shouldn't approve the product without adequate proof of its safety.
>
> The policy of this Nation is, and should always be, that a pesticide should not come on the market until adequate proof of safety has been established and it should not be left for the public to play the role of guinea pig while the true facts of toxicity are brought out. (U.S. House 1963, 5)

Under protest registration, USDA could obtain a court's review of safety and effectiveness but "time often must elapse before a body of evidence is accumulated justifying a seizure action by the Government and a subsequent court case" (U.S. House 1963, 5). Eliminating protest registration would prevent products from appearing on the market before they were proven safe and effective, a significant change in the structure of federal regulation.

Accepting the elimination of protest registration was also the price the industry paid for increased federal preemption of state regulation. The industry was increasingly worried about inconsistent state regulations; forty-seven states required state registration of pesticides by 1963, and industry representatives were concerned about the problem of where to put a long list of state registration numbers on labels (U.S. House 1963, 46). In return for their support for eliminating protest registration, industry sought and received authority for the federal registration number to appear on the label.[14] The industry also obtained a provision requiring a scientific advisory committee, chosen by the National Academy of Sciences and including land grant college representatives, to review registration rejections and cancellations.[15] Since the National Academy of Sciences was known to be hostile to the environmental critique of pesticide use (Hornstein 1993, 429), this was a significant restriction of USDA's new powers.

Although FIFRA remained primarily concerned with efficacy, the elimination of protest registration in 1964 marked a significant change in the character of federal regulation of pesticides. No longer was the federal government simply intervening as a consumer advocate after a product was in the stream of commerce. Registration was transformed from an administrative convenience for USDA into a required license to do business in the national market, and USDA became the first national gatekeeper for pesticides. Thus, after 1964 the principle of national control of a national market was clearly established even though manufacturers and distributors retained the option of registration only at the state level for pesticides not used in interstate commerce until 1972.

Refocusing on the Environment

By the end of the 1960s, public concern over pesticides produced a massive federal effort to evaluate their impact on the environment. The Mrak Commission, dominated by scientists from industry and academia, was appointed in April 1969 and undertook to assess the overall impact of pesticides. The commission's almost 700-page report sought to reassure the public, beginning by noting the "tremendous benefits from the usage of pesticides to prevent disease and to increase the production of foods and fibers" (U.S. HEW 1969, 5). The solution to the uncertainty caused by "recent evidence . . . [of] the unintentional effects of pesticides on various life forms within the environment and on human health" was "[s]ound judgments" (U.S. HEW 1969, 5). To make these judgments "sound" required data, and the report is filled with calls for extensive data collection.[16]

Registration was the Mrak Commission's vehicle of choice for implementing these sound judgments. The commission called for "periodic review and reapproval" by the federal government's technical experts "and in no case should a pesticide registration be effective for a period longer than two years" (U.S. HEW 1969, 238). New pesticides would be registered only "on a provisional basis" while data were developed (U.S. HEW 1969, 238).

Pesticide regulation was transferred from USDA to the newly formed Environmental Protection Agency in December 1970. USDA had not compiled an aggressive record as a regulator; no formal procedure for recall of products was created until May 1969, just days before GAO hearings on USDA's pesticide activities were scheduled to begin; no product had been recalled as dangerous until 1969; and criminal proceedings for violation of FIFRA had been initiated only once (Briggs 1992, 279).[17] Simply transferring administration of FIFRA away from the USDA to a more environmentally oriented agency was not enough, however, because the regulatory structure created by FIFRA was still too focused on efficacy.

The 1972 Federal Environmental Pest Control Act (FEPCA),[18] which revamped virtually every part of FIFRA to focus for the first time on the environment, continued the nationalization of pesticide regulation. The amendments gave the national government authority over pesticides marketed within a single state as well as those sold in interstate commerce. Licensing and use classification expanded national regulation into pesticide use in a significant way for the first time.

The agreement that environmental concerns needed to be incorporated into FIFRA masked both deep divisions over how to do so and agricultural interests' suspicion of EPA. During the congressional hearings on FEPCA, agricultural interests repeatedly attacked EPA for canceling DDT registrations and for restricting eradication campaigns against fire ants and predators. Opponents of pesticide use were just as vocal— the American Honey Producers' Association representative claimed that USDA "has displayed about the same solicitude toward bees as a homicidal maniac with a gun in his hand and an urge to kill" (U.S. House 1971, 442).

The 1972 FEPCA substantially altered registration standards. New pesticides were required to meet standards that included assessment of environmental harm in addition to the traditional efficacy requirement. Older pesticides were to be reregistered by EPA under the new, more stringent standards. In addition, pesticide use was now regulated and users were now restricted to those uses on the labels.

These ambitious goals quickly ran into practical roadblocks. Many users had been accustomed to using pesticides for a wide range of nonlabel uses; they would face the loss of available tools if nothing were done. The Senate agriculture committee was especially concerned about the case of "an entire industry within a single State . . . plagued by a pest for which a perfectly adequate and safe remedy would be available but for the fact that the economic return from the pesticide for such use is not adequate to warrant the cost of Federal registration of the pesticide for such use" (U.S. Senate 1972b, 72). Hawaii, Michigan, and Washington State authorities were particularly vocal on this point (U.S. Senate 1972b, 73).

Moreover, despite its greatly enhanced regulatory authority, it was soon clear that EPA lacked both the political and the administrative resources to carry out the ambitious regulatory program envisioned by the 1972 amendments. In 1975, 46,000 state-registered-only pesticides were awaiting federal reregistration (GAO 1978). Even in March 1986, EPA had not completed even one final reassessment on any pesticide active ingredient and had preliminarily assessed only about 20 percent of the registered active ingredients (GAO 1986, 3).[19] The cost was also high. The review of chlorobenzilate, for example, occupied the time of thirteen EPA staff for three years and cost over $400,000 (National Research Council 1978, 46).

In response to concerns that the 1972 changes overcentralized regulatory authority, Congress made changes in FIFRA in 1975 and 1978, which returned some authority to the states, particularly with respect to enforcement.[20] Federal efforts were now to concentrate on oversight of state activity, registration,[21] labeling, classification compliance monitoring, and investigation of data frauds. The net effect of the changes during the 1970s was to significantly alter the state–national division of labor. Many state programs that had previously been based solely on state authority, such as applicator licensing, now had significant national components as well. Other state programs had their character and goals changed. Thus the EPA's role at the end of the 1970s remained far larger than the national role in the 1960s but significantly smaller than that envisioned in 1972.

FIFRA amendments in the late 1970s and 1980s also sought to increase the role of science (Hornstein 1993, 435–36; National Research Council 1978, 23). EPA was given additional authority to require data, and scientists both inside and outside the agency were given increased roles. This resulted in FIFRA becoming a more a "regularized scientific endeavor" (Hornstein 1993, 435). In addition, EPA was given authority to allow "conditional" registration of pesticides where some health and environmental data were missing. These changes shifted the balance back toward the concerns of agricultural interests.

State Authority

Each version of FIFRA until 1972 was built upon an existing regulatory scheme that depended largely on state level regulation. Much regulation was controlled at the federal level but states could allow additional uses within their borders without federal review, in effect allowing states to opt out of particular federal actions. After the shift of national authority to EPA in 1970, agricultural interests tried unsuccessfully in 1972 to give USDA a veto over EPA's actions as a means of limiting EPA's power. When this failed, they then turned to forcing EPA to continue to share authority with state regulators. One significant way in which they did so was the creation of exceptions to the newly expanded national registration requirement in section 24 of FIFRA.

The National Framework

National registration is now the heart of pesticide regulation, and since 1972 registration incorporates environmental concerns and requires significantly more action by EPA than it did from USDA. Each use, soil treatment of weeds around orange trees for example, must be registered with the EPA and products typically are registered for many different uses. EPA is also now required to classify pesticides for either restricted[22] or general use;[23] many products have both types of uses. In addition, EPA increased the data required for registration substantially after 1970, adding chronic toxicity, mutegenicity, and animal safety tests (Rogers 1994, 448).

In addition, pesticides used on food crops (and EPA takes a broad view of what constitutes a food use) must have a tolerance level for residues set before the pesticide can be registered.[24] EPA sets tolerances on new agricultural produces under the Federal Food, Drug and Cosmetic Act "to the extent necessary to protect the public health," language that EPA has interpreted to allow it to balance the risks and benefits.[25] (Until recently tolerances for food additives fell under the Delaney Clause, which established a zero-tolerance standard for potentially carcinogenic food additives.[26]) Tolerances also raise international trade issues, since they can be used as nontariff barriers to trade (Rosman 1993).

Two major changes in the role of national registration were introduced by FEPCA. First, all uses inconsistent with the federally registered label were made illegal.[27] Many uses had never been registered with state or federal authorities often based on relatively informal recommendations from extension agents and others. These uses were now illegal. Second, state registrations were made federal registrations and, except where the federal law allowed exceptions, had to meet EPA's general registration criteria. Since there were tens of thousands of state-registered-only uses, this created a substantial burden for EPA. For example, Florida alone had two hundred state-registered uses for just one product, Temik (aldicarb), in 1975, which would have to be converted to federal registrations (U.S. House 1975, 212). Florida flower growers worried that sales to them were too small (8 percent of total sales) to justify the manufacturer spending the money on necessary label changes, even if no new data were needed for federal registration (U.S. House 1975, 211).

National registration is a time-consuming and expensive process. It is made all the more difficult by the 1972 FEPCA requirement that pesticides registered under prior versions of FIFRA be reregistered under the new, environmental protection–oriented criteria. The reregistration process has occupied years of EPA's efforts and only recently begun to achieve measurable progress (GAO 1986, 1993). EPA's registration process was also slowed by the 1972 FEPCA provisions on the sharing of data between registrations. EPA reported it was rejecting more than 90 percent of registration applications in 1977 because of the lack of data and lack of authority to use information already on file for similar products to support a registration without the permission of the other registrant (U.S. House 1977a, 165).

The registration provisions of the modern FIFRA are not merely a vestige of the prior consumer protection focus of the earlier statutes. They reflect a vision of environmental protection based on calculation of the costs and benefits of each individual use by an expert gatekeeper.[28] The modified reregistration process created by the 1988 FIFRA amendments provides a good benchmark for the registration process in general, since registration of new products or new uses for old products can be no more efficient than the reregistration of old products or old uses for which there is the added benefit of years of experience with actual use. The General Accounting Office's description suggests the difficulties involved:

> [R]egistration is a lengthy and complex process. The pesticides' registrants must conduct numerous health and environmental studies for EPA's review. Over 100 studies may be required to provide the information EPA needs to assess a food-use pesticide. The studies, some of which take up to 4 years to complete, include information on the chemical and physical characteristics of the pesticides and on their potential to cause adverse effects on human health and/or the environment. EPA is required to review the registrants' studies, determine the acceptability and utility of each piece of information, identify gaps in the information, and, when the information on a pesticide is sufficient, determine whether the pesticide can be used without posing unreasonable health and environmental risks. (1993, 8)

The model suggests that not only is the gatekeeper capable of assessing the complex data needed to understand the impact of individual pesticide use registrations, based upon partial and incomplete data, but that the gatekeeper can act in a timely fashion.

EPA's ability to fulfill this role can be questioned on a number of grounds. Each redesign of the registration/reregistration process brings with it promises of action; each succeeding reinvention of the process reveals how hollow those promises have been. EPA's difficulties with the reregistration process highlight the problems of the gatekeeper approach to regulation. While registration offers the theoretical opportunity to catch problem products before they enter the stream of commerce, the resource demands to successfully implement it suggest it can achieve only limited effectiveness. The heavy premarket focus of a registration-based regulatory framework also neglects the provision of incentives for potential pesticide users. Finally, the resource demands of evaluating even a single pesticide product divert attention from discovering methods of resolving the underlying pest problems that create the demand for chemical controls.

Perhaps most importantly, national regulation is an appropriate means to address only the national concerns raised by pesticide use. It is a strikingly inappropriate means to address local concerns. National registration was initially introduced to address efficacy and acute poisoning concerns, both of which are arguably uniform across the United States. The environmental impact of pesticides is much more varied, however, and a pesticide's use can have dramatically different impacts in different locations. For those products used under more or less uniform conditions nationwide, such as household pest control products, national registration may be a reasonable first approximation of appropriate regulations. For agricultural pesticides, however, uniform national registrations are far more problematic, even without considering possible regional differences in attitudes toward risk.

Special Local Needs Registrations

The original proposals for FEPCA did not include provisions for state registrations to meet local needs and state officials were not reluctant to complain (U.S. House 1971, 821, 851, and 857). States argued they had the expertise and resources to handle regulation. Scientists from Florida's Department of Agriculture, for example, testified:

> We have been controlling pesticides since 1939. We feel that we have a very effective program. We feel that our control of pesticides in Florida is adequate at the present time. We have 25 laboratory personnel who are involved in chemical examination of pesticides and pesticide residues. We have 13, the equivalent of 13, full-time pesticide researchers. We have a central laboratory in Tallahassee, the state capital. We have a branch laboratory in Sanford. We have two mobile laboratories, all of which are engaged in the control of pesticides.
>
> We have a pesticide technical council which advises the commissioner on the adoption of regulations pertaining to pesticides. . . .
>
> We feel that we have the best technical brains in the State, the most knowledgeable people, to advise the commissioner in this area. (U.S. House 1971, 513)

As a companion to the tightening of federal registration requirements and elimination of intrastate, nonfederal registration in the 1972 FEPCA, section 24 was created to allow states to register pesticides for intrastate use under certain conditions[29] (U.S. Senate 1972a, 29). This authority was the subject of a struggle between the Senate Agriculture and Commerce Committees with the more environmentally oriented Commerce Committee proposing an amendment to severely restrict this authority (U.S. Senate 1972b, 22). If, as agricultural interests feared, environmentally oriented regulators were to become the national gatekeepers for pesticides and slam shut the door on pesticide use, state regulators, who tended to be much closer to agricultural interests, could keep the gate open at least a bit. The states prevailed in Congress and the battle shifted to implementation of the new language.

States were unhappy with EPA's implementation of section 24(c), calling the interim regulations so restricted as to make the authority "useless" (U.S. House 1977a, 34–35; U.S. Senate 1977, 110). EPA was making 24(c) too much like section 3, they argued, and a registrant "gains no advantage by requesting a state registration vs. a federal registration if EPA has required the systems to be essentially equal" (U.S. House 1977a, 42). Delays by the agency in implementing 24(c) prompted a Washington State agriculture official to claim "[t]here are those within EPA who obviously distrust the competency and integrity of state control officials to carry out [24(c)]" (U.S. House 1975, 351). Requiring full data and barring registration of competing products were preventing 24(c) from relieving the pressure caused by EPA's delays in proceeding under section 3 (U.S. House 1977a, 82). One particularly sore point was the 1972 FEPCA version of section 24(c)'s requirement that states be certified by the EPA administrator as "capable of exercising adequate controls to ensure that such registration will be in accord with the purposes of this Act." Also, when states issued SLN registrations, the EPA administrator had ninety days to disapprove it.

The 1977 amendments strengthened state authority by removing the certification requirement. EPA unsuccessfully defended its certification authority by arguing that it placed only "reasonable restraints" on the states, restraints necessary to "assuring that pesticide decisions, at whatever level of government they are made, adequately reflect the broad public interest" (Costle 1977). The 1978 amendments strengthened state authority by replacing the EPA certification requirement with a default grant of authority, which EPA could suspend under limited conditions.[30] They also strengthened state authority by restricting the EPA administrator from disapproving an SLN registration on the basis of "lack of essentially" or if "its composition and use patterns are similar to those of a federally registered pesticide," except when the registration is inconsistent with the Food and Drug Administration's residue tolerances for food or feed.[31] EPA did successfully fight off attempts to remove its veto power over SLN registrations, which agricultural interests had argued was necessary to make the states "true partners" in pesticide regulation (U.S. House 1977a, 43).

Environmentalists were also unhappy with the implementation of 24(c), particularly after 1978. States registered pesticides under 24(c) that

EPA "had determined . . . may have an unreasonable adverse effect on man or the environment" (GAO 1978, 42). Approximately 20 percent of 24(c) registrations fell into this category (GAO 1978, 42). When the GAO questioned EPA about these registrations, EPA responded that it "did not believe it could restrict the states from registering those pesticides" and that it did not plan to address this issue in its final regulations[32] (GAO 1978, 45).

SLNs represent much more than a division of labor between federal and state regulators. Arguing for removal of the EPA veto, Florida Congressman Richard Kelly asked, "[D]on't you think it is important for the Federal Government not to divorce itself from the real world and for us to trust the State agricultural establishment?" (U.S. House 1976, 245). Kelly's question captured the essential difference between federal and state registration. Federal registration was focused on preventing bad products, whether ineffective, acutely toxic, or environmentally hazardous, from reaching the market. State SLN registrations were meant to provide a tool to solve a pest control problem. State regulators were asking "what tool is available to solve this pest problem?" rather than "what are the environmental impacts of this pesticide?" In the highly polarized 1970s debate over pesticide regulation, there was little trust to go around.

SLN Regulation Today

Under the current versions of FIFRA and SLN regulations, states have broad authority under 24(c) to expand the registration of pesticides.[33] Most importantly, a registration under 24(c) is effectively a section 3 registration within the state for which it is issued. EPA's recently issued guidance document and the current 24(c) regulations defer authority to the states to register pesticides under a wide range of circumstances.[34] Not only may states register products under 24(c), but 24(c) registrations can negate restrictions imposed on federal labels, impose more restrictive measures than are on section 3 labels, and limit use of a product to a subset of section 3 uses. EPA currently rejects only 3 to 4 percent of 24(c) applications for nonadministrative reasons. Those rejected fall largely into two categories: registrations for treated seed uses[35] and attempts to register a distributor product rather than the basic ingredient.[36]

States may register new products or additional uses of federally registered products if (1) there exists a pest problem within the state for which the state has determined that an appropriate federally registered product is not available; (2) for food crops, there is a tolerance or other clearance for the pesticide on the crop; and (3) registration for the same use has not previously been denied, disapproved, suspended, or canceled by the administrator or voluntarily canceled by the registrant after EPA has issued a notice of intent to cancel the use based on health or environmental concerns about an ingredient.[37] In addition, the state must determine that the product's use will not cause unreasonable adverse effects on man or the environment if the product has a composition not similar to a federally registered product, involves a use pattern not similar to a federally registered product, or has had other uses of either the same or a similar product canceled, suspended, disapproved, or denied by EPA. The cost of a 24(c) registration varies from state to state. In the most restrictive states, such as California, pest control specialists estimate the cost of preparing an application to be between $10,000 and $25,000.[38]

EPA exercises relatively limited review of 24(c) applications. In contrast to the extensive data required for a section 3 registration, data requirements are minimal. For amendments to federal products or new products that are substantially similar to currently registered products in composition and use, EPA does not require additional data. Even for products that are not substantially similar to registered products, "EPA will ask for only a brief summary of the data, the state's conclusions, and a certification that the product will not cause unreasonable adverse effects as defined in FIFRA." In addition to review of individual applications, EPA also periodically reviews the records generally.

The new guidance document, developed with extensive consultation with the states, resolves several policy questions that had plagued the program for years. A "special local need" exists when a pest problem exists, or is likely to exist, for which a state can document that (1) a federally registered product is not available in the state for the desired sites; (2) the federally registered products that are available cannot be applied without "causing unacceptable risks to human health or the environment"; (3) the registration is necessary to maintain an integrated pest management, resistance, or minor use pest control program; or 4) the existing federally registered product can be reduced by a formulation that poses less risk to man or the environment. Price is generally not an acceptable measure of a special local need. EPA rarely, if ever, has disputes with states over the states' implementation of the definition of special local need.[39]

EPA's formulation of these guidelines is particularly significant since it delegates more authority to the states than some states had previously claimed under the regulations.[40] For example, California, which has the most extensive state pesticide regulatory apparatus and one of the more restrictive views of state authority, had previously refused to issue 24(c) registrations where any federally registered product was available within the state, even if the product were not available at the location of need.[41] Most important is the broadening of the definition of special local need to consider pest resistance, reducing hazard, and providing users with choice. Products with a different mode of action on the pest can help prevent the development of resistant populations.

For food crops, the most critical issue is the existence of a tolerance.[42] USDA funds the IR4 program to assist in provision of tolerances for minor uses. The requirement of a tolerance is less of a burden than it might appear, however, because EPA classifies crops into broad groups and accepts a tolerance on one for use on others. Thus a pesticide registered under section 3 for almonds could be registered under section 24(c) for use on pecans based on the almond tolerance.

The history of pesticide regulation in the United States leads to the conclusion that there has been a general recognition of the need for efforts at both the national and state levels. The setting of tolerance levels for pesticide residues on crops is an effort to regulate an externality that crosses state boundaries. Federal registration suffices for most states, reducing the costs of registration for pesticide manufacturers. However, the provision for Special Local Needs registrations by the states is an implicit acknowledgment that a centralized registration process is extremely cumbersome and cannot take account of the particular circumstances of time and place. The question is, how well has this combination of federal and state regulation worked?

The evidence is quite compelling that the state and federal regulatory mix has not resulted in excessive dangers to consumers of fruits and vegetables. The federal government sets the tolerance levels, and, under 24(c), the states can approve pesticides for uses not approved by the EPA. However, the federal tolerance levels cannot, in any case, be exceeded. A 1996 study by the National Research Council finds that

> based on existing exposure data, the great majority of individual naturally occurring and synthetic chemicals in the diet appears to be present at levels below which any significant adverse biologic effect is likely, and so low that they are unlikely to pose an appreciable cancer risk. . . .
> . . . natural components of the diet may prove to be of greater concern than synthetic components with respect to cancer risk. (1996, 5–6)

However, more explicit evidence on the SLN exception available to states would be helpful. The next section develops such evidence.

SLN Use

In this section I analyze SLN use by statistically examining the pattern of adoption. The results suggest that SLN registrations are not generally abused, although several particular products have such widespread use that their SLN registrations could be argued to be bypassing the section 3 registration requirements.

Patterns of SLN Use

One function of SLN registrations is to provide for lowered entry barriers for pest control needs that could not justify the costs of a section 3 registration. The lower cost and faster response time of the 24(c) procedures could provide growers of specialty crops with access to pesticides that would be unavailable if the registrant were required to conduct the full section 3 registration process. Similarly, section 24(c) registrations provide a means for growers of any crop to obtain pesticides to address pest problems that are insufficiently widespread to justify a registrant obtaining a section 3 registration. SLN registrations are also used as a means of limiting manufacturers' liability. Where a manufacturer has decided that the potential sales for a particular use do not justify the potential liability from adverse effects on the crop, a 24(c) registration can include as a condition that the user has signed an indemnification agreement with the manufacturer.[43]

Section 24(c) registrations might also be used to circumvent section 3's requirements, however. A pesticide could be registered in the primary states where a crop is grown under 24(c) and a vast majority of the market covered without an additional section 3 registration. To the extent that the crop faces essentially the same pests in each state, the 24(c) registration would substitute for a section 3 registration. Citrus, for example, is grown commercially primarily in California, Florida, Texas, and Arizona. A 24(c) registration in those four states would provide a registrant with access to substantially all of the market for citrus pesticides. Moreover, the potential avoidance of section 3 registration costs would be a significant incentive to devote research and development resources to finding new uses for existing pesticides rather than finding new active ingredients.

Criticism of the use of section 24(c) registrations began in earnest in 1983 when the Rural Advancement Fund of the National Sharecroppers Fund (RAF/NSF), a North Carolina-based farm advocacy group, published a critique (Spalt 1983a). The RAF/NSF study made three major criticisms of SLNs:

- Most registrations were neither "special" nor "local" but dealt with major crops and widespread pest problems.
- A few products made up the bulk of the SLN registrations.
- EPA performed inadequate review of SLN registrations.

It concluded that

> SLN pesticide registration is a giant loophole. In the vast majority of
> cases, SLN pesticides are not being used for special pest problems in
> local situations. Instead, a limited number of chemical products are being
> used on major crops, to control general problems, in many regions of the
> country. Clearly, pesticide products used in this magnitude, which bear
> little or no relation to "special local needs" should be subject to standard
> registration procedures to determine if and how they can be safely used.
> (Spalt 1983b, 6–7)

The RAF/NSF study based these conclusions on an analysis of SLN
registrations in twenty-five states during 1981 and 1982. They found that
the top ten crop/site uses accounted for 62.7 percent of SLN registrations, that the top five registrants accounted for 46 percent of SLN registrations studied, five pesticide products accounted for 23 percent of
SLN registrations studied, and the top five generic chemical ingredients
accounted for 32.7 percent of SLN registrations studied (Spalt 1983a).
Somewhat similar patterns in SLN use exist today. Tables 5.1 and 5.2
list SLN registrations by state, registrant, and "parent" EPA registration.[44]
SLN registrations are issued primarily by a few states: the top five account for over 40 percent of all active SLN registrations.

There are several possible explanations for the concentration of SLN
registrations in a few states. First, those states may have more diverse
agricultures than others. Second, those states may have more organized
grower groups or more effective state regulators who aggressively seek
SLN registrations to benefit their growers. Third, those states may be
more susceptible to pest outbreaks requiring chemical control.

It is not clear whether these patterns indicate that SLNs are being used
as an inappropriate end run around section 3 registration or whether they
represent an appropriate expansion of registration to meet state needs.
The relatively small number of SLN registrations per section 3 ("parent") EPA registrations does suggest that most of the pesticides involved
are not receiving registrations equivalent to a national registration by
obtaining multiple SLN registrations. Since some crops may require registration in only a few states to ensure near complete market share, this
is not a completely satisfactory test. In addition, because pests may differ across states on the same crop, a series of 24(c) registrations for a
particular product could represent appropriate registrations to address
different local pest conditions.

Although EPA rarely disputes states' characterizations of special
local needs,[45] EPA has taken steps to limit the ability to use 24(c) to circumvent section 3. In 1996 EPA began a policy of questioning applica-

tions which cover five or more states and denying applications when there are fifteen registrations for the same product and use (U.S. EPA 1996). In addition, where a commodity is grown in a limited number of states, EPA will seek consultation with the registrant if there are registrations covering almost all of the relevant states[46] (U.S. EPA 1996). EPA's own preliminary search has found only ten to fifteen products where the number of registrations indicated a potential problem,[47] and some of these may be related to the ability to use a particular product in a wide variety of applications (U.S. EPA 1996).

One version of a successful SLN program, and one implicit in the RAF/NSF study, is that SLN registrations exist for specialty crops, such as taro or pineapples. Crops grown in only a few states, with relatively minor market impact, could not support the registration costs of a new section 3 registration. Nor would the additional marketing allowed by section 3 registration be useful to a registrant for many

Table 5.1
Top 15 Issuers of SLN Registrations

State	Number of SLNs	Percent of Total	Cummulative Percent
Washington	354	13	13
California	337	12	24
Oregon	263	9	34
Florida	149	5	39
Texas	125	4	43
Idaho	103	4	47
Mississippi	101	4	51
Arizona	94	3	54
North Carolina	76	3	57
Louisiana	73	3	59
Virginia	71	3	62
Georgia	65	2	64
Oklahoma	62	2	66
Arkansas	56	2	68
South Carolina	54	2	70

Sources: USDA (various years); Council of State Government (various years); Pest-Bank™ data provided by Silver Platter International N.V., Norwood, Massachusetts.

Table 5.2
Number of SLNs per Parent Registration

Number of SLN Registrations per Parent Registration	Number of Parent Registrations
1	227
2	238
3	198
4	152
5	85
6	114
7	133
8	88
9	108
10	40
11–20	49
21–40	18
41–100	4
100+	1

Note: Median number of SLN registrations per parent EPA registration = 2.
Source: National Pesticide Information Retrieval System (NPIRS).

of these crops: ginger, for example, is grown commercially in only a few states.

Other crops, like cotton or alfalfa, however, are grown in many states. A pattern of SLN registrations for these crops covering the major states in which these crops are grown might indicate that companies are forgoing section 3 registration and achieving high market coverage without submitting the safety data required by section 3. The limit on this type of behavior is the requirement of a tolerance for registration under section 24(c).

The difficulty lies in defining what is success for the SLN program. In conversations with people on both "sides" of the SLN issue, I found similar views. Neither side views the program as successful and neither sees refining the statute as a solution. Instead both voice a desire for EPA and state regulatory authorities to stand up to those on the other side, who they view as overly influential, and make more "right" decisions.

If we observed registrations in most states for a particular dangerous product, for example, that would indicate use of the SLN registration procedure to subvert national registration. Control of flies, for example, in animal facilities is a need that does not appear to be either special or local. On the other extreme, a registration for a product for taro or ginger, crops grown in only a few states, would appear to be both special and local.

Between those extremes, however, lie the bulk of SLN registrations and it is much more difficult to determine whether registrations for these products constitute an abuse. Both environmentalists and pesticide users see problems with SLN use. Not surprisingly these perceived problems tend to mirror each other. Environmentalists complain that EPA is allowing too many SLN registrations, not imposing sufficient offsetting restrictions, and generally being overly driven by political pressures. Pesticide users and others who consider pesticide use essential to modern agriculture argue that EPA is overly strict, crimping state authority through onerous informal guidelines and long delays.

Empirical Analysis

Examination of the states' experience with SLNs offers an opportunity to test several hypotheses about SLN use. The first result of such an examination is to reveal how poor the data on pesticides are. The data collected in computerized form have serious inadequacies; important information is often not available or missing from a substantial number of observations. For example, some of the most interesting data would be data on toxicity and pesticide use. Toxicity data are simply not available for many pesticides and use data are not collected.

The limited data available allow some analysis, however. The ideal test would be to regress a set of independent variables describing the pesticide (categorizing its use, toxicity, cost, etc.) and the states (categorizing the importance of agriculture in the economy, the influence of agricultural interests on state government, the crops grown, the diversity of the state's agriculture) on a dependent variable indicating whether a particular pesticide had a SLN registration in that state. Data limitations preclude such a test, however.

The data that are available are taken from the Census of Agriculture, the Book of the States, the Statistical Abstract, and Pest-Bank™, a commercial repackage of federal and state data.[48] The data allow categorization of the pesticides in three ways. First, pesticides are assigned one of three label signal words: caution, warning, and danger, in order of increasing hazardousness. Second, pesticides may be categorized by the pest group to which they apply: disinfectants, plant pathogenic fungi, insects and other invertebrates, plant pathogenic nematodes, weed plants, protozoa and other unicellular organisms, vertebrates, and undefined.

Third, pesticides can be classified by target pest type (algaecides, anti-fouling compounds, bactericides, defoliants, desiccants, disinfectants, fungicides, herbicides, insecticides, nematicides, poisons, repellents), use classification, requirement of child-resistant packaging, and product registration status.

The data available permit a series of simple tests. I first compare the group of section 3 registered pesticides for which SLN registrations have been issued with those for which SLN registrations have not been issued. I next compare section 3 registered pesticides with SLN-registered pesticides to those without SLN registrations. In table 5.3, I list the proportions that meet the various categorizations and report significance levels for differences in means.

These comparisons reveal a number of significant differences between section 3 and SLN registrations. SLN registrations are more likely to be classified with one of the higher level of hazardousness signal words than section 3 registrations. With respect to pest groups, SLN registrations are more concentrated on pests in the weed, insect, nematode, and vertebrate pest groups than section 3 registrations; a similar concentration is shown by the type data. SLNs are less likely to involve conditionally registered pesticides and less likely to be required to have child-resistant packaging.

The differences between section 3 registrations and SLN registrations suggest that the SLN process is being used to meet different needs from the section 3 process. The differences in means tests do not allow us to choose between benign and malignant explanations, however. The pattern shown here is consistent with both a careful use of the SLN process to meet specific needs, while avoiding national registration of more hazardous uses, and abuse of the process to register more dangerous uses under a lower level of regulatory scrutiny.

To distinguish between these explanations we can examine the pattern of registration by state. If the SLN process is being misused, it is likely that it is being misused because state regulatory agencies have been captured by agricultural interests. Agricultural interests can capture state regulatory agencies in two ways. First, agricultural interests may have significant political power because of the importance of agriculture in a state's economy. For example, agriculture contributed approximately 14 percent of South Dakota's gross state product in 1991. Second, agriculture may be relatively unimportant to a state's economy but the state pesticide regulatory apparatus may be structured to allow capture by agricultural interests. In Texas, for example, which has a much more diversified economy than South Dakota, pesticides are regulated by an elected agriculture commissioner who is also responsible for promoting state agriculture. Table 5.4 summarizes the variables used below and table 5.5 gives descriptive statistics for each.

States' agriculture is measured in four ways: state share of total agricultural income; state share of total government agricultural payments to farmers; the proportion of agricultural income contributed by livestock; and total spending on fertilizer.[49] As a state's share of national agricultural income rises, the state becomes a more important independent market.[50] States that receive significant amounts of federal government agricultural payments are likely to have less diverse agricultural economies, and hence less need for "special local need" pesticide registrations if these are not being used to meet truly local needs. On the other hand, if they are being used to meet major crop producers needs in an end run around EPA, one would expect those states where agriculture is sufficiently politically powerful to extract rents on a national scale to obtain a significant share of SLN registrations. States that derive significant portions of their agricultural income from livestock would, all else equal, have less demand for pesticides than states where agricultural income derives from crops.[51] Finally fertilizer spending serves as an extremely rough proxy for overall pesticide demand, figures for which are not available.

The state governments are described by four variables. State agriculture agencies are the most common regulatory body that handles section 24(c) requests. The head of these agencies is often elected. One would expect an elected agency head to be more responsive to agricultural interests than an appointed head because ballot races for agriculture commissioner are more likely to attract interest in the agricultural community. Appointed heads are responsible to the governor, who has a broader constituency. ELECT is 1 when the head is elected and 0 otherwise. I also included the ratio of the head of the agriculture department's salary to that of the governor (SRATIO) as a proxy for the relative political importance of agricultural interests.[52]

The political groups most often concerned with potential abuse of the 24(c) process are environmentalists, and two variables are included to capture their influence. First, a dummy variable (CKNOW) is 1 if the state has a community right to know law mandating public disclosure of the use or presence of hazardous materials and 0 if it does not. The presence of such a law indicates well-organized environmental groups operating on the state level. Second, a dummy variable (GWATER) is 1 if the state has been listed by EPA as having extensive groundwater pollution, a condition that would raise the level of concern about abuse of pesticides and provide environmentalists with evidence to support their calls for restricting pesticide use and 0 if it has not.

Table 5.3
Difference in Means Tests

	Variable	All §3	All SLNs	Active § 3 without SLN	Active § 3 with SLN
Signal Word	Caution	0.5674	0.4308[a]	0.5689	0.5094[a]
	Warning	0.1759	0.2743[a]	0.1750	0.2139[a]
	Danger	0.2566	0.2935[a]	0.2562	0.2767[b]
Pest Group	Undefined pest	0.1469	0.3368[a]	0.1384	0.4986[a]
	Disinfectant organism	0.2441	0.0048[a]	0.2493	0.0297[a]
	Plant pathogenic fungi	0.1916	0.1304[a]	0.1913	0.2042
	Insects and other invertebrates	0.3922	0.4172[a]	0.3910	0.4438[a]
	Plant pathogenic nematodes	0.0063	0.0492[a]	0.0054	0.0411[a]
	Protozoa and other unicellular organisms	0.0008	0.0002[b]	0.0007	0.0051[a]
	Vertebrates	0.0342	0.0964[a]	0.0337	0.0536[a]
	Weed plants	0.2232	0.3007[a]	0.2199	0.3577[a]
	Algaecide	0.1064	0.0083[a]	0.1084	0.0240[a]
	Antifouling	0.0148	0.0010[a]	0.0151	0.0029[a]
	Bacteriocide	0.0256	0.0023[a]	0.0261	0.0046[a]
	Disinfectant	0.1620	0.0061[a]	0.1655	0.0183[a]

– continued –

Table 5.3
(continued)

Variable	All §3	All SLNs	Active § 3 without SLN	Active § 3 with SLN
Type				
Fungicide	0.1976	0.1363[a]	0.1975	0.2025
Herbicide	0.1357	0.2825[a]	0.1315	0.3092[a]
Nematicide	0.0092	0.0691[a]	0.0083	0.0468[a]
Insecticide	0.4192	0.4399[a]	0.4399	0.4398
Poison	0.0292	0.0899[a]	0.0289	0.0439[a]
Repellent	0.0265	0.0101[a]	0.0269	0.0080[a]
Conditional Registration	0.4104	0.2957[a]	0.4079	0.5157[a]
Child-Resistant Packaging	0.0280	0.0045[a]	0.0281	0.0262

[a] Difference in means significant at 1% level.
[b] Difference in means significant at 5% level.

Sources: USDA (various years); Council of State Government (various years); Pest-Bank™ data provided by Silver Platter International N.V., Norwood, Massachusetts.

Table 5.4
Regression Variable Definitions

Variables	Definitions
Fertilizer	Total spending on fertilizer by agriculture sector in 1988 / 1,000
NATSHARE	State share of national agricultural sector income in 1988
GRATIO	Proportion of total agricultural sector income due to government transfer payments
LRATIO	Ratio of total agricultural income from livestock to total agricultural income
Right to Know	1 if state had a community right to know law governing toxics in 1988, 0 otherwise
SRATIO	Ratio of salary of highest paid state government agricultural official to governor's salary (>1 means ag official is paid more than governor)
ELECT	1 if state directly elected head of state agriculture department, 0 otherwise
GWATER	1 if state was on groundwater pollution list, 0 otherwise

Sources: USDA (various years); Council of State Government (various years); Pest-Bank™ data provided by Silver Platter International N.V., Norwood, Massachusetts.

The independent variables defined above are regressed on a series of dependent variables using OLS: the total number of SLNs issued by each state; the number of SLNs issued in each of the three label warning categories (caution, warning, and danger); the number of SLNs issued to the top twenty SLN registrants nationally; and the number of SLNs issued in each of the pest group categories for which there were sufficient registrations (fungi, weeds, and insects). If the SLN process is being abused, abuse is likely to appear in these areas for several reasons. If the abuse is the result of a small group of registrants making an end run around the section 3 requirements, looking at the top twenty SLN registrants is a means of examining whether those who register approximately half of all SLNs are a group particularly likely to be abusing the process. If the abuse is that more dangerous uses are being diverted into SLN registrations, using the warning and danger SLNs may reveal the problem. If the problems lie with the shift into the major pest groups (insects, weeds, and fungi) then examining those groups may reveal the problem. The results of the regressions are given in table 5.6.

Table 5.5
Regression Variable Descriptive Statistics

Variable	Mean (Standard Deviation)
CKNOW	0.40 (0.49)
SRATIO	0.78 (0.23)
GWATER	0.50 (0.51)
ELECT	0.26 (0.44)
NATSHARE	0.02 (0.02)
LRATIO	0.50 (0.18)
Fertilizer	978 (1044)
GRATIO	154 (197)

The regressions have several interesting results. The state share of total agricultural income and LRATIO have the expected signs and are consistently significant: as a state's share of national agricultural income increases, so does the number of SLNs; as livestock constitutes a larger proportion of agricultural income, the number of SLNs declines. Fertilizer sales and government agricultural payments have an inverse relationship to the number of SLNs and are both significant in all but the case of weed SLNs, where government payments are not significant. These results are evidence, albeit not conclusive, that SLNs are not being used to circumvent the section 3 process, at least not by agricultural interests with sufficient political power to obtain large amounts of government agricultural spending (e.g., corn growers). The possibility remains, however, that agricultural interests with significant state-level political influence, but with less national political power (e.g., potato growers), are misusing the process.

Interestingly, none of the variables that measured the susceptibility to capture of states' agricultural regulatory agencies were significant for any

Table 5.6
Regression Results

					Dependent Variable			
Variables	All SLNs	Caution Labeled SLNs	Warning Labeled SLNs	Danger Labeled SLNs	SLNs of Major Registrants	Plant Pathogenic Fungi SLNS	Weed SLNs	Insect SLNs
Constant	249.6 (195.5)	101.7 (90.77)	91.15 (48.60)	62.14 (63.17)	174.0 (94.70)	32.98 (29.80)	120.0 (63.53)	119.3 (72.25)
CKNOW	92.16 (72.77)	38.49 (33.78)	24.70 (18.09)	31.82 (23.51)	49.40 (35.24)	16.17 (11.09)	26.21 (23.64)	34.75 (26.89)
SRATIO	249.4 (188.7)	122.9 (87.61)	38.57 (46.90)	79.66 (60.97)	84.29 (91.39)	41.84 (28.76)	40.61 (61.31)	67.70 (69.73)
GWATER	-46.95 (72.48)	-22.74 (33.65)	-12.79 (18.01)	-12.60 (23.42)	-21.83 (35.10)	-0.1101 (11.05)	-17.80 (23.55)	-11.43 (26.78)
ELECT	56.77 (82.93)	22.85 (38.50)	12.76 (20.61)	25.07 (26.79)	29.08 (40.16)	1.939 (12.64)	22.35 (26.94)	26.74 (30.64)
NATSHARE	35775.2[b] (6186.2)	16983.6[b] (2871.8)	6592.4[b] (1537.4)	12526.2[b] (1998.5)	12899.0[b] (2995.8)	3852.4[b] (942.7)	6263.3[b] (2009.8)	12631.7[b] (2285.7)

– continued –

Table 5.6
(continued)

Variables	Dependent Variable							
	All SLNs	Caution Labeled SLNs	Warning Labeled SLNs	Danger Labeled SLNs	SLNs of Major Registrants	Plant Pathogenic Fungi SLNs	Weed SLNs	Insect SLNs
LRATIO	-699.3^b (212.1)	-322.5^b (98.46)	-161.8^b (52.71)	-220.1^b (68.52)	-327.6^b (102.7)	-103.9^b (32.32)	-199.9^b (68.91)	-254.0^b (78.37)
Fertilizer	-0.3498^b (0.0957)	-0.1690^b (0.0444)	-0.0654^b (0.0238)	-0.1188^b (0.0309)	-0.1285^b (0.0463)	-0.0362^a (0.0146)	-0.0773^a (0.0311)	-0.1217^b (0.0354)
GRATIO	-1.352^b (0.3217)	-0.6295^b (0.1494)	-0.2350^b (0.0800)	-0.5030^b (0.1040)	-0.4949^b (01.558)	-0.1611^b (0.0490)	-0.1465 (0.1045)	-0.4813^b (0.1189)
Adjusted R^2	0.613	0.622	0.455	0.646	0.462	0.499	0.284	0.582

[a] significant at 5% level.
[b] significant at 1% level.

of the specifications. Although we cannot exclude the possibility that there are better measurements of susceptibility to capture, which might have been significant, these variables spanned a sufficiently wide range of state characteristics to provide some limited support for the notion that there is not a link between susceptibility to capture and SLN use.

Finally, comparing the various specifications also suggests areas in which we might look in the future for additional evidence. SLNs for use in combating weeds produced the smallest adjusted R^2. This relatively small amount of explained variance suggests that other factors play a relatively important role here.

Conclusion

Pesticide regulation in the United States has evolved from limited state regulation at the turn of the century to broad-based federal regulation at century's end. The goals of regulation have shifted from efficacy to environmental protection. Despite these significant changes and despite concerted efforts to take away their authority, states have continued to play an important role. Federal regulators' inability to successfully implement their role as gatekeepers has forced them, sometimes reluctantly, to allow states to exercise considerable authority even in the central area of registration. If success is measured by state participation, then pesticide regulation is at least a qualified success as an example of environmental federalism.

Shared authority is successful on a broader scale as well. States appear to exercise real authority to vary pesticide registrations from the national standard and to exercise it in a fashion at least broadly consistent with their differing interests. Washington, Oregon, and California in particular have used the 24(c) authority to foster diverse agricultural sectors, for which national registration would be a significant burden. The statistical results tend to confirm what the pattern of registrations discloses; aside from a few pesticides with unusually widespread SLN registration activity, there does not appear to be significant overregistration of pesticides through 24(c) to bypass section 3 and use of 24(c) procedures is not significantly correlated with measures of susceptibility of state regulatory agencies to capture.

If 24(c) is successful, however, it is successful primarily at ameliorating the problems caused by the national registration scheme under section 3. Even if we were to accept that EPA has finally, more than twenty-four years after the 1972 FEPCA changes to FIFRA, gotten the section 3 registration program "right" (and it is far from clear that they have), regulating pesticide use as pesticide use rather than treating it as part of a broader pest control decision through the use of incentives and information spreading devices is a failure.[53] Building a regulatory scheme on premarket regulation avoids "really bad stuff" and allows for satisfying public actions such as banning DDT, however. National registration under FIFRA constitutes a significant barrier to entry in the pest control market and even good regulations implementing it cannot avoid distorting use decisions. By the time the potential pesticide user is considering a pest control strategy FIFRA's regulatory scheme is notable largely by its absence. Perhaps the most encouraging development is the use of SLNs to shift liability risks—an indication that users and manufacturers can successfully allocate such risks by contract.

There are three important lessons from the pesticide regulatory experience with shared national and state authority. First, national regulation needs to be focused on national concerns. The information problems for a national regulator attempting to license every use of every pesticide are so overwhelming that the national government can never hope to meaningfully solve them. Second, states have the potential to play a significant role in adapting environmental regulation to local conditions without the development of a race to the bottom. Third, our experience with FIFRA suggests where the demand for local variance in policy is strong enough, national policy makers may be forced to share meaningful authority even within a regulatory framework that is built around a national gatekeeper.

Notes

1. The extent to which FIFRA preempts state common law claims is unresolved. The 1992 Supreme Court decision in *Cipollone v. Liggett Group, Inc.*, 112 S.Ct. 2608 (1992), suggests FIFRA may preempt a number of common-law claims. Both the 10th and 11th Circuits have found that FIFRA preempts some common-law tort claims. *Arkansas-Platte & Gulf Partnership v. Van Waters & Rogers, Inc.*, 981 F.2d 1177 (10th Cir.) *cert. denied*, 114 S.Ct. 60 (1993) (failure to warn); *Papas v. Upjohn Co.*, 985 F.2d 516, *cert. denied*, 114 S.Ct. 300 (1993) (inadequate labeling). An earlier decision by the D.C. Circuit Court found no preemption in an inadequate labeling case. *Ferebee v. Chevron Chemical Co.*, 736 F.2d 1529 (D.C. Cir.) *cert. denied*, 469 U.S. 1072 (1984). Since *Ferebee* was decided before *Cipollone*, however, its continued validity is questionable. Users can also bring state law claims for ineffective products and for products that are alleged to damage the crop, these are generally not preempted. See, e.g., *Southland Farms, Inc. v. Ciba-Geigy Corp.*, 575 So.2d 1077 (Ala. 1991) (ineffective) and *Herrick v. Monsanto Co.*, 874 F.2d 594 (8th Cir. 1989) (crop

damage). See Grossman (1996, 286–95) for a general discuss of tort law preemption issues.

2. There are many others, including applicator licensing, preemption issues concerning state liability laws, and emergency exemptions from federal regulation. States also have the authority to impose additional restrictions on pesticide use.

3. The insecticide was even used to "replace rice at wedding ceremonies" (Wharton 1974, 248). Paul Müller, a Swiss chemist, received the Nobel Prize in Medicine in 1948 for his 1938 discovery (Graham 1970, 211).

4. Regulatory policies have important implications for innovation, a topic beyond the scope of this chapter.

5. In addition to the broadness of the effectiveness of a pesticide, many other characteristics jointly affect the product's usefulness and its environmental impact: (1) degree of sorption to and within soil surfaces; (2) persistence; and (3) volatility (Gustafson 1993, 82–101). Degradation of pesticides is the result of physical, chemical, and biological processes that vary significantly among use locations (Coats 1991, 11). Light and heat, for example, are two central factors in determining degradation rates.

6. 33 U.S.C.A. § 1251(a)(1) (1986).

7. 36 Stat. 331 (1910).

8. 61 Stat. 163 (1947).

9. 61 Stat. 163, 165 (1947).

10. The most significant state action in this period was the Wisconsin DDT proceeding, which prompted a ban. The environmentalists' success was partly due to the failure of DDT's defenders to anticipate significant consequences from a state proceeding and consequent lack of preparedness (Dunlap 1981, 159).

11. Remarkably, a few lines later the USDA testimony notes that "It will be necessary to follow up [registration] by collecting samples in the field and submitting them for tests . . ." (U.S. House 1946, 4).

12. The agricultural pesticide industry also opposed indicating registration on the label (U.S. House 1946, 42). By 1963 these concerns had faded and even a strong supporter of agricultural interests admitted he was "at a loss to understand" that provision (U.S. House 1963). Registration numbers were finally added to labels in 1963 when FIFRA was amended to require inclusion of the registration number to facilitate poison control centers' determining the appropriate antidote (U.S. House 1963, 15).

13. In 1954, authority to establish tolerances for pesticide residues on raw agricultural goods was shifted from USDA to the Food and Drug Administration (68 Stat. 511 [1954]). As with registration, the manufacturer was responsible for generating detailed data, which the agency experts would interpret to set a tolerance "to the extent necessary to protect the public health" (68 Stat. 511 [1954]).

14. 78 Stat. 190 (1964).

15. 78 Stat. 190, 191 (1964).

16. For example, the report argued that "The continuous analysis of data gath-

ered in a comprehensive monitoring system would reveal points of potential danger and permit regulatory control measures to be instituted before permanent damage is done" (U.S. HEW 1969, 170).

17. The other major change in the 1960s was the 1966 abandonment of "no residue" tolerances for pesticides on food. Advances in scientific techniques meant that lower levels of residue could be detected and now the Food and Drug Administration was called upon to determine a safe level of residues (Alford 1970, 301–2).

18. 86 Stat. 973 (1972).

19. Even in 1993, only 8 percent of active ingredients had been reregistered (Grossman 1996). EPA's registration program was inadequate even for those substances it managed to complete, as it generally does not consider the potential toxicity of the "inert" ingredients in pesticides (40 C.F.R. § 158.155 (b) [1996]). Since inert ingredients can have environmental effects alone or in combination with the active ingredients, this is a serious gap (Hogan 1990).

20. The Maryland secretary of agriculture, testifying on behalf of the National Association of State Departments of Agriculture in 1977, said the association was "appalled at the limited understanding that EPA demonstrates in the development and implementation of regulations under the amended FIFRA. . . . EPA has failed to carry out the original intent of Congress" (U.S. House 1977a, 25). Witnesses testifying before Congress "asked the Committee to amend Section 24(c) to allow the states to be the sole authority in determining registration for special local needs (U.S. House 1977b, 5).

21. States, of course, remain free to require registration of pesticides sold within their borders. In most states, with the notable exception of California, state registration is not a significant barrier to entry for a manufacturer, since federally registered users are easily registered. California, on the other hand, requires significant independent data submission to obtain state registration. See Calif. Food and Agric. Code § 12811 (Deering 1994); 3 Cal. Code Regs. §§ 6170.5, 6172.

22. Restricted-use pesticides may be applied only by a certified applicator, except that some may be applied under other restrictions as specified by the administrator (7 U.S.C. § 136a(d)(1)(C)(ii) [Supp. 1996]).

23. General-use pesticides are those for which the administrator "determines that the pesticide, when applied in accordance with its directions for use, warnings and cautions and for the uses for which it is registered, or for one or more of such uses, or in accordance with a widespread and commonly recognized practice, will not generally cause unreasonable adverse effects on the environment" (7 U.S.C. § 136a(d)(1)(B) [Supp. 1996]).

24. 21 U.S.C.A. §§ 342, 346a, 348 (1972 & Supp. 1996).

25. 21 U.S.C. § 346a(b) (1992); Regulation of Pesticides in Food: Addressing the Delaney Paradox, 53 Fed. Reg. 41, 104 (1988).

26. 21 U.S.C. § 348 (c)(3)(A) (1972); The 1996 Food Quality Protection Act eliminates the Delaney Clause, but also lowers tolerance levels for pesticides.

27. § 17(a)(2)(g) of 1972 FEPCA, 86 Stat. 973, 989–991 (1972).

28. Ironically, many critics of pesticide use recognize the extraordinary de-

mands this approval places on the regulatory apparatus when they consider regulation in developing countries. For example, one author argued that "Many developing countries do not have the legal, technical, and administrative resources to control the sale and use of pesticides and thus can not protect the health and environment of their people" (Uram 1995, 469).

29. States may not impose additional labeling or packaging requirements or permit uses prohibited by the federal government (7 U.S.C.A. § 136v a-b). States were also limited to registrations for uses not previously denied, disapproved, or canceled by the administrator (86 Stat. 973, 997 [1972]).

30. The final limitation imposed upon state authority to issue SLNs is that the EPA administrator may suspend a state's authority to register pesticides if the administrator finds that a state "is not capable of exercising adequate controls" or has not exercised adequate controls to assure that registrations issued under this authority "will be in accord with the purposes" of FIFRA (7 U.S.C.A. § 136v(c)(4) [Supp. 1996]).

31. 7 U.S.C.A. § 136v(c)(2)-(3) (Supp. 1996).

32. States operated under 24(c) with a high degree of independence from EPA during the 1970s. The following example illustrates this independence (GAO 1978, 47–48). The state of Tennessee had an infestation of 5 million blackbirds in a state park. EPA recommended two avicides for use, but Tennessee chose to issue 24(c)s for two other products, fenthion and methyl parathion. EPA considered both these products inefficacious and believed that fenthion would cause unreasonable adverse effects. EPA contacted Tennessee state employees several times to determine what Tennessee was doing about the bird problem. According to EPA documents, these inquiries were ignored or evaded; after Tennessee began spraying, only one individual was available to EPA and he stated he was "not allowed" to discuss the spraying. The documents also say that after Tennessee's registration and use of fenthion, a Tennessee Department of Agriculture employee admitted that if EPA had been aware of the state's intent to register fenthion, EPA would have disapproved the registration.

Subsequent surveys of the sprayed area by an EPA inspector and a Tennessee State employee showed that the fenthion killed only 88 birds in an estimated 10,800-square-foot area where bird mortality should have been heaviest. Methyl parathion was similarly ineffective, and the state canceled both registrations (GAO 1978, 48).

33. Unless otherwise noted, this section is based upon EPA (1996) and the current 24(c) regulations published at 40 C.F.R. §§ 162.150–162.156 (1996).

34. States have additional authority, subject to EPA oversight, to register pesticides for emergency uses under section 18. These registrations last only up to a year, however.

35. EPA has classified treated seed (where the pesticide is directly applied to the seed before planting) as a food use requiring a tolerance unless a radiotracer study shows no uptake of the tracer into the crop, something that is unlikely. (The aerial portion for nonroot crops or the root in the case of root crops are examples of these.) Uses on crops grown for seed use do not require tolerances if no part of the crop will be used for human food or livestock feed and there is

no likelihood of residues in crops grown from the harvested seed. Some states have previously sought to register products for these types of seed uses without tolerances, arguing they were not food uses.

36. EPA requires 24(c) registrations to be based on a basic section 3 registration rather than on a distributor registration to protect basic ingredient manufacturers. If distributor products could serve as the basis for registrations, manufacturers could be unaware of new uses of their products. Since the manufacturer is potentially liable for harm from use, requiring 24(c) registrations to be based on section 3 registrations ensures that registrants are aware of the uses of their products, allowing them to withhold consent. This information is from the author's interview of James Tompkins, deputy branch chief, Registration Support Branch, U.S. EPA, Washington, D.C., April 1996.

37. New data can be submitted to resolve such concerns and then a 24(c) registration may be permitted (U.S. EPA 1996).

38. Reed Smith, pesticide consultant, interview by author, April 1996.

39. James Tompkins interview, April 1996.

40. Rick Melnicoe, regional coordinator, Interregional Project No. 4, Department of Environmental Toxicology, University of California-Davis, interviewed by author, April 1996.

41. Rick Melnicoe interview, April 1996.

42. Where no tolerance exists, a section 18 emergency registration is still possible.

43. Rick Melnicoe interview, April 1996.

44. Most SLNs are simply additional uses for pesticides already registered under section 3. A given "parent" section 3 registration could have multiple "child" 24(c) registrations in a given state for different uses, "child" registrations in multiple states for a single use, or a combination.

45. James Tompkins interview, April 1996.

46. This policy change was partially brought about by the experience with Furadan, an insecticide and nematicide manufactured by the FMC Corporation, as noted by James Tompkins in an April 1996 interview. FMC Corporation has over 130 SLN registrations.

47. James Tompkins interview, April 1996.

48. I am grateful to Silver Platter International N.V., Norwood, Massachusetts, for providing me with the Pest-Bank™ data CD.

49. All variables are for 1988 data unless otherwise noted. I used 1988 data since 1988 was roughly the midpoint between 1978 and 1996.

50. An alternative approach would have been to use the percentage of gross state product represented by agriculture. This measure proved resolutely insignificant, suggesting that it is the relative importance of the state as a market rather than of agriculture within the state that matters.

51. I would have liked to be able to include a measure of the diversity of states' agriculture akin to the Herfindahl Index used in the industrial organization literature. Unfortunately the manner in which agricultural data are collected precludes calculation of such a measure from published data. (In particular,

many states are listed by USDA as having "greenhouse" as one of their top four crops, a category for which there is little data and less consistency across states.) Indeed, virtually everyone I spoke with in my search for such a measure asked me to let them know if I ever found one.

52. This variable was inspired by the information conveyed by the ratio of college football coaches' salaries to college presidents' salaries.

53. USDA found that paying farmers to provide vegetive "filter strips" along bodies of water significantly reduced the environmental impact of pesticide use (Gustafson 1993, 167). Focusing on similar incentive programs or on production decisions that affect pesticide use (such as crop choice, tilling methods, crop rotation) is a potentially effective alternative strategy.

References

Alford, Harold G. 1970. Appendix 2: Federal Requirements for Pesticide Products. In *Since Silent Spring*, by Frank Graham Jr. Boston: Houghton Mifflin, 299–303.

Briggs, Shirley. 1992. *Basic Guide to Pesticides: Their Characteristics and Hazards*. Washington, DC: Taylor and Francis.

Coats, Joel R. 1991. Pesticide Degradation Mechanisms and Environmental Degradation. In *Pesticide Transformation Products: Fate and Significance in the Environment*, ed. L. Somasundaram and Joel R. Coats. Washington, DC: American Chemical Society, 10–30.

Costle, Douglas M. 1977. Letter to Rep. Thomas Foley, October 4. In *House Report No. 95-663*. Washington, DC: U.S. House, Committee on Agriculture, 95th Congress, 1st session.

Council of State Governments. Various years. *Book of the States*. Lexington, KY: Council of State Governments.

Dunlap, Thomas R. 1981. *DDT: Scientists, Citizens, and Public Policy*. Princeton: Princeton University Press.

General Accounting Office (GAO). 1978. *Special Pesticide Registration by the Environmental Protection Agency Should Be Improved*. CED-78-9.

———. 1986. *Pesticides: EPA's Formidable Task to Assess and Regulate Their Risks*. RCED-86-125.

———. 1993. *Pesticides: Pesticide Reregistration May Not Be Completed Until 2006*. GAO/RCED-93-94.

Georghiou, George P., and Charles E. Taylor. 1986. Factors Influencing the Evolution of Resistance. In *Pesticide Resistance: Strategies and Tactics for Management*. Washington, DC: National Academy Press, 157–69.

Graham, Frank, Jr. 1970. *Since Silent Spring.* Boston: Houghton Mifflin.

Grossman, Margaret Rosso. 1996. Environmental Federalism in Agriculture: The Case of Pesticide Regulation in the United States. In *Environmental Policymaking with Political and Economic Integration,* ed. John B. Braeder et al. Brookfield, VT: Edward Elgar, 274–304.

Gustafson, David I. 1993. *Pesticides in Drinking Water.* New York: Van Nostrand Reinhold.

Hogan, Kevin M. 1990. Note: Inert Ingredients and Pesticide Registration Data Requirements: EPA's Complacency Compounds FIFRA's Inadequacies. *Vermont Law Review* 15: 265–99.

Hornstein, Donald T. 1993. Lessons from Federal Pesticide Regulation on the Paradigms and Politics of Environmental Law Reform. *Yale Journal on Regulation* 10: 369–446.

McCabe, Martha. 1989. Pesticide Law Enforcement: A View from the States. *Journal of Environmental Law and Litigation* 4: 35–54.

National Research Council. 1978. *Regulating Pesticides.* Washington, DC: National Academy Press.

———. 1996. *Carcinogens and Anticarcinogens in the Human Diet.* Washington, DC: National Academy Press.

Rogers, William. 1994. *Environmental Law,* 2d ed. St. Paul, MN: West.

Rosman, Lewis. 1993. Note: Public Participation in International Pesticide Regulation: When the Code Commission Decides, Who Will Listen? *Virginia Environmental Law Journal* 12: 329–65.

Spalt, Allen. 1983a. *A Report on "Special Local Need" Pesticide Registrations Section 24(c) of FIFRA.* Pittsboro, NC: Rural Advancement Fund of the National Sharecroppers Fund.

———. 1983b. Testimony on Behalf of the Rural Advancement Fund/ National Sharecroppers Fund before the House Committee on Agriculture, Subcommittee on Department Operations, Research and Foreign Agriculture. Typescript copy, July 27.

U.S. Department of Agriculture (USDA). Various years. *Agricultural Statistics.* Washington, DC: U.S. Government Printing Office.

U.S. Department of Health, Education, and Welfare (HEW). 1969. *Report of the Secretary's Commission on Pesticides and Their Relationship to Environmental Health.* Washington, DC: U.S. Government Printing Office.

U.S. Environmental Protection Agency (EPA). 1996. Guidance on FIFRA sec. 24(c) Registrations. February 9.

U.S. House of Representatives. 1946. Committee on Agriculture. *Federal Insecticide, Fungicide, and Rodenticide Act: Hearings.* 79th Congress, 2d session, February. Washington, DC: U.S. Government Printing Office.

————. 1963. Committee on Agriculture, Subcommittee on Departmental Oversight and Consumer Relations. *Registration of Economic Poisons.* 88th Congress, 1st session, August. Washington, DC: U.S. Government Printing Office.

————. 1971. Committee on Agriculture. *Federal Pesticide Control Act of 1971.* 92d Congress, 1st session, February and March. Washington, DC: U.S. Government Printing Office.

————. 1975. Committee on Agriculture. *Federal Insecticide, Fungicide, and Rodenticide Act Extension.* 94th Congress, 1st session, May. Washington, DC: U.S. Government Printing Office.

————. 1976. Committee on Agriculture. *Business Meetings on Federal Insecticide, Fungicide, and Rodenticide Act Extension.* 94th Congress, 1st session, part 2, February. Washington, DC: U.S. Government Printing Office.

————. 1977a. Committee on Agriculture, Subcommittee on Department Investigations, Oversight, and Research. *Extending and Amending FIFRA.* 95th Congress, 1st session. Washington, DC: U.S. Government Printing Office.

————. 1977b. Committee on Agriculture. *House Report 95-343(I).* 95th Congress, 1st session. Washington, DC: U.S. Government Printing Office.

U.S. Senate. 1970. Committee on Commerce. Subcommittee on Energy, Natural Resources, and the Environment. *Pesticides Amendments to Hazardous Substances Act.* 91st Congress, 2d session, May and September. Washington, DC: U.S. Government Printing Office.

————. 1972a. Committee on Agriculture and Forestry. *Senate Report 92-838.* 92d Congress, 2d session. Washington, DC: U.S. Government Printing Office.

————. 1972b. Committee on Commerce. *Senate Report 92-970.* 92d Congress, 2d session. Washington, DC: U.S. Government Printing Office.

————. 1977. Committee on Agriculture, Nutrition, and Forestry, Subcommittee on Agricultural Research and General Legislation. *Extension of the Federal Insecticide, Fungicide, and Pesticide Act.* 95th Congress, 1st session, June. Washington, DC: U.S. Government Printing Office.

Uram, Charlotte. 1995. International Regulation of the Sale and Use of Pesticides. *Northwestern Journal of International Law and Business* 10: 460–78.

Wharton, James. 1974. *Before Silent Spring: Pesticides and Public Health in Pre-DDT America.* Princeton: Princeton University Press.

Chapter 6

Water Federalism: Governmental Competition and Conflict over Western Waters

Barton H. Thompson Jr.

The natural and political geography of the western United States, combined with water's fluidity, virtually ensured that federalism would be a central issue in western water policy. Despite the size of western states, most major rivers in the West are interstate; three are international (the Columbia in the North and the Colorado and Rio Grande in the South). The Colorado and Snake Rivers not only cut through multiple states but form state borders; the Rio Grande comprises almost half of the nation's border with Mexico. Numerous aquifers also cross state lines and international boundaries.

Even if rivers were nicely confined to individual states, the national government's ownership of or, in the case of Indian reservations, trust responsibility over 45 percent of the land in the seventeen western states would have generated federalism issues. The aridity of large swaths of the West, sometimes encompassing prime agricultural and residential sites, also meant that many local water users ultimately would need to import water from great distances to survive and develop. And this almost guaranteed that water users would turn to the national government, the ultimate deep pocket, for help in reconstructing the West's hydroscape and that, at some point, the national government would have to decide whether interstate transfers were permissible.

Yet we lack an overarching framework or set of frameworks for evaluating federalism issues in the water field. Most general treatments of federalism have focused on the role that a federal system plays in determining the size of government and the mix of public services—all of

175

which is relevant but does not speak directly to the regulatory and inter-state issues that dominate water federalism. The federalism literature of greatest relevance has examined the relative consequences of state and national control of environmental policy. That literature, however, has primarily focused on pollution questions and ignored resource allocation issues, even though the issues are closely tied.

The water literature has examined federalism issues only in discrete contexts. Numerous articles have examined such issues as how inter-state rivers should be apportioned, whether federal lands should enjoy unique federal rights, and whether national regulatory and programmatic schemes should override state law. Most of these articles, however, have been heavily doctrinal: few have delved with any rigor into the policy underpinnings of competing national and state claims to comparative advantages or competence over particular water issues; none has tried to develop an overarching set of principles.

This chapter takes a step back and examines water federalism in a broad context. The first section provides a brief history of federalism conflicts over water in the western United States and suggests how the nation's constitutional structure has influenced the relative power of states and the national government. The second section then appraises the appropriate role of states and the national government in setting wa-ter policy and allocating water resources.

By looking at water federalism from a broad perspective, this chapter abstracts from many of the difficult complexities that plague water poli-cy and only touches on some of the relevant issues and history. Various themes in the history of water federalism, however, appear only when one looks at water issues at a general level. A broader normative inquiry can also highlight various issues that cut across specific water issues. This chapter, in short, tries to draw out general themes that illuminate issues of water federalism, in full recognition that the themes and issues need further development in individual contexts.

A Historical Overview

A history of water federalism in the western United States can be divid-ed usefully into four separate periods. During the Gestation Period of the latter half of the nineteenth century, states assumed principal control over water resources and successfully fought off alternative governance based on national regulation, a common market, or watershed management. Most western states, in turn, delegated considerable discretion to local water districts or similar organizations. This basic structure—primary state control with considerable local discretion—continues through today. During the Embryonic National Period (1902 to 1914), the national government continued to defer to state policy but positioned itself to assume a potentially larger role in water policy through its new reclamation program, the Supreme Court's creation of "federal reserved rights," and the Court's entry into the apportionment of interstate rivers. During the National Empire Period (1914 to 1968), the national government actively sought and largely won expanded powers over western water. As described below, however, neither Congress nor national administrative agencies used that power to displace the states' central role in water policy. The current Environmental Period, beginning with the passage of the Wild and Scenic Rivers Act of 1968, has brought the greatest national displacement of state water authority. Although the Supreme Court has reduced the national government's authority to supplant state water law through reclamation and federal reserved rights, Congress has asserted growing powers over western water resources—often without forethought and design—through environmental legislation.

The likely future structure of water federalism in the United States is unclear. There is a great deal of discontent over the current decision-making authority. The increase in national powers has brought a strong backlash from the West that, with a modicum of success, is insisting on a devolution of decision making to states and local communities. Growing concerns over the balkanization of watersheds among state and local jurisdictions, combined with an increasing awareness of the externalities that individual watershed activities can impose on the health of the watershed as a whole, has led to renewed interest in watershed management. Finally, after years of analysis demonstrating the advantages of robust water markets, some states have finally begun to take the necessary steps to unfetter and promote water transfers.

The Gestation Period, 1849 to 1901

Formulation of U.S. water policy in the West dates to the discovery of gold in California in 1849 and California's admission to the Union a year later. For the first two decades, neither the states nor the national government took an active role in shaping water rules; instead they largely deferred to the customs and rules that were developing in local communities and mining camps. Judicial resolutions of local conflicts often paralleled these differences in local water customs, giving the appearance of judicial indecision but merely reflecting the community-specific norms.

Early legislative statements of water policy were vague and relatively noncommittal.[1] As prior appropriation began to take hold across a broad set of communities, however, state legislatures codified the system statewide. California enacted the first detailed appropriation code in 1872. When Colorado entered the Union in 1876, its constitution expressly embraced the prior appropriation system.[2] By the turn of the century, all states and territories had adopted either a pure prior appropriation system or a hybrid scheme of appropriative and riparian rights (Dellapenna 1990). In the next several decades, most of the hybrid states limited or abolished riparian rights.

While state legislatures established uniform water systems, they continued to permit some local variation both on purpose and by default. Local water companies and irrigation districts provided the principal means of achieving local diversity. From the outset, these local institutions permitted their members or customers to "customize" water rights to their own needs and interests (Thompson 1993b). In 1886, for example, the California Supreme Court held that riparians generally had rights superior to those of appropriators—seriously threatening local farming regions built around irrigation and prior appropriation.[3] Unable to convince the state legislature to abolish riparian rights, irrigators settled instead for legislative authorization of irrigation districts that had the authority to condemn or purchase riparian rights and thus eliminate the riparian threat (Worster 1985; Malone 1965). Although local irrigation districts and water companies often played an important role in customizing local policy to local needs, states retained the primary power over water resources.

As western states began to impose the prior appropriation doctrine, some water users challenged the states' power to allocate and regulate water. The national government initially owned the vast majority of land in the western territories and states. By natural extension, some people suggested that the national government also owned most of the water. Riparians who had acquired their land from the national government under preemption or other provisions and who often preferred riparian to appropriative rights argued that water rights were a matter of national, not state, law and should follow the traditional common law.[4] If these arguments had been accepted, the national courts and Congress might have played the principal role in defining western water law.

The national government responded at both the legislative and judicial levels, however, by supporting state and territorial efforts to impose a prior appropriation system. In the Mining Act of 1866, for example, Congress agreed to recognize and protect prior possessory rights "to the use of water for mining, agricultural, manufacturing, or other purposes" where "recognized and acknowledged by the local customs, laws, and the decisions of courts."[5] In amendments to the mining act four years later, Congress emphasized that people acquiring land from the national government took the land subject to such water rights.[6] The Supreme Court further strengthened state authority by holding that the congressional mining provisions were a "recognition of a preexisting right of possession": the national government "had, by its general conduct, recognized and encouraged and was bound to protect" local water claims.[7] Finally, when admitting new states to the Union, Congress often implicitly approved state control by approving state constitutions that asserted that water was owned or held by the state in trust for its citizens (Thompson 1996a).

State and territorial claims to general regulatory authority, nonetheless, were always a bit precarious. In the latter decades of the nineteenth century, states and territories had to fight off a number of serious challenges to their authority. To begin, a number of policymakers, including some members of Congress, continued to advocate a nationally imposed, westwide water system. Several Congressional bills in the 1880s would have established a national licensing system for portions of the West's waters (Pisani 1992). Discussions at the 1898 National Irrigation Congress also surfaced the idea of creating a national water law system, an idea seconded by *Scientific American* in an editorial two years later. None of these proposals, however, came close to passage by Congress.

Even the statutes that Congress did pass were not clear victories for state or territorial rights. Although often superficially deferential to local water rights, the language of the statutes suggests that Congress was more interested in supporting the prior appropriation system than in permitting state discretion. The 1866 Mining Act provisions, for example, recognized locally created water rights but only when based on "priority of possession."[8] More troubling yet was the Desert Land Act of 1877 that permitted patenting of 640-acre tracts of public land upon proof of irrigation and payment of 25 cents per acre.[9] The California congressional delegation took the lead in passing the Desert Land Act, apparently at the behest of James Ben-Ali Haggin, a California lawyer and entrepreneur who was busy trying to amass an immense land empire and saw the act as a useful means of doing so. Haggin was a leading irrigator, and the act, perhaps only coincidentally, enshrined the prior appropriation system. After providing that land claimants were entitled only to as much water as they appropriated and needed for irrigation, the act mandated that all other nonnavigable waters "shall remain and be held free for the appropriation and use of the public for irrigation, mining and manufacturing purposes subject to existing rights."[10]

Here, as in other early contexts, the U.S. Supreme Court provided essential support to state power and discretion. In 1899, the Court affirmed the general authority of state and territorial governments to dictate water policy within their borders, although leaving the national government with some authority where national interests were at stake.[11] In response to the national government's claim of plenary power over west-

ern rivers, the Court held that states, not the national government, enjoyed general authority over their waterways and could determine their
own systems of water rights—with two exceptions. First, Congress could
regulate navigable streams to ensure navigability. Second, absent congressional permission, states could not "destroy the right of the United States,
as the owner of lands bordering on a stream, to the continued flow of its
waters, so far at least as may be necessary for the beneficial uses of the
government property." When the Supreme Court finally interpreted the
1877 Desert Land Act three decades later, it ignored the act's "appropriation" language and held that Congress had given the states "plenary
control" over their water resources "with the right in each to determine
for itself to what extent the rule of appropriation or the common-law rule
in respect of riparian rights should obtain."[12]

States successfully fought off not only the nationalization of water
policy but alternative forms of regional management. The political
geography of states does not well match the ecological geography of
waterways. States are at once both too big, encompassing dozens of individual watersheds each with its own idiosyncratic natural and societal
characteristics, and too small, fracturing individual watersheds among
states. Recognizing this fact, John Wesley Powell urged Congress to divide the West into one hundred fifty separate regions corresponding to
natural drainage basins. In Powell's vision, these regions, rather than the
national or the state governments, would allocate and regulate water resources (Powell 1890a, 1890b).

Both political reality and Powell himself assured defeat of his watershed approach. By the time Powell fully laid out his proposal in 1890,
thirteen of the western states were already admitted to the Union, and
political borders were largely set for the other four future states. Neither
states nor territorial governments were eager to cede control over water
resources to new governmental units, many of which would have crossed
state borders. Powell, however, was his idea's worst enemy. At the same
time he was promoting his "natural districts," Powell was also staking
out other policy positions guaranteed to offend all significant western
water interests. To the dismay of irrigationists, Powell opposed federal
funding of water projects; to the dismay of cities and private water developers, he opposed transbasin water transfers (Pisani 1992).

States also fought off a final competitor for control over water resources, the private market. Under a market model, the states would have
played a limited role by establishing the initial property right to water,
but the market would have "regulated" use, fostered reallocation, and
developed storage and delivery systems. The market model stood a good
chance of prevailing in the early formulation of western water policy.
With the blessing of state courts, miners frequently transferred water as

one claim played out or failed and another claim struck pay dirt (Sax, Abrams, and Thompson 1991). Where water users needed storage or delivery projects, private companies, both commercial and mutually owned, met the need—ensuring the early irrigation of millions of acres.

Several factors, however, conspired against the market model. First, natural disasters, regional and worldwide financial crises, and sometimes just poor planning undercut the financial attractiveness of private water projects (Pisani 1992). One agricultural economist at the turn of the century estimated that only about 5 percent of the capital invested in private canal projects between 1885 and 1895 ever generated any return; investors lost most of their capital entirely (Fortier 1907).

States, moreover, acted to undercut or bar the market from playing a significant role in allocating and reallocating water. Fed by populist concerns over monopolies and speculative "profiteering" in other natural resources, Wyoming prohibited water transfers at the start of the twentieth century, and nine other western states ultimately followed Wyoming's lead (Thompson 1993a). Even where transfers were permissible, states often opposed and impeded interstate transfers (Thompson 1997). Beginning with California's Wright Act in 1887, states also undercut private water developers by fostering governmental irrigation districts and providing them with taxation and condemnation powers that private developers did not enjoy (Sax, Abrams, and Thompson 1991).

Here again, the Supreme Court, although at the pinnacle of its protection of private property, not only supported but endorsed state efforts to suppress the market's role in water allocation and development. In 1896, the Court upheld California's Wright Act against claims that the taxation power of irrigation districts violated the due process clause of the Fourteenth Amendment.[13] In response to the argument that irrigation districts served no real public use, the Court responded that "no general scheme of irrigation [could] be formed or carried into effect" without irrigation districts; private companies were not up to the task. Twelve years later, the Court ruled that New Jersey could bar a water company from purchasing and exporting water to Staten Island, New York, rejecting a variety of constitutional challenges.[14] The plaintiffs argued in part that New Jersey's ban violated the "dormant commerce clause," which generally prevents a state from banning or otherwise directly discriminating against interstate commerce. In a complete rejection of the market model, however, Justice Oliver Wendell Holmes wrote for a unanimous Court that

few public interests are more obvious, indisputable and independent of particular theory than the interest of the public of a State to maintain the rivers that are wholly within it substantially undiminished, except by such drafts upon them as the guardian of the public welfare may permit for the purpose of turning them to a more perfect use.[15]

Congress played a more ambiguous role in shaping the role that the market would play in western water policy. Congress rejected early pleas for national reclamation projects, partly on the ground that the private sector could meet the West's water development needs (Pisani 1992). In 1888, however, Congress appropriated funds for a national irrigation survey that most officials believed was simply the precursor to a national reclamation program.[16] And in 1894 Congress passed the Carey Act that contemplated a mixed national–state–private system of development in which private companies would often develop and build irrigation works, but the state and federal governments would closely supervise planning, pricing, and water distribution (Pisani 1992). Congress also shaped the market's role at a more subtle level. In the Desert Land Act of 1877, for example, Congress effectively barred the use of foreign capital to construct canals to irrigate the desert-act lands even though foreign investment was then the principal source of funding water projects.[17]

The Embryonic National Period, 1902 to 1914

Although states enjoyed relatively strong control over western water policy at the start of the twentieth century, the seeds were being laid for a stronger national role. As local water sources became fully appropriated, western farmers and politicians began to dream of monumental projects involving long-distance water transport. Because states and private companies found few of these projects financially feasible, farmers and politicians began to call on the national government to enter the field and subsidize the projects. As competition for the West's limited water supplies grew, the chances of conflicts among states, or between states and the national government in its role as land owner and trustee, also increased.

Congress finally answered western petitions for a national reclamation program with the 1902 Reclamation Act.[18] Reflecting the consensus at the century's turn in favor of state allocation and regulation of water, Congress demanded surprisingly little in the way of increased federal authority in return for the reclamation program; in some senses, state regulatory authority ended up stronger as a result of the Reclamation Act. Congress, for example, rejected any role for the market by mandating that the right to use any water delivered through the reclamation program would be "appurtenant to the land irrigated."[19] According to one of the principal sponsors of the act, this provision was critical to "prevent all the evils . . . certain to result from unlimited authority to transfer water" and represented an "advance" over earlier law that permitted market transfers.[20]

Congress used its financial leverage in the Reclamation Act to dictate several discrete elements of water policy: users of reclamation water could receive water only for "beneficial" uses on 160 acres or less of land and only if they lived on or in the "neighborhood" of the land.[21] Otherwise, however, Congress expressly deferred to state water authority:

> [N]othing in this Act shall be construed as affecting or intended to affect or to in any way interfere with the laws of any State or Territory related to the control, appropriation, use, or distribution of water used in irrigation, or any vested right acquired thereunder, and the Secretary of the Interior, in carrying out the provisions of this Act, shall proceed in conformity with such laws. . . .[22]

According to supporters of the act, states and territories were the appropriate foci for generating water policy; it was "right and proper" that states and territories should control water distribution. "The conditions in each and every State and Territory are different. What would be applicable in one locality is totally and absolutely inapplicable in another."[23]

Congress relinquished its most direct means of intervening in local water policy by exempting individual reclamation projects from the need for specific congressional authorization and appropriation. As originally structured, the reclamation program relied on a trust fund supported from sales of public domain lands.[24] The newly created Reclamation Service (later to become the Bureau of Reclamation) did not need to consult with Congress before pursuing a reclamation project. And the Reclamation Service generally acceded to state wishes in the construction and operation of projects. In fact, many of the early projects were projects that states or local districts had once contemplated building but were only too eager to turn over to the national government (Dunbar 1983). The national government's nose, nonetheless, was in the tent and, as discussed in the next section, the reclamation program ultimately would prove to be a vehicle for reshaping western water policy.

The Supreme Court also opened several doors to a greater national role in western water policy. In its 1908 decision in *Winters v. United States*,[25] for example, the Court created a system of national water rights, to be defined and enforced as an initial matter by federal courts, in rivalry with state water rights. In a case pitting an irrigation project financed by the Bureau of Indian Affairs (BIA) against earlier state appropriators, the Court held that Indian tribes enjoy water rights for use on their reservations as a matter of national law. The case was a victory not so much for Native Americans as for nationalism. The author of the Court's majority opinion, Justice Joseph McKenna, was seldom a friend of Native Americans, but strongly favored the national government; Justice David Brewer, the lone dissenter, was one of the Court's strongest protectors of minorities but favored states' rights.

As in other settings, the federal Constitution's system of checks and balances helped blunt *Winters'* impact on state water policy. The Supreme Court could create a form of national water right, but Native Americans could not use their water rights without funding for irrigation projects— which meant BIA money. Although the *Winters* decision cast a cloud of uncertainty over state water rights, state water users effectively lobbied to shut down Indian reclamation projects. Although the Bureau of Indian Affairs was devoting increasing sums of money to reclamation projects prior to *Winters*, the sums leveled off and ultimately decreased after the Supreme Court's decision (McCool 1987).

A year prior to *Winters*, the Supreme Court also assumed the power to divide interstate waters among states. In *Kansas v. Colorado*,[26] Kansas complained that upstream diversions from the Arkansas River by Colorado users were injuring Kansas users. As the Court recognized, the case squarely presented the question of "national control": Did the national government have the power to resolve disputes of this nature and, if so, how? The Supreme Court rejected the U.S. Department of Justice's argument that the national government owned and could decide legislatively how to allocate interstate waters (Pisani 1982).

Borrowing the concept of "equitable apportionment" from disputes over fisheries, however, the Court concluded that it had the power and the right to allocate the water among the states, after which each state could exercise authority over its share. The Court turned to federal "common law," best translated as judicial policy making, to resolve interstate disputes. Rather than relying on any specific rule for dividing interstate waters among the states, the Court concluded that it would consider the equities on a case-by-case basis with "equality of right" as a "cardinal rule."

The possibility of a free-ranging Supreme Court resolving interstate disputes was as disturbing to many states as congressional intervention was. States therefore began looking for a mechanism of resolving interstate disputes without submitting to the jurisdiction of the national judiciary—and found it in interstate compacts. In calling for compact negotiations over the Colorado River in 1922, delegates of the seven Colorado basin states urged that the states' relative rights "should be settled and determined by compact or agreement between said States," rather than by the Supreme Court (Dunbar 1983). Although states continued to resort to judicial apportionment when all else failed, compacts became the principal means of resolving interstate water disputes and remain so today (Muys 1971).

The National Empire Period, 1914 to 1968

From 1914 through 1968, the national government's power over western water policy grew considerably, but the growth was not always steady, and local users were often able to discourage the national government from fully exercising its new power. A major vehicle for expanding national power was the national reclamation program. From the outset, the reclamation program ran into financial trouble. Although Congress had contemplated that the program would be financially self-supporting, the high local demand for nationally subsidized projects, joined by the Reclamation Service's own interest in maximizing its role, led the service to undertake economically nonviable projects. In 1911, farmers receiving water from the reclamation program began to lobby for an extension of the period over which they could repay the capital costs of their projects. The post–World War I depression of 1921–23 and the Great Depression both generated pleas for further extensions in and relaxation of payback terms (Dunbar 1983).

As the national government assumed more of the cost and risk of reclamation projects, it insisted on greater control over the projects and water uses. Although Congress had initially forsworn any role in evaluating and approving individual reclamation projects, Congress in 1914 demanded that projects obtain annual appropriations (and thus undergo annual legislative oversight) as the quid pro quo for extending the payback period (Chan 1981). Over time, Congress increasingly used its authority to dictate the design and operational details of reclamation projects.

Ironically, the reclamation program's greatest impact was to increase the importance of local irrigation districts—and thus ultimately to balkanize western water policy. Because of the fiscal strength that districts' taxing power provides, Congress began to insist that most regions form irrigation districts as a prerequisite for receiving national reclamation water. Even where Congress did not insist that districts be formed, the Bureau of Reclamation encouraged their formation (Sax, Abrams, and Thompson 1991). Largely as a result, states such as California that receive sizable quantities of reclamation water are dominated by large water districts, while smaller mutual water companies provide the vast majority of water to farmers in other western states such as Utah (Thompson 1993c). This policy has had a cascading effect on western water policy. As I have elaborated elsewhere, water districts and mutual water companies, which are the dominant forms of local water organizations in agricultural regions, often behave quite differently. Water districts, for example, typically have been more resistant than mutuals to external water marketing (Thompson 1993b).

Both Congress and the Bureau of Reclamation continued to defer to the states on most issues not linked to the financial viability of the reclamation program. Their clients, after all, were local water users who wanted the federal largesse but generally favored state and local control over water policy. Competition within the national government for the opportunity to build new water projects strengthened the hand of states and local communities. Beginning in the 1930s, the Army Corps of Engineers sometimes competed with the Bureau of Reclamation for new water projects in the West, permitting local communities to choose the federal agency that provided them with the greatest leeway and the best financial arrangement. Because the corps and the bureau reported to different congressional committees, members of Congress also joined in the competition. When California looked to the federal government to take over its Central Valley Project during the Great Depression, local farmers did not want to comply with the acreage limitation and residency requirement of the 1902 Reclamation Act. By pitting the Army Corps of Engineers (which was not subject to similar constraints) against the bureau, Central Valley farmers were able to gain informal administrative relief from the bureau that enabled many farmers to effectively avoid the reclamation limitations for almost half a century (McCool 1987; Worster 1985).

Most policymakers, moreover, agreed as a normative matter that states and local regions faced widely differing water environments and needs and should play the principal role in setting water policy. Proposals to institute national water planning and regulation occasionally surfaced but were never widely supported. When President Franklin Roosevelt urged national water planning in the midst of the Great Depression, even his own Natural Resources Planning Board disagreed (Shallat 1992). According to the board, the national government should limit its role to the supervision and coordination of local policy making: "Planning does not involve the preparation of a comprehensive blueprint of human activity to be clamped down like a steel frame on the soft flesh of the community" (Natural Resources Planning Board 1934).

In the courts, nonetheless, the Justice Department sought greater national authority over western water even if for political or policy reasons the national government did not always exercise that authority to displace local policies. In the Supreme Court, the Justice Department continued to argue that the national government owned and enjoyed plenary power over all unappropriated waters in the West.[27] On this issue, the Court held firm, unanimously holding in 1935 that, at least subsequent to the Desert Land Act of 1877, the states rather than the national government had plenary control.[28]

On other judicial fronts, however, the Justice Department experienced more success. The Supreme Court, for example, held that the national government possesses "federal reserved water rights" not only for Indian reservations (as *Winters* had recognized) but for all the lands it has reserved from the public domain. In a watershed 1955 decision, the Court concluded that Oregon could not object to the construction of the Pelton Dam, a private hydroelectric project, on the Deschutes River because the dam was to be built on lands reserved by the national government for power development.[29] Eight years later, in *Arizona v. California*,[30] the Court ruled that national forests, wildlife refuges, recreation areas, and other reservations all held federal reserved water rights sufficient to meet their needs.

In the same decision, the Supreme Court also expanded national powers over interstate waters. Although the Court had earlier indicated that Congress did not have the authority to apportion interstate waters, the Court in *Arizona v. California* concluded not only that Congress enjoyed the authority but that Congress had actually apportioned the waters of the Lower Colorado River in the 1928 Boulder Canyon Act. Congress expressed deference to state water law in the 1928 act, but the Court determined that Congress had given the secretary of the Interior virtually unfettered discretion to apportion water during periods of shortage without regard to state law.

Arizona v. California also represented the culmination of a series of cases in which the Supreme Court expanded the Bureau of Reclamation's authority to dictate water policy in connection with its projects. Section 8 of the 1902 Reclamation Act, as already noted, provided that the bureau would "proceed in conformity" with state laws and that state law would govern the "control, appropriation, use, [and] distribution" of water.[31] Beginning in the late 1950s, however, the Court whittled away at section 8—ultimately reducing it to a requirement that the bureau comply with state law merely when *acquiring* water rights.[32]

During this period, the Supreme Court awarded power to the national government even when neither Congress nor the executive branch sought it. Soon after World War II, for example, the Federal Power Commission (FPC) dismissed the application of a private company seeking to build a hydroelectric project in Iowa because the state had not yet approved the project. Sensitive to state water interests, Congress had expressly provided in the 1920 Federal Power Act that hydroprojects had to comply with state water laws.[33] Yet when the hydro-developer challenged the FPC's dismissal of its application in *First Iowa Hydro-Electric Cooperative v. Federal Power Commission*,[34] the Supreme Court effectively gutted these provisions and held that hydroprojects need comply with state law only when they interfere with vested state water rights. Convinced that state water policy threatened the national interest in maximizing the development of inexpensive hydropower (Plouffe 1986), the Court was willing to take the national government where Congress had been afraid to tread.

The Supreme Court similarly created a national water program where none existed in *Arizona v. California*. As noted, the Court held that Congress, in the 1928 Boulder Canyon Project Act, had apportioned the waters of the Colorado River among the lower basin states and had given the secretary of the Interior broad authority to allocate water in times of shortage. As the dissent observed, the language and history of the act provided no support for either proposition. Whatever one might believe is Congress's power to apportion and regulate an interstate river, Congress did not try to exercise that power in the act (Hundley 1975).

The Supreme Court's varied decisions emboldened national agencies to ignore state water authorities where the states stood in the way of the agencies' agendas. Prior to the Pelton Dam decision, for example, the Department of Defense and other federal agencies routinely sought state permits for new water diversions. Within weeks after the Pelton Dam decision, federal agencies were notifying states that they were withdrawing their permit applications because the Supreme Court had made it clear they did not need state permission to divert water.[35] In light of the Court's reading of the 1902 Reclamation Act, the Bureau of Reclamation also started ignoring state water policies and determinations that hindered projects it was developing (Worster 1985). Nonetheless, the bureau remained more sympathetic to local views than did agencies like the Department of Defense that did not have local "clients."

Despite considerable bluster and outrage from western members, Congress chose not to statutorily relinquish the national government's newfound water authority (Morreale 1966). In the afterglow of Pelton Dam, a number of western senators introduced a bill to reestablish state domination and effectively reverse the Supreme Court's nationalistic revisions of federal law. One bill would have reserved "all navigable and nonnavigable waters . . . for appropriation and use of the public pursuant to State Law."[36] The bill also would have required all national agencies, "permittees, licensees, and employees" who needed water in connection with national programs to "acquire rights to the use thereof in conformity with State laws and procedures relating to the control, appropriation, use, or distribution of such water." Opposed by the Defense and Justice Departments (although acceptable to the Bureau of Reclamation and Department of the Interior), the bill never passed; nor did various compromise efforts, which inevitably alienated one group in trying to please another.

Yet the "nationalization" of western water policy during the middle of the twentieth century should not be overstated. Political reality and caution constrained the degree to which national agencies took advantage of their new power. Although the Bureau of Reclamation could have ignored state law in the distribution and regulation of federal reclamation water, the political need to please the bureau's constituents generally led the bureau to bow to state and local policy. Various national agencies like the Department of Defense did begin to claim water without complying with state appropriation procedures, but they very seldom exercised that power to override state appropriative rights that predated the federal claim (Romm and Fairfax 1985). Even the most self-interested agencies were politically astute enough to recognize that any sizable displacement of state water rights or policy might have provoked Congress to reverse the Supreme Court's positions.

Congress also did not exercise its power to allocate interstate water rights until 1990 when it apportioned the Truckee and Carson Rivers and Lake Tahoe between California and Nevada.[37] Although *Arizona v. California* established Congress's power, Congress has been naturally reluctant to take sides in interstate disputes over a matter as sensitive as water. If any state feels slighted, its senators will inevitably oppose the congressional apportionment and, as a matter of comity, the Senate is unlikely to approve the apportionment over the opposition of those senators. Even Congress's 1990 apportionment was effectively a congressional ratification of an agreement already worked out with California and Nevada (Reid 1995).

The National Empire Period, in short, saw a substantial expansion of national power over western water but not a concomitant exercise of that power. Where state law threatened national programs or policy, the national government would flex its muscles. The Supreme Court supported this emerging nationalism and even reached out to give the national government power it had never sought and sometimes expressly disavowed. In most matters, however, Congress and national administrative agencies continued to defer to the states. The Supreme Court loosened the constraints and prodded the national government, but politics still prevailed in most instances to maintain state primacy.

The Environmental Period, 1968 to Present

The past quarter-century has seen both a contraction and an expansion of national authority over western water issues. While the Supreme Court has retreated from many of its centralizing decisions of the mid-twentieth century, Congress has passed a number of general environmental laws that threaten far greater national intervention in western water policy than even the most fervent nationalist ever urged during the National Empire Period. In most situations outside water quality, Congress almost certainly did not contemplate the significant impact that most of its environmental statutes would have on western water policy. But the breadth of the statutory provisions, combined with citizen suit provisions that gave environmental groups the opportunity to seek judicial intervention, assured that the statutes would ultimately collide with state water authority.

In a flurry of judicial revisionism, the Court has reduced or restricted many of the powers that the national government appeared to enjoy at the end of the National Empire Period and has threatened to whittle away even further. Although none of the decisions has been constitutionally based, the opinions together reflect a strong belief in the importance of maintaining state primacy in the water field. In its 1978 decision in *California v. United States*,[38] for example, the Supreme Court reconsidered its reclamation decisions and held that the Bureau of Reclamation must comply with state water law except where state law is inconsistent with an explicit congressional directive. In doing so, the Court engaged in a lengthy historical survey of congressional legislation designed to prove a "consistent thread of purposeful and continued deference to state water law by Congress." The Court used this history to suggest that the national government should avoid interfering with state policy in light of varying local conditions, local decision makers' better grasp of local conditions and needs, and the likelihood of confusion and conflict if there were multiple sets of law. The Court also noted early views that Congress could not constitutionally intervene in western water policy (except to protect navigation and national property interests). Although the Court ultimately conceded that reclamation law preempted state law in some contexts (e.g., in the application of national acreage limitations), *Cali-fornia v. United States* tried to establish a bulwark against national intrusion by establishing both a historical presumption against and a constitutional suspicion of congressional interference.

In a decision handed down the same day, the Court also cut back on federal reserved water rights.[39] First, the Court limited the lands entitled to reserved rights to those "*appurtenant* lands *withdrawn* from the public domain for *specific federal purposes*" (emphasis added). More importantly, the Court held that even these lands are entitled to reserved water only where necessary to fulfill the primary purposes for which the lands were withdrawn. The Court then displayed its antipathy toward reserved rights by giving the primary purposes of national forests a stingy reading (Fairfax and Tarlock 1979). Here again, the Court tried to influence future national policy by emphasizing the problems that it believed flowed from federal reserved water rights. To the Court, federal reserved rights were inevitably disruptive to carefully structured state water systems and to western water users reliant on state rights. Over a decade later, in an opinion that the Supreme Court ultimately did not deliver for procedural reasons, the Court also would have cut back dramatically on the amount of water that Native American tribes could claim as a matter of federal reserved rights (Getches and Williams 1994).

The Supreme Court also has restricted its own discretion in apportioning the waters of interstate rivers. In *Colorado v. New Mexico*, the Court considered whether it should depart from prior appropriation in apportioning water between two appropriation states. Colorado argued that the Court should reduce New Mexico's apportionment, even though prior in time, because of "wasteful" water uses. After initially suggesting a willingness to engage in a roving inquiry of the relative equities of alternative apportionments,[40] the Supreme Court retreated two years later and held that Colorado could obtain more water only on "clear and convincing evidence" that New Mexico could reduce its water needs through "financially and physically feasible" conservation measures.[41] The Court thereby signaled that it would not normally use its power of equitable apportionment to displace state law with its own concept of good water policy. In line with its other pro-state decisions, the Court emphasized the importance of not undercutting the certainty of state water law systems.

The Court has not been unfailing in its support of state over federal authority. In 1990, for example, the Court affirmed its earlier rulings that the Federal Energy Regulatory Commission (formerly the Federal Power Commission) generally does not have to comply with state law in licensing hydroelectric dams—even though the relevant provisions of the Federal Power Act are almost identical to Section 8 of the Reclamation Act.[42] Even in the hydropower context, however, the Court ultimately awarded the states considerable authority over the operational features of hydroelectric dams through state certification provisions in the Clean Water Act.[43]

For most of the Environmental Period, politics has also continued to deter the national government from launching a direct assault on state supremacy regarding water issues. President Jimmy Carter's failed efforts to develop a comprehensive national water policy illustrates the political barriers. At Carter's request in 1977, the Office of Management and Budget, the Council on Environmental Quality, and the Water Resources Council reviewed existing water policies and concluded both that state water systems were deficient and that a "national perspective" was imperative. Faced by a storm of protest, Carter retreated and reassured states that they "must be the focal point for water resource management" (Matheson 1979; Dunbar 1983).

Yet the national government has incidentally backed into considerable power over western waters through congressional passage of broad environmental legislation. Most of the national government's increased authority has come from expanding application of the Clean Water Act and the Endangered Species Act. Section 404 of the Clean Water Act, for example, specifies that anyone discharging material into navigable waters must first obtain a national permit and show that the discharge will not have adverse environmental consequences.[44] When Congress passed this provision in 1972, most members of Congress saw it as directed toward water quality and the protection of navigation. No one suggested that section 404 would give the national government authority to scrutinize and bar state-authorized water diversions on environmental grounds. When Congress revisited the Clean Water Act in 1977, moreover, Senator Malcolm Wallop of Wyoming tried to forestall any such reading of section 404 by adding a new policy statement to the act:

> It is the policy of Congress that the authority of each State to allocate water within its jurisdiction shall not be superseded, abrogated or otherwise impaired by this Act. It is the further policy of Congress that nothing in this Act shall be construed to supersede or abrogate rights to quantities of water which have been established by any State.[45]

Most major water projects, however, require section 404 permits for dams or diversion works. And lower federal courts have read section 404 to require the Army Corps of Engineers, which administers the permit system, to probe the environmental effects not only of structures built in a waterway but of the water diversions themselves.[46] The same courts have dismissed the Wallop Amendment (quite correctly from a pure legal standpoint) as a mere "policy statement" that cannot override substantive provisions. As a consequence, section 404 has given the corps and the Environmental Protection Agency (EPA), which has veto power over corps permits, tremendous authority over state water decisions. EPA's 1990 disapproval of Denver's proposed Two Forks Dam and Reservoir is illustrative. EPA refused to let the project go forward in part because it concluded that Denver had other, less environmentally damaging means of meeting its population's water needs, including groundwater, conservation, leasing, and exchanges (U.S. EPA 1990).

EPA also enjoys some leverage over state water quantity decisions through its responsibility under the Clean Water Act to set ambient water quality standards for foot-dragging states. EPA's authority here is limited and indirect. Although water diversions can reduce downstream water quality, Congress has refused to give EPA direct regulatory authority over instream flows. When the U.S. Water Resources Council recommended in 1977 that Congress consider such regulation, Congress responded by passing the Wallop Amendment and asking EPA to study the issue. When EPA circulated a draft report suggesting that "minimum flows in themselves may be necessary to meet the objectives of the Clean Water Act," western criticism forced EPA to deep-six the study (Sax, Abrams, and Thompson 1991).

EPA, however, is learning to use its power over ambient water quality standards to influence instream flow decisions. Where states such as California have statutes or other legal doctrine linking water allocation decisions and water quality, tough ambient quality standards can force states to reduce diversions. In the case of California's Sacramento–San Joaquin Delta, for example, EPA has used its authority to adopt salinity standards for the delta to force California to address the delta's serious instream flow problems. Because point sources technically must reduce their discharges under the Clean Water Act to meet ambient standards, a state's failure to address instream flows also can force additional reductions on point sources—generating political pressure to increase instream flows.

Unless amended by Congress, the Endangered Species Act (ESA) poses the greatest threat to state authority over western water policy.[47] Under section 7 of the ESA, federal agencies must ensure that any action that they authorize, fund, or carry out "is not likely to jeopardize the continued existence" of an endangered or threatened species.[48] The Army Corps of Engineers thus cannot issue a section 404 permit for any water project that threatens an endangered species.[49] In operating federal water projects, the Department of the Interior and Army Corps of Engineers also must protect endangered species before pursuing other water-related goals, even if states and local residents would favor different priorities.[50]

Sections 9 and 10 of the ESA pose an even broader threat to state authority by directly regulating state, local, and private water activities. Section 9 prohibits any public or private action that would "take" an endangered species; the ESA in turn defines "take" to include actions that would kill or harm an endangered species or that would modify a species' habitat in a harmful fashion.[51] Section 10 authorizes the Department of the Interior to issue "incidental take permits," but only where a nonfederal party develops a "Habitat Conservation Plan" that the department believes minimizes the risk to the species to the maximum degree feasible. Sections 9 and 10 therefore give the Department of the Interior the power to regulate diversions and withdrawals that might harm an endangered species. Unlike section 7, moreover, sections 9 and 10 give the Department of the Interior direct authority over nonfederal entities and over existing as well as new diversions.[52]

Few, if any, members of Congress contemplated this use of the ESA when it was enacted in 1973. The ESA, however, promises national oversight of a large segment of western waterways. Virtually every major river in the West contains endangered species of fish, although many have not yet been listed, giving the Department of the Interior broad authority over western surface waters (see, e.g., Bolin 1993). The ESA also offers the Department of the Interior authority over many instances of groundwater overdraft: Lower groundwater tables can threaten overlying vegetation and can diminish natural springs to the detriment of wildlife dependent on those springs. The department has frequently identified groundwater threats in listing specific endangered species, particularly endangered plants (Thompson 1995).[53] Over the past several years, the Department of the Interior has used the ESA to help force states to address specific water problems that states appeared to be neglecting, such as excessive withdrawals from the Sacramento River in California (Gray 1994) and mining of the Edwards Aquifer in Texas (Batt 1995; Ruhl 1995).

Congress blindly stumbled into expanded national authority over water policy in passing the Clean Water Act and the ESA. On occasion, environmental considerations also have stimulated Congress to explicitly enlarge the national government's role. The Environmental Period began with Congress's straightforward protection of wild and scenic rivers in 1968.[54] Although Congress emphasized that it was not generally displacing state jurisdiction over wild and scenic rivers, the 1968 act makes it quite clear that a state cannot permit diversions that interfere with the purposes of including a river in the national wild and scenic rivers system (Gray 1988). In the early 1990s, Congress also decided to take a more active role in regulating the use of water from two major federal reclamation projects. As noted earlier, Congress historically has let the states regulate how reclamation water is used. In the Central Valley Project Improvement Act of 1992,[55] however, Congress intervened in what historically would have been considered California's province— reallocating 800,000 acre-feet of water, for example, to instream flow, and requiring all water districts to use increasing block rate structures, develop water conservation plans, and implement best management practices (Mecham and Simon 1995). In authorizing completion of the Central Utah Project,[56] Congress similarly mandated a variety of conservation goals and procedures (Melling 1993 and 1994).

At the same time as states are facing a major national challenge to their water authority, the other two major competitors to state regulation are also enjoying a rebirth. First, the national government has shown new interest in the possibility of watershed management, resurrecting in a slightly different and less revolutionary form John Wesley Powell's visions of regional authorities based on natural drainage basins. Current efforts to restore and manage the Colorado and Columbia Rivers are principal examples of the current fascination with watershed management (Keiter 1996a and 1996b). Unlike Powell's proposals a century ago, modern watershed management generally does not displace the existing authority of national, state, and local agencies but instead attempts to coordinate the authority and move toward more unitary visions.

Second, there is growing interest in using market forces in place of or as a supplement to elements of state water regulation. States themselves have recognized the importance of at least limited forms of water markets. All western states have either eliminated their historic prohibitions on water transfers or riddled them with loopholes (Thompson 1997). Western states have also tried to ease administrative barriers to market transfers and have developed governmentally run "water banks" to promote short-term transfers (Thompson 1993a). Despite this pro-market trend, however, parochial concerns continue to shape state policies and restrict robust markets. Most western states impose special conditions on interstate water transfers (Thompson 1991 and 1993a). States also have refused to permit members of irrigation districts to sell their water to external users over the opposition of their district (Thompson 1993b).

Since the early 1980s, the national government has taken initial steps to break down these parochial barriers to active water markets. The Supreme Court, for example, has reconsidered its earlier interstate commerce decisions and ruled that states generally cannot discriminate against interstate water transfers.[57] In the Central Valley Project Improvement Act, Congress limited the ability of irrigation districts to veto proposed transfers of project water by their members (Thompson 1993b). The Bureau of Reclamation also has adopted more liberal policies generally with respect to the transfer of reclamation water (although the bureau's policy is still best described as "cautious") (National Research Council 1992; Thompson 1993b).

Summary: An Institutional Perspective

Although there have been significant national incursions into western water policy, particularly over the past quarter-century in the environmental arena, states still retain a surprising degree of supremacy over western water policy. The checks and balances built into the U.S. Constitution have served as a major constraint on national intrusions, as the framers in part intended. As one would expect, the executive branch, which reports to the only two nationally elected officials, has shown the greatest interest in central control of water resources. The executive branch, however, can accomplish little by itself—as shown by the abortive attempts by both Presidents Franklin Roosevelt and Jimmy Carter to assert greater national authority. Where national agencies are themselves in competition for local "clients," as the Bureau of Reclamation and Army Corps of Engineers have been at times in the western United States, this competition also can drive the executive branch to greater solicitude toward state control. Local clients appreciate federal largesse, but typically they heavily favor deference to state and local policies.

Congress, reflecting constitutional design, has often hesitated to assert significant national control over western water resources. National concerns over such issues as the environment or power development have led Congress to intervene on particular issues. But even here Congress has often included language in its legislation protecting state authority to significant degrees (although this language has sometimes been effectively read out of the statutes by the courts). Of the two houses, the Senate has typically been the most concerned about protecting state authority and, given its conservative rules, has served as a major obstacle to nationalization efforts.

The federal judiciary has played a major role in determining the relative *authority* of the national and state governments. Little of this role has flowed from constitutional interpretation. Except for passages from the earliest interstate apportionment cases in the Supreme Court, the courts have never suggested that the national government is limited in its constitutional power over western waters (although the current Court's fascination with the limitations of national authority stands a slight chance of ultimately becoming an issue in the water field). The courts, however, have strongly influenced the relative balance of authority through their interpretation of federal statutes and their creation of purely judicial doctrines, such as federal reserved water rights and equitable apportionment.

Because the Constitution is not directly implicated, Congress could reverse the courts' determinations, but it has not. Each time the courts have dramatically switched their views on such issues as federal reserved water rights or relative federal–state powers under the national Reclamation Act, members of Congress and others have urged congressional reversal. But Congress has consistently failed to act—regardless of whether the courts' decisions have undermined or supported state authority. The courts, in short, appear to have very broad leeway to define the extent and nature of national authority over western water resources.

An interesting question is why Congress has not overridden the courts' decisions more frequently, particularly given the gyrations in the courts' holdings. Perhaps the courts have simply stayed in tune with Congress's views over time. More likely Congress's failure to act has reflected two other factors. First, the courts' decisions often have not made that much of a difference in actual water policy. When the Supreme Court recognized national water rights for all federal reservations, federal agencies carefully avoided using these rights to override existing state water rights in most cases. The Supreme Court's later retreat in *United States v. New Mexico* therefore did not affect a major change in actual practice. Second, inertia is a much stronger element of the congressional process than is frequently suggested. Many of the water issues that the federal courts have addressed generate strong political views on both sides of the question. Under these circumstances, the best course of action for a risk-averse Congress is to leave the issues to the courts.

Normative Considerations

What should be the relative roles of national, state, and local governments in the formulation of western water policy? As described above, the states still retain primary authority over western water policy, although they have delegated a good deal of power to local water agencies, and the national government has slowly eroded the states' plenary control. Numerous policymakers and academics, however, continue to argue for greater national involvement—both over specific issues such as groundwater extraction and use (Blomquist 1991)[58] and over western water policy generally (Long Peak's Working Group 1992; Foster and Rogers 1988). Other policymakers and academics increasingly call for the devolution of authority to watershed defined entities (Adler 1995; Goldfarb 1994).

General federalism discussions outside the water context have suggested a diverse set of advantages to state over national primacy, including customization of policies to regional differences, enhanced democratic input, and policy competition (Ostrom 1987, 1994; Wildavsky 1990). At

the same time, analysts have identified various problems with state primacy ranging from local provincialism to the critical role of the national government in supporting free market capitalism (Dorn 1990; Weingast
1995). Applying these general analyses to water policy is not a simple
matter; water resources frequently cross state borders and give rise to
significant externalities, complicating the question of the optimal allocation of authority between states and the national government. To sim-
plify federalism issues in the water context, this section examines the
optimal allocation question in steps. The section begins by considering
the appropriate role of state and national governments if water resources
were contained wholly within island states with no opportunity for moving water among states. The section then examines how the policy prescriptions of an island model change when the realities of potential
interstate water transfers, interstate waters, interstate externalities, and
federal land interests within state borders are added. Finally, the section
briefly considers two alternatives to pure state or federal control: control
by local water districts and watershed management.

An Island Model

Start for analytical simplicity by assuming that (1) the only governmental entities of relevance are the state and national governments, (2)
all surface waterways and aquifers are located wholly within state borders, and (3) each state is a geographic island. Water cannot be moved
from one state to another, and water use in one state does not impose
any physical externality on residents of other states. The states, however, are confederated as a union in which citizens engage in trade and
move freely among states. Under these assumptions, how would an ideal
constitution allocate authority over water policy between the states and
the national government? Although the assumptions are obviously unre-
alistic, they permit us to scrutinize both the general arguments for state
primacy and several of the arguments that have been made for greater
national authority over water resources.

Authority over Water Use and Quality

In the island model, a number of considerations militate strongly in
favor of awarding states principal authority over water allocation and
quality. To begin, each state is likely to face different water conditions,
demands, and policy preferences. Overall annual renewable supplies of
water will vary among states, as will the comparative mix of groundwater and surface water, the characteristics of those sources (e.g., an aquifer's relative recharge, the timing of river flows, the natural salinity of
a waterway, or a stream's aesthetic value), and threats to those sources

(e.g., the potential for saltwater intrusion). The public's policy preferences also will differ. Some populations, for example, will prefer greater economic output, while others will prefer more environmental or recreational amenities.

State control of water policy also enables crucial testing and comparison of alternative approaches. Local policy discretion, for example, drove development and adoption of the modern permit-based appropriation system. At various points, western states tried various forms and combinations of riparian, community-based, preferential, and appropriative systems, as well as different forms of administrative implementation (Sax, Abrams, and Thompson 1991). Although variations remain among states, experience and competition ultimately led virtually all western states to quite similar systems. Similar testing and borrowing now appears to be occurring in state programs addressing groundwater overdraft (Smith 1986), water conservation, nonpoint pollution, and preservation of instream flows (Sax, Abrams, and Thompson 1991).

Citizens may also believe that they have more direct input into state decisions. If so, water users are likely to be more accepting of state policy and perhaps more willing to let the government address water problems. Consider the problem of groundwater overdrafting. Because groundwater is a critical means of adjusting to changing surface water conditions, farmers have long been politically terrified of groundwater regulations that might strip them of the power to decide how much groundwater to use (Bowman 1990). Farmers, however, have accepted some state regulatory systems, particularly where the systems have delegated considerable authority to local entities. Where authority is localized, farmers have felt more comfortable with a regulatory regime that they believe is responsive to their needs and less subject to capture by environmental and other interests. Farmers, by contrast, have been adamantly opposed to national groundwater regulation.

In the island model, with no physical externalities or shared waterways, the case for a significant national role by contrast is weak. The greatest debate is likely to center on whether national regulation is needed of water quality, instream flows, groundwater overdrafting, and other environmental aspects of water policy. The most common claim is that a "race to the bottom" among states will lead the states to provide suboptimal environmental protection. Because states compete economically, the argument goes, states will suffer from a perverse incentive to permit excessive pollution and water diversions in order to attract businesses away from other states. Some have also claimed that environmental and conservation interests are systematically underrepresented in state legislatures relative to user interests.[59]

Proponents, however, have not offered empirical support for a "race to the bottom" in either the water or general environmental context. Economic models suggest that interstate economic competition will not necessarily lead to a race to the bottom on environmental amenities (Revesz 1992). Assuming that people are mobile and have different tastes in income and environmental amenities, they will sort themselves by state policy with some states appealing to those who prefer higher income and other states to those preferring higher instream flows (Tiebout 1956). Where the population is not mobile but states can compete for capital through tax and environmental policies, states are likely to set a zero net tax on capital and protect the environment to the degree that the marginal cost of that protection corresponds to the marginal decrease in wages—both of which are optimal economic results (Oates 1990; Oates and Schwab 1988).

The models are not decisive. For example, if states impose a positive net tax on capital (and the empirical evidence is inconclusive on this point) (see Mieszkowski and Zodrow 1989), the tax benefits of attracting more capital will lead states to set suboptimally low environmental protections (Oates and Schwab 1988). The models are also inconclusive if the population is not mobile and is fractured within each state into dissident groups with different tastes for income and other amenities (Oates 1990). Given the benefits of state policy making, nonetheless, the models impose an obligation on proponents of national environmental decision making to produce greater evidence of a race to the bottom.

Empirical support for a systematic antienvironmental or anticonservation bias at the state level is also weak. Some states like California have often led the federal government in various environmental or conservation measures. The most comprehensive study of environmental policy making at the state level showed that the relative strength of polluting industries within a state (measured by the industries' contribution to gross state product) was actually correlated with *stronger* regulation of air and water quality (although a high concentration of extractive industries correlated with weaker water quality laws) (Ringquist 1993).

Proponents of national regulation often assume a systematic bias at the state level where it appears that states are not addressing a particular environmental or conservation problem. An instructive example of the problem of this approach is groundwater overdrafting. Proponents of national groundwater legislation frequently note the lack of effective groundwater management in many states as proof of the need for national intervention. As William Blomquist (1991) has reported, however, fifteen states adopted programs for groundwater supply management during the 1980s. The severity of groundwater problems in a state, rather than the political power of water users or the state's political culture, provided the best explanation for why particular states regulated groundwater extraction while others did not. Of the explanatory factors studied, only gross measures of groundwater dependency and use were statistically significant. Although some states can clearly be faulted for failing to address critical groundwater overdrafts, there is no evidence that states ignore the need to address groundwater withdrawals when mining becomes extensive enough to justify governmental intervention.

Many environmentalists have also argued that the national government must protect water quality, instream flows, and other environmental amenities as a moral imperative. Moral imperatives, like equality, are antithetical to federalism (Wildavsky 1990). Some policies (slavery is the most obvious example) are morally unacceptable and require national uniformity. We should be careful, however, not to confuse moral imperatives with strong policy preferences. A majority of the nation might prefer to see significant instream flows in all waterways; some citizens might even base their preference on ecomoralism. Yet such preferences do not justify a national instream flow standard. As I have elaborated elsewhere, few of our national environmental policies currently rise to the level of moral imperatives (Thompson 1996a). Although the nation strongly supports environmental protection, the debates over environmental policy illustrate that most environmental policies ultimately involve trade-offs.[60]

National Reclamation

Given that the U.S. government's first major foray into western water policy was the 1902 reclamation program, one might expect that the justification for national reclamation is fairly strong. Yet as the island model reveals, national involvement in reclamation is not only unnecessary but counterproductive. Both of the two principal rationalizations of national reclamation fail scrutiny. First, proponents of the federal reclamation program have often argued that many valuable projects were beyond state or private financial means and that the national government could profit from economies of scale. Empirical studies, however, do not back up these claims. Although state and private companies failed to pursue many large-scale projects that the United States ultimately constructed, state and private companies generally passed on the opportunity for the simple reason that the projects were economically unjustifiable (Dunbar 1983). Second, proponents of national projects have also argued that reclamation benefits "inure to the nation as a whole" (U.S. Advisory Commission 1991). Economists, however, have been quite skeptical of such spillover claims.

Water users lobbied for a national reclamation program not for these reasons but for the simple and pernicious reason that the national government enjoys a greater ability than states to subsidize water projects. It can do this because of its ability to engage in deficit financing and because it can more readily hide subsidy schemes from voters. Federal reclamation subsidies by now are legendary. The few sizable state water projects, by contrast, largely pay their own way (although they enjoy the luxury of federal tax-exempt financing). The most obvious consequences of the federal reclamation subsidies are also well known—induced demand for economically inefficient and environmentally damaging water projects, reduced conservation efforts, and often significant return flow problems (LeVeen and King 1985). The ill consequences of federal subsidies, however, do not stop here. Consider groundwater overdrafting again. By offering the hope of new, subsidized sources of water, the national government historically undermined incentives to resolve groundwater overdrafting through conservation. Federal subsidies in effect created a moral hazard. Farmers could deplete local groundwater resources with the realistic expectation that the national government would help pay for a substitute supply (Reisner 1993). Groundwater users thus favored groundwater regulation only where justified by the prevention of collateral damages such as subsidence or saltwater intrusion.

Beyond Islands

By minimizing the interactions among states and the interconnectedness of their populations, the island model establishes the strongest case for state jurisdiction over water policy. This section examines how the federalism analysis changes if one assumes that there is a physical potential for interstate water transfers, that some water bodies are interstate, and that the national government needs water for lands that it owns within the borders of the states. As explained below, these more realistic assumptions justify limited national intervention into western water policy both to foster interstate transfers and to resolve externalities on interstate waterways. States, however, should still retain primary authority over intrastate policy issues.

Interstate Commerce in Water

Start by eliminating the assumption that water cannot physically be transported from one state to another (while retaining for the moment the assumed lack of interstate waterways). The nation then has an interest in promoting an interstate market in water just as in other resources and goods (Gergen 1988). Absent effective markets, the marginal value of water will vary among states, and the total national value of water will be suboptimal. Interstate markets permit the water to flow from economically low-value to higher-value uses and increase national wealth (Booker and Young 1994).

Direct state restrictions on interstate water markets. As discussed above, however, western states historically have restricted water exports to other states (Thompson 1991). These state restrictions are often mirrored in export restrictions imposed by local water districts, which generally prohibit their members from selling conserved or unused water to outsiders (Thompson 1997).

Parochial economic concerns have frequently motivated these restrictions (Thompson 1993b). With restricted markets, local residents can obtain water at a lower price determined by the price of an appropriation permit if unappropriated water is still available or by the local marginal value of water in other uses. If out-of-staters can obtain local water, unappropriated water will be depleted sooner, and local users will be forced to pay a higher price reflecting the greater multistate demand. Although some local owners of water rights might favor interstate markets because of the increased opportunity to sell water, residents who contemplate demanding more water in the future will generally prefer a protected market.

Such parochialism is a traditional justification for national intervention. If the United States is to be an economic union and not simply a military confederation, a major purpose of the national government must be to ensure that local self-interest does not impede national markets. The Constitution thus awards Congress the power to regulate interstate commerce and implicitly limits the authority of the states to restrict such commerce.

Even the most cogent arguments made in favor of such restrictions are meritless. Some policymakers and academics have asserted that state and local restrictions are necessary to protect local communities (Chan 1988, 1989; Utton 1985). According to the most common version of the argument, failure to restrict interstate markets will permit "deep-pocketed industrial" regions to acquire water from their poorer rural neighbors, threatening the lifestyle and future of the rural areas and sowing dissension. The argument, however, assumes that the nation should preserve the current distribution of water resources even if citizens' tastes, as revealed through the market, call for reallocation. It also assumes unrealistically that market transfers are one-way streets and that rural areas cannot buy water back if they later need it.[61]

Healthy societies are dynamic and fluid. Over time, geographic regions will experience different economic vectors. For example, one region might initially grow, as local farming or mineral operations prosper, then shrink as local resources play out; other regions prove more productive, or economic demands change, and then grow again as a site for new industry or perhaps for vacation homes. The market supports this dynamism by permitting resources, including water, to move in response to changing demands. Even if a state or local government decides that it should try to preserve particular regional characteristics (e.g., small family farming) for sound policy reasons, the government should do so directly through subsidies or broader structural changes rather than by regulating a single input such as water. By trying to preserve a region through water, a government distorts the market in an important economic resource while not effectively dealing with the underlying weaknesses of the region and thus merely delaying the day of reckoning. Water transfers are only a manifestation of economic change rather than the cause of that change.

The Supreme Court, as well as at least one policy analyst (Levmore 1983), has suggested that a state program that encourages water conservation might sometimes justify restrictions on water exports.[62] The argument appears to be both that states will not engage in optimal water conservation if other states can then take the conserved water and that states deserve the fruits of their conservation efforts. Both arguments assume that states encourage conservation by directly restricting use. In this case, if a state imposes conservation mandates on local users and does not proscribe exports, citizens of other states can appropriate the conserved water and defeat the state's ultimate conservation goals.

States, however, also can encourage conservation through taxes or fees. If everyone were charged or taxed for their use of a state's water, the charge or tax would encourage both local and foreign users to conserve water. Indeed, such a system is likely to be more effective than an administrative mandate. Where water is currently being used, moreover, interstate markets would directly encourage conservation by providing existing users with a financial incentive, and the financial means, to conserve water. Interstate markets, in short, need not undercut, and are more likely to encourage, conservation.

Indirect policy barriers. Other aspects of state water policy can also impede interstate markets. Some forms of water rights, such as riparian rights or correlative groundwater rights, directly preclude trade by tying water to particular units of land. The state process for changing water rights and wheeling privileges in intrastate aqueducts are other polices that can restrict transfers (Thompson 1993a). Such restrictions beg the question of the degree to which the national government should intervene to eliminate these bar-riers.

Case-by-case balancing is essential and inevitable. Weighing in favor of national intervention is the value of interstate trade, combined with a lingering fear that many obstacles are parochially inspired. In each case, however, the national government must also evaluate the degree to which nonparochial concerns support the state policies and to which the national government can effectively intervene without becoming enmeshed in general state water policy. Most elements of state water policy, ranging from the determination of instream flows to the individual characteristics of water rights, affect interstate markets to one degree or another. Although interstate markets are valuable, the national desire to foster markets should not automatically override the significant interest in preserving state and local authority over water policy.

Consider, for example, correlative groundwater rights. In the half-dozen states including California that recognize correlative rights, owners can claim the rights only if they own land overlying an aquifer, and they must use the water on the overlying land. Eliminating these limitations could increase the amount of water available for interstate trade, and parochial concerns over city demands on aquifers helped influence original adoption of the restrictions. Nonparochial considerations, however, also support the restrictions if they reduce the risk of overdraft by increasing return flow to an aquifer or if they provide a relatively simple and administratively low-cost means of allocating groundwater. A national override would reduce the experimentation and competition that federalism enhances. If the national government were to eliminate the overlying use requirement, moreover, the government also would have to address how the new tradable right would relate both to other forms of groundwater rights and to interrelated surface water. Absent evidence that a state policy hinders a significant quantity of interstate trading, the national government thus would do best by permitting policies that only indirectly restrict interstate markets.

Interstate Water Bodies and Externalities

Next, relax the critical assumption that no water bodies are interstate. As noted in the introduction, most major rivers and a number of significant aquifers in the western United States are interstate. Such interstate water bodies raise difficult federalism issues. Assuming that states are to retain at least some authority over interstate waters, for example, how should authority be allocated among the competing states? Interstate waters also inevitably give rise to externalities, in the form of pollution, reduced instream flows, which itself can lower water quality (Miller, Weatherford, and Thorson 1986), and withdrawals from aquifers.

The need for national intervention. Interstate rivers dictate at least some national intervention. Although the issues theoretically could be left to the states to resolve, the result is likely to be neither efficient nor fair. Consider, for example, the likely result if the national government played no role in allocating an interstate river. Upstream states would control the river ab initio. Indeed, if the state farthest upstream on the river wished to divert all the water from the river or to use it as a cheap sewage system, that state would enjoy the geographic power to do so. Downstream states could try to negotiate treaties or compacts with the upstream states by offering to pay for reductions in overall diversions or pollution, but there is little reason to believe that such negotiations would be successful, let alone yield an efficient level of instream flow and quality.[63] States that have been involved in water compact negotiations in the western United States have faced intense political pressure not to give away any of the state's water rights. States have typically reached agreement only under the threat of judicial action and then only by leaving key issues open or vaguely resolved (Reid 1995). Even if states could negotiate efficient levels of instream flow and pollution, a few states would end up with immense power over what are typically the major rivers in arid regions, raising serious fairness concerns in a federalist system.

Absent national involvement, interstate aquifers initially would be common with each state having an incentive to let its users pump the aquifer dry before another state's users did the same. Given the inefficiencies of a commons to all the states overlying an aquifer, chances are likely to be greater here of a treaty or compact dividing the aquifer. In Southern California, for example, private and public entities have succeeded in negotiating effective aquifer control measures where state law did not provide them (Blomquist 1992). Other local regions, however, have been less successful in negotiating agreements among overlying users, and in one of the few currently existing disputes over an interstate aquifer, New Mexico and Texas have been unable to negotiate an effective resolution of their competition for the Hueco Bolson (Tarlock and Frownfelter 1990).

The limited role for national control. Although some degree of national intervention is necessary, complete national control of interstate water bodies is neither necessary nor beneficial. The Department of Justice has argued for years that the national government owns and should control interstate surface waters. The Justice Department's principal constitutional basis for its position—that diversions should be closely coordinated with navigational needs—is weak in the West, where most interstate rivers are not commercially navigable, and is totally inapplicable to interstate aquifers. Navigational needs, moreover, might justify national authority to set minimum instream flows but not control over other aspects of water policy.

National control of interstate water bodies would carry some advantages. National control would avoid the difficult, perhaps intractable problem (discussed below) of how to divide interstate water bodies among states. National control, moreover, would better promote interstate water markets. Interstate trades are most likely among users from the same river or aquifer system because of the physical ease of moving the water. Even if the national government ensures that states do not openly discriminate against interstate trade, dividing control of an interstate water body among states is likely to impede such interstate trades. Traders will have to deal with at least two water agencies rather than one. And because exporting states will still be motivated by parochial concerns, subtle or covert discrimination remains likely through unique water rules or implementation.

Despite the potential advantages of national control, the disadvantages cumulatively outweigh them. National control of interstate waters would strip states of authority not only over issues that could impose externalities on other states (such as water quality and total diversions) but over other issues of primarily or entirely local interest (such as the allocation of water among local users). Nationalization of interstate water bodies would thus unnecessarily eliminate the advantages of state control. Dual national and state water systems, where the national government would control interstate waters and states would control intrastate waters, also would require careful coordination. Because intrastate and interstate waters are perfect substitutes, national policies could undercut state policies and vice versa. Finally, giving regulatory oversight to existing state water agencies avoids the administrative duplication of creating a separate national water agency.

The national government, however, can play a valuable role in regulating specific externalities, especially water quality. Even though the justification for significant national intervention is greater here than in the case of purely intrastate water pollution, the United States has largely ignored the issue. A principal reason has been the nation's preoccupation under the Clean Water Act with uniform technological standards for pollution discharges (Tarlock 1991). Since the act was passed, EPA has focused on the comparatively simple administrative task of setting and enforcing technological standards. So long as point sources meet these technological standards, EPA has largely ignored ambient water quality standards in both interstate and intrastate waters. The Clean Water Act has also slighted nonpoint causes of water pollution such as agricultural return flow or diversions that do not have ready technological fixes. A final reason why the nation has neglected pollution externalities has been the scientific difficulty of determining the effect of one state's actions on water quality in another. The biological, chemical, and physical interactions within waterways are exceptionally complex and have made it difficult historically to clearly identify and manage interstate externalities.

None of these explanations is a justification for not intervening at the national level. The Clean Water Act's technological focus on point sources has long been criticized (Pederson 1988; Ackerman and Stewart 1985). And the difficulties of determining and resolving externalities does not undercut the advantage that the national government has in resolving interstate disputes. Because multilateral negotiations among states are seldom likely to resolve interstate water quality issues effectively, national intervention is essential.

Yet in addressing interstate water quality, the national government must again be mindful of the benefits of state policysetting. If water quality standards could be reduced to a common metric to which the populations of all states could agree, the national government could set a common water quality standard for an entire interstate water body employing that criterion. In fact, however, the appropriate water quality standard is a complex policy issue on which the polity of different states are likely to adopt different answers. Any water quality standard mandated by the national government thus is likely to interfere with one or more states' individual policy preferences. To minimize this inevitable interference, the national government might consider several actions.

First, the national government should avoid imposing its own standards except where a downstream state has expressly asked the government to intervene and can demonstrate that water pollution from upstream states is reducing downstream quality to a level below that which the downstream state itself has adopted for comparable intrastate waters. Initially, moreover, the national government should encourage states to try to negotiate their own resolution of the externality. The resolution could take the form of either specific water quality standards or an institution, such as a watershed commission, that would formulate the standards. Although such negotiations are difficult, the threat of greater national intervention can help drive an effective resolution. After EPA ordered the Colorado River basin states to develop numeric stateline standards for total dissolved solids, for example, the states were able to successfully agree on numeric standards for three locations on the river and the basics of an implementation plan (Miller, Weatherford, and Thorson 1986).

Second, the national government must stand willing to impose national water quality standards where individual states cannot agree, but the national standards should strive for a middle ground that reflects the different policy preferences among states. The national government should set a standard that (1) ensures downstream states a minimum water quality that permits its residents to use the waterway for basic consumptive, recreational, and aesthetic uses and (2) guarantees the downstream state at least the same quality of water that the upstream state insists upon for its comparable intrastate waters. The second criterion ensures that no state can impose a burden on the residents of another state that it has decided its own residents should not bear. Combined with the principle that downstream states should not be permitted to complain about water quality that is no lower than the water quality of its own instate streams, the second criterion could be dubbed the Golden Rule of interstate pollution: Do unto others how you do unto yourself (Merrill 1993).

Finally, the national government could increase both state latitude and efficiency by fostering an interstate market in water quality. The national government should ensure that all major sources of pollution be given specific emission allocations (cumulatively satisfying the water quality standards) and then foster their tradability. If any states or their citizens wanted to decrease pollution below the threshold standard, they could buy and retire pollution rights from individual polluters. If any states or their citizens wanted to increase their pollution discharges, they could buy and use pollution rights. Given the varied biological, chemical, and physical interactions in any waterway, a market system would be far more complicated to design than current air pollution markets (Thompson 1996b). The national government indeed might decide that some forms of trade are too difficult to evaluate and therefore outlaw them. Any steps toward a market, however, would permit greater economic flexibility and state discretion.

Apportionment among states. The national government must not only help in resolving externalities but also apportion interstate waters among riparian states. Several factors inform this task and unfortunately do not always point to the same solution. First, the apportionment system should provide as much predictability and stability as possible—both to reduce apportionment disputes and, more importantly, to provide secure property rights and thus facilitate market trading. Second, the system should not be biased toward one state policy or another. Third, the system should not create any perverse incentives such as overuse of water resources. Finally, the character of a national union requires that states view the apportionment system as fair. Although an interstate water market will permit water to flow to the area of highest need, the original apportionment determines who will enjoy the initial scarcity rents.

Possible apportionment systems are infinite, but several have proven prominent in surface water disputes. The Supreme Court often has claimed that it is engaged in an "equitable" apportionment of interstate waters requiring a "delicate adjustment" of all relevant factors.[64] In the western United States, however, the Supreme Court in practice has typically relied on the prior appropriation doctrine, refusing to depart from strict priority except when confronted by clear evidence of inequity.[65]

If the choice is limited to these two basic approaches, the prior appropriation system has the edge, both for its crystalline character and for its almost uniform adoption in the West at the state level. Although a pure equitable apportionment system might best promote fairness by permitting the Court to engage in a broad-ranging inquiry into relative equities, such a balancing approach would leave interstate rights both uncertain and insecure. Where all relevant states employ prior appropriation for intrastate waters, water users also are likely to perceive the system as a fair means of apportioning waters. Departing from a temporal priority rule for users who are drawing from the same interstate water body (and perhaps live in close proximity to each other) merely because the users live on different sides of a state border would generate serious horizontal equity concerns where priority is the prevailing interstate norm.

The prior appropriation system, however, poses two problems as a system for apportioning interstate waters—one rooted in federalism and the other rooted in economic efficiency. First, unless states are permitted to appropriate water for instream flow, upstream states by appropriating and consuming all unused water can foreclose the ability of lower states to choose a water policy that favors preservation over use. Second, the Court's use of the prior appropriation system raises all of the system's traditional efficiency problems. The system encourages states to appropriate interstate waters quickly before their neighbors do. As applied historically in most states and by the Supreme Court, the system does not even recognize the need to preserve instream flow for environmental, recreational, aesthetic, and water quality purposes. During droughts, the system also cuts back junior uses before even touching senior uses, which is likely to be far less efficient than proportional reductions in water use. Although interstate markets can help reduce any inefficiencies resulting from the latter problem, the prior appropriation system unnecessarily creates a need for market transfers and their attendant transaction costs.

If the Supreme Court were starting over again in deciding how to apportion surface water, some form of crystalline sharing rule would reduce these problems (although at the risk, as discussed above, of some horizontal inequities among neighboring water users in different states). Factoring in hydrologic complexities such as tributaries, evaporation, and differing instream needs, the Court could divide a river's flow equally among all riparian states or proportionate to the percentage of the river's watershed found in each state. Having adopted the prior appropriation system, however, the Court could abandon it today only with considerable disruption to western water systems and economies.

The principal issue today, when many interstate streams are already fully appropriated, is the degree to which the Court will use judicial apportionment to require conservation and other equitable reallocations of water. In an interstate dispute over the Vermejo River, for example, Colorado argued that the Court should award it more than the prior appropriation system would mandate because New Mexican users were wasting water.[66] As noted in Part I, the Court initially indicated a strong inclination to agree with Colorado if the state could show that New Mexican users could reduce their diversions through "reasonable conservation measures."[67] Two years later, however, the Court backed away and, while not foreclosing a departure from prior appropriation, suggested that it would abandon priority only on exceptionally strong evidence of significant waste.[68]

The Court was correct to be cautious and indeed should forswear any free-roving equitable inquiry. As the Court observed, ad hoc departures from the prior appropriation system can result in significant uncertainty and disrupt established water rights.[69] By scrutinizing alleged inefficiencies in a state's water system, moreover, the Court inevitably reduces that state's sovereignty and the advantages of a federal system. Finally, interstate water markets provide a more effective and less intrusive means of encouraging conservation and economically beneficial reallocations. If users in one state can readily conserve water, the opportunity to sell the water to users in other states will encourage an efficient level of conservation without imposing national consumption standards on that state's users.

Division of interstate waters unfortunately has cast in question the interstate marketability of those waters. Some analysts, for example, have suggested that judicial apportionment of a set quantity of water to a state should entitle the state to prohibit out-of-state use of the water. The Supreme Court has not addressed the issue. Although the logic of the Court's dormant commerce clause opinions seems equally applicable to interstate waters, the Court has emphasized that its equitable apportionment decrees have "fostered" the "legal expectation that under certain circumstances each State may restrict water within its borders."[70]

Even more troubling are the numerous compacts among states that divide interstate waters. Many interstate compacts bar or partially restrict interstate transfers (Thompson 1991). And lower federal courts have held that congressionally approved interstate compacts are federal law and thus not subject to the dormant commerce clause.[71] Even where an interstate compact does not expressly limit interstate trade, the compact's division of water among the signatory states can implicitly raise questions regarding the transferability of the water (Thompson 1997; Holme 1987).

The national government must resolve these questions if it is to promote interstate water markets. The Supreme Court must clarify that judicial apportionment decrees do not exempt states from the dormant commerce clause. Congress, moreover, must ensure that it does not undermine interstate markets by approving compacts that explicitly or implicitly restrict interstate trade or by apportioning water on terms that could be interpreted to prevent such trade. To quickly eliminate all uncertainty, Congress could enact blanket legislation specifying that all waters of the United States are transferable no matter what the terms of judicial apportionment decrees, interstate compacts, or earlier congressional legislation.

Protecting National Interests

Yet a final complication to consider is the presence of national property within state borders. Almost half of all western lands consists of national parks, forests, wilderness areas, military reservations, and other federal lands, much of which, like any other land, needs water. The Supreme Court has held that reserved federal land enjoys an implied right to as much water as is needed to fulfill the reservation's primary purposes. Although the Court has repeatedly reaffirmed the existence of federal reserved water rights, debate still rages over the validity and proper scope of such rights.

Assuming that the national government should own and manage western lands, the national government should be able to override any aspects of state law that would prevent it from using the lands for their legitimate functions. Facing different political interests, state governments will not always be inclined to provide water for national lands. The national government should be able to insist at a minimum on the same water entitlements as private property owners or the states enjoy.[72] The national government should also be able to override state water policies, such as bans on instream appropriations, that would prevent the national government from fulfilling the purposes of a particular reservation. Although national water rights ideally should be integrated with state water systems for both federalism and practical reasons, excusing the national government from having to comply with state procedures should not pose serious concerns so long as the national government follows the substance of state water law wherever possible.

Federal reserved water rights, however, serve a quite different function. When the national government created most western reservations, it might have but typically did not claim a national right to any water. Indeed, as the Supreme Court has admitted, Congress often expressly instructed the government's land agencies to acquire any necessary water rights under state law, and this was the practice that the land agencies followed for years.[73] If the national government had continued to follow this route or even overridden state law in those infrequent cases where necessary to achieve its purposes, there would have been little controversy.

The Court-created doctrine of federal reserved water rights has provoked debate because it performs two more radical functions. First, federal reserved rights permit the national government to set aside potentially large quantities of water for possible future use. A key feature of the prior appropriation system is that water rights are lost if the water is not used. Concomitantly, water cannot be held for speculative future use. Although one might disagree with the value of the rule, it certainty has often been touted as a critical and valuable feature of prior appropriation (Trelease 1957). Federal reserved water rights survive even if not used and thus directly undermine the prior appropriation system. This might be tolerated to carry out the national government's purposes, but it is not necessary. If water is already appropriated by the time the government needs water for a particular use, the government can always buy or condemn the necessary water.

Second, and in a related fashion, the courts have used the federal reserved rights doctrine to meet new governmental demands without forcing the government to purchase or condemn the necessary water. In many reserved right cases, the national government has recognized, decades after reserving land, that it needs additional water rights either because of increased demand on a waterway that has reduced the amount of instream flow otherwise available to the government or because of newly recognized governmental uses for the water. In these situations, Congress could authorize the purchase or condemnation of the necessary water. By creating implied reserved rights, however, the Supreme Court created a method by which the national government can belatedly claim additional water without paying compensation. Although the Court's creation of implied federal reserved rights might itself be considered an unconstitutional taking of displaced state water rights, the Court is guardian of its own actions and thus can get away with what Congress cannot (Thompson 1991).

Alternative Levels of Authority

Most of the above analysis also speaks to the advantages and disadvantages of giving authority over water policy to local entities such as irrigation districts. Local authority, even more than state authority, permits water policy to be contoured to local conditions and encourages direct democratic input into policy decisions. Local authority, however, is typically exercised without consideration of the interests of a state or the nation as a whole (Thompson 1993b). For example, irrigation districts for purely parochial reasons have often opposed water exports. Ir-

rigation districts also have been slow to impose conservation requirements unless the district itself is facing shortages.

As at the state–national level, an unfettered water market is of particular importance, both to promote more efficient use of water and to encourage valuable conservation. At the state–local level, however, there
is no constitutional provision equivalent to the dormant commerce clause.
So long at least as only intrastate transfers are involved, one irrigation
district can prevent water from being transferred to another water district without running afoul of either the state or the national constitution. This means that state or national legislatures must protect against
parochial obstacles to water transfers and, to date, legislatures have seldom intervened (Thompson 1997).

Watershed Management

Interest in watershed management is increasing for good reason (Adler
1995; Keiter 1994; Goldfarb 1994). Our political boundaries, as already
emphasized, do not correlate well with natural boundaries. Imposing
multiple policies on the same waterway or watershed, based purely
on where one state or local border begins and another ends, makes no
policy sense. Externalities are also most likely to arise where different
jurisdictions have authority over parts of the same waterway or watershed. In a similar fashion, water policy needs to be integrated with other
resource and environmental issues within a relevant geographic region.
Policy suffers when decisions are unnecessarily divided substantively or
geographically.

The difficult issue is how best to move toward watershed management. The best solution at the moment appears to be the formation of
partnerships among relevant governmental entities around specific policy issues or sets of issues (Goldfarb 1994; Harrison 1980). The partnerships can be ad hoc or can be formalized into watershed commissions.
One alternative—the formation of a watershed management authority
with independent power—suffers from a variety of problems: the additional entity can create new problems of duplication and overlap; the
appropriate geographic boundaries for each specific issue can often vary,
making it difficult to determine universal boundaries for a watershed
management authority; and authorities with independent power typically
lack valuable checks and balances. The other principal alternative—national regulation at a watershed level—raises the various concerns with
national power discussed earlier.

Partnerships, however, generate their own problems. The governmental agencies and entities that participate are often reluctant to give up
any power or even to cooperate with each other, making it difficult to

achieve concrete progress. Even in the best of worlds, moreover, agreement on particular policies and implementation schemes is time- and re-
source-intensive. At the moment, however, partnerships appear to be the
most workable system and the system that best preserves the values of
federalism.

Conclusion

Although this chapter has not attempted a detailed study of the individual issues involved in water federalism, a number of initial conclusions
can be drawn. First, states' current primacy in water policy appears to
be appropriate and beneficial. State authority (particularly when delegated in part to local entities) carries a variety of advantages over national
regulation. Proponents of extended national authority over such traditional state issues as instream flow in intrastate streams have not made a
convincing case that there are any systematic deficiencies in state policy
making that justify displacing state authority.

The above discussion emphasizes that the national government does
have a role in western water policy. Indeed, in some cases, the national
government has not been aggressive enough. None of the three branches
of the national government, for example, has taken sufficient steps to
open up interstate water markets and eliminate parochial state barriers.
Indeed the national government has often been as much a part of the
problem as a part of the solution. Although the Supreme Court has finally subjected state barriers to the dormant commerce clause, the Court
has also suggested that states might enjoy greater leeway in regulating
interstate water transfers than in regulating other interstate markets. Congress also has approved compacts that directly or indirectly impede interstate sales.

The Supreme Court also has not addressed the constitutionality of direct export restrictions by local water districts. On a purely doctrinal
basis, the Court might conclude that such restrictions do not discriminate against interstate commerce since they apply equally to intrastate
trades, but the Court has rejected a similar distinction in invalidating
county bans on the importation of hazardous waste for local disposal. If
the Court does not act, Congress justifiably should intervene to remove
parochial barriers at both the state and local levels.

The national government also must make greater strides in addressing
interstate water pollution. Although this would seem to be the most logical area for national intervention, both the complexities of the issue and
the national government's myopic focus on technological approaches to
water quality have dissuaded the national government from aggressively

dealing with this issue. As the nation begins to focus more on ambient water quality and nonpoint contributions to water pollution, the national government will, one hopes, focus more attention on interstate quality.

There are other areas, however, where the national government has intruded too far or with insufficient appreciation for state and local discretion. An area where the national government should look for ways of returning some authority to the states is intrastate environmental policy. On many water issues, the argument for comprehensive national mandates remains weak.

Federal reserved water rights are also unnecessarily intrusive on state water policy. The national government should normally obtain needed water through state water systems. Because state water policies might often be motivated by different goals than underlie national lands, the national government should have the ability to override state law where necessary to carry out the purposes of the national lands. As constructed by the Supreme Court, however, federal reserved water rights undercut the certainty that is a key ingredient of the prior appropriation system and permit the government to displace state water rights without compensation. Thankfully, in practice, the national government has typically asserted federal reserved water rights cautiously and with sensitivity to the concerns of state water right holders.

Finally, the national government should get out of the reclamation business. The federal reclamation program, which was inspired from the outset by questionable goals, has done more harm than good overall. Congress has already taken major strides toward reducing the historical subsidy (Wahl 1989) and should phase out the subsidy entirely. Congress should also devolve ownership of water projects to the state or local level. Although the Bureau of Reclamation defers to state policies on many issues, its operation of reclamation projects creates dual policies on other issues and unnecessarily interferes with state policy discretion.

Notes

1. See, for example, 1861 Colo. Session Laws 67, § 1.
2. See Colorado Constitution, art. 16, § 6.
3. See *Lux v. Haggin*, 69 Cal. 255, 10 P. 674 (1886).
4. This was the principal argument of the defendants in *Coffin v. Left Hand Ditch Co.*, 6 Colo. 443 (1882).
5. *Act of July 26, 1866*, 14 Stat. 253, § 9.
6. *Act of July 9, 1870*, 16 Stat. 218, § 17.
7. See *Broder v. Natoma Water & Mining Co.*, 101 U.S. (11 Otto) 274 (1879).

8. See *Act of July 26, 1866*, 14 Stat. 253, § 9.

9. *Act of March 3, 1877*, 19 Stat. 377.

10. *Act of March 3, 1877*, 19 Stat. 377, § 1.

11. See *United States v. Rio Grande Dam & Irrigation Co.*, 174 U.S. 690 (1899).

12. See *California Oregon Power Co. v. Beaver Portland Cement Co.*, 295 U.S. 142 (1935).

13. See *Fallbrook Irrigation District v. Bradley*, 164 U.S. 112 (1896). Two justices dissented, including Justice Stephen Field who had served on the California Supreme Court and understood western water issues better than any of the other justices serving at the time.

14. See *Hudson County Water Co. v. McCarter*, 209 U.S. 349 (1908).

15. *Hudson County Water Co. v. McCarter*, 209 U.S. 349, 356 (1908).

16. 25 Stat. 618.

17. 19 Stat. 377.

18. 32 Stat. 388.

19. 43 U.S.C. § 372.

20. 35 Cong. Rec. 6679 (June 2, 1902).

21. 32 Stat. 388, §§ 5, 8.

22. 43 U.S.C. § 383.

23. 35 Cong. Rec. 6770 (1902).

24. See 32 Stat. 388.

25. 207 U.S. 564 (1908).

26. 185 U.S. 125 (1907).

27. The Justice Department continued to push the argument in both *Wyoming v. Colorado*, 259 U.S. 419 (1922) and *Nebraska v. Wyoming*, 325 U.S. 589 (1945).

28. See *California Oregon Power Co. v. Beaver Portland Cement Co.*, 295 U.S. 142 (1935).

29. See *Federal Power Commission v. Oregon*, 349 U.S. 435 (1955).

30. 373 U.S. 546 (1963).

31. 43 U.S.C. § 383.

32. See *City of Fresno v. California*, 372 U.S. 627 (1963); *Ivanhoe Irrigation District v. McCracken*, 357 U.S. 275 (1958).

33. 16 U.S.C. §§ 803, 821.

34. 328 U.S. 152 (1946).

35. The change in agency behavior is documented in U.S. Senate (1956). Evidence of federal agencies' earlier practice of obtaining needed water rights in compliance with state law is provided in *United States v. New Mexico*, 438 U.S. 696 (1978).

36. See, for example, S. 863, 84th Cong., 2d Sess. (1956).

37. See P.L. 101-618, 104 Stat. 3289, tit. II.

38. 438 U.S. 645 (1978).

39. See *United States v. New Mexico*, 438 U.S. 696 (1978).

40. See *Colorado v. New Mexico*, 459 U.S. 176 (1982).

41. See *Colorado v. New Mexico*, 467 U.S. 310 (1984).

42. See *California v. Federal Energy Regulatory Commission*, 495 U.S. (1990).

43. See *PUD No. 1 v. Washington Dept. of Ecology*, 114 S.Ct. 1900 (1994).

44. 33 U.S.C. § 1344.

45. 33 U.S.C. § 1251(g).

46. See, for example, *Riverside Irrigation District v. Andrews*, 758 F.2d 508 (10th Cir. 1985).

47. See, for example, Estes (1992).

48. 16 U.S.C. § 1536.

49. See *Riverside Irrigation District v. Andrews*, 758 F.2d 508 (10th Cir. 1985).

50. See *Carson-Truckee Water Conservancy District v. Clark*, 549 F.Supp. 704 (D. Nev. 1982), *aff'd in part & rev'd in part*, 741 F.2d 257 (9th Cir. 1984), *cert. denied*, 470 U.S. 1083 (1985).

51. 16 U.S.C. §§ 1532(19), 1538.

52. See, for example, *United States v. Glenn-Colusa Irrigation District*, 788 F.Supp. 1126 (E.D. Cal. 1992).

53. At the moment, however, the "habitat modification" proscriptions of section 9 of the ESA extend only to endangered fish and wildlife, not endangered plants. Compare 16 U.S.C. § 1538(a) (prohibitions applicable to endangered fish and wildlife) with 16 U.S.C. § 1538(b) (prohibitions applicable to endangered plants).

54. 16 U.S.C. §§ 1271 et seq.

55. 106 Stat. 4706.

56. 106 Stat. 4600.

57. See *Sporhase v. Nebraska ex rel. Douglas*, 458 U.S. 941 (1982).

58. For an example of a recent bill that would have provided for national regulation of groundwater extraction, see S. 1992, 100th Cong., 2d Sess. (1988).

59. Stewart (1977) provides a fairly comprehensive list of factors that might justify national regulation in the environmental field.

60. Some environmental laws are supported by stronger moral claims than others. For example, laws governing the conservation of depletable natural resources, such as endangered fish species. Conservation of resources for future generations has a strong moral basis in both our societal norms and philosophy (Rawls 1971; Thompson 1996a).

61. The argument also constitutes a general challenge to a national market economy and fails to justify imposing unique restrictions on water. The community-based justification for preventing interstate movement applies equally well to energy resources, capital, labor, and other mobile resources.

62. *Sporhase v. Nebraska ex rel. Douglas*, 458 U.S. 941 (1982).

63. Such treaties or compacts, moreover, would themselves need national enforcement to be effective.

64. See *Nebraska v. Wyoming*, 325 U.S. 589 (1945).

65. See *Colorado v. New Mexico*, 467 U.S. 310 (1984); *Wyoming v. Colorado*, 259 U.S. 419 (1922).

66. See *Colorado v. New Mexico*, 467 U.S. 310 (1984) and 459 U.S. 176 (1982).

67. See *Colorado v. New Mexico*, 459 U.S. 176 (1982).
68. See *Colorado v. New Mexico*, 467 U.S. 310 (1984).
69. See *Colorado v. New Mexico*, 467 U.S. 310 (1984).
70. See *Sporhase v. Nebraska ex rel. Douglas*, 458 U.S. 941 (1982).
71. See *Intake Water Co. v. Yellowstone River Compact Commission*, 590 F.Supp. 293 (D. Mont. 1983), *cert. denied*, 469 U.S. 925 (1984).
72. This was the holding of the Nevada Supreme Court in *State v. Morros*, 104 Nev. 709, 766 P.2d 263 (1988).
73. See *United States v. New Mexico*, 438 U.S. 696 (1978).

References

Ackerman, Bruce, and Richard Stewart. 1985. Reforming Environmental Law. *Stanford Law Review* 37(5): 1333–65.

Adler, Robert. 1995. Addressing Barriers to Watershed Protection. *Environmental Law* 25(4): 973–1106.

Batt, Kevin D. 1995. Above All, Do No Harm: Sweet Home and Section Nine of the Endangered Species Act. *Boston University Law Review* 75(4): 1177–231.

Blomquist, William. 1991. Exploring State Differences in Groundwater Policy Adoptions, 1980–1989. *Publius* 21(2): 105–15.

———. 1992. *Dividing the Waters*. San Francisco: ICS Press.

Bolin, James H., Jr. 1993. Of Razorbacks and Reservoirs: The Endangered Species Act's Protection of Endangered Colorado River Basin Fish. *Pace Environmental Law Review* 11(1): 35–87.

Booker, J. F., and R. A. Young. 1994. Modeling Intrastate and Interstate Markets for Colorado River Water Resources. *Journal of Environmental Economics and Management* 26(1): 66–87.

Bowman, Jean A. 1990. Ground-Water-Management Areas in United States. *Journal of Water Resources Planning and Management* 116(4): 484–502.

Chan, Arthur. 1981. The Structure of Federal Water Resources Policy Making. *American Journal of Economics and Sociology* 40(2): 115–27.

———. 1988. Policy Impacts of *Sporhase v. Nebraska. Journal of Economic Issues* 22(4): 1153–67.

———. 1989. To Market or Not to Market: Allocation of Interstate Waters. *Natural Resources Journal* 29(2): 529–47.

Dellapenna, Joseph W. 1990. Riparian Rights in the West. *Oklahoma Law Review* 43(1): 51–70.

Dorn, James. 1990. Introduction: Federalism and the Economic Order. *Cato Journal* 10(1): 1–15.

Dunbar, Robert G. 1983. *Forging New Rights in Western Waters.* Lincoln and London: University of Nebraska Press.

Estes, Melissa K. 1992. The Effect of the Federal ESA on State Water Rights. *Environmental Law* 22(3): 1027–66.

Fairfax, Sally, and A. Dan Tarlock. 1979. No Water for the Woods: A Critical Analysis of *United States v. New Mexico. Idaho Law Review* 15(3): 509–54.

Fortier, Samuel. 1907. The Greatest Need of Arid America. *Official Proceedings of the Fifteenth National Irrigation Congress.* Sacramento, 67–74.

Foster, Charles H. W., and Peter P. Rogers. 1988. *Toward an Agenda for Action.* Cambridge: Harvard University Energy and Environmental Policy Center.

Gergen, Mark P., 1988. The Selfish State and the Market. *Texas Law Review* 66(6): 1097–153.

Getches, David H., and Susan M. Williams. 1994. Winters Rights: What We (Think We) Know, What We Don't Know. Paper presented at Indian Water Rights Conference sponsored by the Stanford Law School and Native American Rights Fund, September 9–10, Stanford University.

Goldfarb, William. 1994. Watershed Management: Slogan or Solution? *Boston College Environmental Affairs Law Review* 21(3): 483–509.

Gray, Brian. 1988. No Holier Temples: Protecting the National Parks through Wild and Scenic River Designation. *University of Colorado Law Review* 58(4): 551–98.

———. 1994. The Modern Era in California Water Law. *Hastings Law Journal* 45(2): 249–308.

Harrison, David C. 1980. Basinwide Perspective: An Approach to the Design and Analysis of Institutions for Unified River Basin Management. In *Unified River Basin Management,* ed. Ronald M. North, Leonard B. Dworsky, and David J. Allec. Minneapolis: American Water Resources Association, 427–37.

Holme, Howard K. 1987. Obstacles to Interstate Transfers of Water: Many a Slip 'Twixt the Cup and the Lip. In *Tradition, Innovation, and Conflict: Perspectives on Colorado Water Law,* ed. Lawrence J. MacDonnell. Boulder: Natural Resources Law Center, University of Colorado Law School, 267–86.

Hundley, Norris, Jr. 1975. *Water and the West: The Colorado River Compact and the Politics of Water in the American West.* Berkeley: University of California Press.

Keiter, Robert B. 1994. Beyond the Boundary Line: Constructing a Law of Ecosystem Management. *University of Colorado Law Review* 65(2): 293–333.

————. 1996a. Ecosystems and the Law: Toward an Integrated Approach. Working Paper. University of Utah, College of Law, Salt Lake City.

————. 1996b. Toward Legitimizing Ecosystem Management on the Public Domain. *Ecological Applications* 6(3): 727–30.

LeVeen, E. Phillip, and Laura B. King. 1985. *Turning Off the Tap on Federal Water Subsidies.* San Francisco: Natural Resources Defense Council.

Levmore, Saul. 1983. Interstate Exploitation and Judicial Intervention. *Virginia Law Review* 69(4): 563–631.

Long Peak's Working Group of National Water Policy. 1992. *America's Waters: A New Era of Sustainability.* Boulder: Natural Resources Law Center, University of Colorado School of Law.

Malone, Thomas E. 1965. *The California Irrigation Crisis of 1886: Origins of the Wright Act.* Ph.D. dissertation, Stanford University.

Matheson, Scott M. 1979. President Carter's Water Policy: Partnership or Preemption? *Rocky Mountain Mineral Law Institute* 25: 1-1–1-25.

McCool, Daniel. 1987. *Command of the Waters: Iron Triangles, Federal Water Development, and Indian Water.* Berkeley: University of California Press.

Mecham, Duane, and Benjamin M. Simon. 1995. Forging a New Federal Reclamation Water Pricing Policy: Legal and Policy Considerations. *Arizona State Law Journal* 27(2): 507–57.

Melling, Tom. 1993. The CUP Holds the Solution: Utah's Hybrid Alternative to Water Markets. *Journal of Energy, Natural Resources, and Environmental Law* 13(1): 159–207.

————. 1994. Dispute Resolution within Legislative Institutions. *Stanford Law Review* 46(6): 1677–715.

Merrill, Thomas. 1993. Transboundary Pollution, the Supreme Court, and the Reverse Golden Rule. Northwestern University School of Law, Chicago.

Mieszkowski, Peter, and George R. Zodrow. 1989. Taxation and the Tiebout Model: The Differential Effect of Head Taxes, Taxes on Land Rents, and Property Taxes. *Journal of Economic Literature* 27(3): 1098–146.

Miller, Taylor, Gary Weatherford, and John Thorson. 1986. *The Salty Colorado.* Washington, DC: Conservation Foundation.

Morreale, Eva Hanna. 1966. Federal–State Conflicts Over Western Water—A Decade of Attempted "Clarifying Legislation." *Rutgers Law Review* 20(3): 423–526.

Muys, Jerome C. 1971. *Interstate Water Compacts: The Interstate Compact and Federal–Interstate Compact.* Legal Study 14. Washington, DC: National Water Commission.

National Research Council. 1992. *Water Transfers in the West: Efficiency, Equity, and the Environment.* Washington, DC: National Academy Press.

Natural Resources Planning Board. 1934. *A Plan for Planning.* Washington, DC.

Oates, Wallace E. 1990. Economics, Economists, and Environmental Policy. *Eastern Economic Journal* 16(4): 289–96.

Oates, Wallace E., and Robert M. Schwab. 1988. Economic Competition Among Jurisdictions: Efficiency Enhancing or Distortion Inducing? *Journal of Public Economic* 35(3): 333–54.

Ostrom, Vincent. 1987. *Garcia*, the Eclipse of Federalism, and the Central-Government Trap. In *Federalism and the Constitution: A Symposium on Garcia.* Washington, DC: U.S. Advisory Commission on Intergovernmental Relations, 35–53.

———. 1994. *The Meaning of American Federalism: Constituting a Self-Governing Society.* San Francisco: ICS Press.

Pederson, William. 1988. Turning the Tide on Water Quality. *Ecology Law Quarterly* 15(1): 69–102.

Pisani, Donald J. 1982. State vs. Nation: Federal Reclamation and Water Rights in the Progressive Era. *Pacific History Review* 51(2): 268–81.

———. 1992. *To Reclaim a Divided West: Water, Law, and Public Policy, 1848–1902.* Albuquerque: University of New Mexico Press.

Plouffe, William L. 1986. Forty Years after First Iowa: A Call for Greater State Control of Water Resources. *Cornell Law Review* 71(4): 833–49.

Powell, John Wesley. 1890a. The Irrigable Lands of the Arid Region. *Century Magazine* 39: 766–76.

———. 1890b. Institutions for the Arid Lands. *Century Magazine* 40: 111–16.

Rawls, John. 1971. *A Theory of Justice.* Cambridge: Belknap Press of Harvard University Press.

Reid, E. Leif. 1995. Ripples from the Truckee: The Case for Congressional Apportionment of Disputed Interstate Water Rights. *Stanford Environmental Law Journal* 14(1): 145–79.

Reisner, Marc. 1993. *Cadillac Desert: The American West and Its Disappearing Water*, revised and updated edition. New York: Penguin Books.

Revesz, Richard. 1992. Rehabilitating Interstate Competition: Rethinking the "Race-to-the-Bottom" Rationale for Federal Environmental Regulation. *New York University Law Review* 67(6): 1210–54.

Ringquist, Evan J. 1993. *Environmental Protection at the State Level: Politics and Progress in Controlling Pollution.* Armonk, NY: Sharpe.

Romm, Jeff, and Sally K. Fairfax. 1985. The Backwaters of Federalism: Receding Reserved Water Rights and the Management of National Forests. *Policy Studies Review* 5(2): 413–30.

Ruhl, J. B. 1995. Biodiversity Conservation and the Ever-Expanding Web of Federal Law Regulating Nonfederal Lands: Time for Something Completely Different? *University of Colorado Law Review* 66(3): 555–673.

Sax, Joseph L., Robert H. Abrams, and Barton H. Thompson Jr. 1991. *Legal Control of Water Resources*, 2d ed. St. Paul, MN: West.

Shallat, Todd. 1992. Water and Bureaucracy: Origins of the Federal Responsibility for Water Resources. *Natural Resources Journal* 32(1): 5–25.

Smith, Paula. 1986. Coercion and Groundwater Management: Three Case Studies and a "Market" Approach. *Environmental Law* 16(4): 797–882.

Stewart, Richard. 1977. Pyramids of Sacrifice? Problems of Federalism in Mandatory State Implementation of National Environmental Policy. *Yale Law Journal* 86(6): 1196–272.

Tarlock, A. Dan. 1991. Upstream, Downstream: Rationalizing Different State Water Quality Standards on Interstate Streams. *Rocky Mountain Mineral Law Institute* 37: 23-1–23-48.

Tarlock, A. Dan, and Darcy A. Frownfelter. 1990. State Groundwater Sovereignty after *Sporhase*: The Case of the Hueco Bolson. *Oklahoma Law Review* 43(1): 27–49.

Thompson, Barton H., Jr. 1991. Interstate Transfers: *Sporhase*, Compacts, and Free Markets. In *Western Water Law in the Age of Reallocation*. Philadelphia: American Law Institute, 81–102.

———. 1993a. *The Future of Water Markets: Emerging Institutions, Shifting Paradigms, and Organizations*. Discussion Paper 387. Stanford: Center for Economic Policy Research, Stanford University.

———. 1993b. Institutional Perspectives on Water Policy and Markets. *California Law Review* 81(3): 671–764.

———. 1993c. Water Organizations in the West. Readings for Water Organizations in a Changing West conference, sponsored by the Natural Resources Law Center, University of Colorado School of Law, Boulder, June 14–16.

———. 1995. Legal Disconnections between Ground and Surface Water. In *Making the Connections: Proceedings of the Twentieth Biennial Conference on Ground Water*. Davis: Center for Water and Wildland Resources, University of California, 19–30.

———. 1996a. Environmental Policy and State Constitutions: The Potential Role of Substantive Guidance. *Rutgers Law Journal* 27(4): 863–925.

———. 1996b. Foreword. *Stanford Environmental Law Journal* 15(2): viii–xxi.

———. 1997. Water Markets and the Problem of Shifting Paradigms. In *Water Marketing: The Next Generation*, ed. Terry L. Anderson and Peter J. Hill. Lanham, MD: Rowman and Littlefield, 1–29.

Tiebout, Charles. 1956. A Pure Theory of Local Expenditures. *Journal of Political Economy* 64(5): 416–24.

Trelease, Frank J. 1957. A Model State Water Code for River Basin Development. *Law and Contemporary Problems* 22(2): 302–22.

U.S. Advisory Commission on Intergovernmental Relations. 1991. *Coordinating Water Resources in the Federal System: The Groundwater-Surface Water Connection*. Washington, DC.

U.S. Environmental Protection Agency (EPA). 1990. *Recommended Determination to Prohibit Construction of Two Forks Dam and Reservoir Pursuant to Section 404(c) of the Clean Water Act*. Denver: Region 8.

U.S. Senate. 1956. Committee on Interior and Insular Affairs, Subcommittee on Irrigation and Reclamation. *Water Rights Settlement Act: Hearings on S. 863*. 84th Congress, 2d session. Washington, DC: U.S. Government Printing Office.

Utton, Albert E. 1985. In Search of an Integrating Principle for Interstate Water Law: Regulation versus the Market Place. *Natural Resources Journal* 25(4): 985–1004.

Wahl, Richard W. 1989. *Markets for Federal Water: Subsidies, Property Rights, and the Bureau of Reclamation*. Washington, DC: Resources for the Future.

Weingast, Barry. 1995. The Economic Role of Political Institutions: Market-Preserving Federalism and Economic Development. *Journal of Law, Economics, and Organization* 11(1): 1–31.

Wildavsky, Aaron. 1990. A Double Security: Federalism as Competition. *Cato Journal* 10(1): 39–58.

Worster, Donald. 1985. *Rivers of Empire: Water, Aridity, and the Growth of the American West*. New York: Pantheon Books.

Chapter 7

Western States and Environmental Federalism: An Examination of Institutional Viability

Karol Ceplo and Bruce Yandle

Since 1970, statutory responsibility for protecting and managing environmental assets in the United States has rested with the national government. The U.S. Environmental Protection Agency (EPA) was formed that year, and major environmental statutes were passed that ended a long era of state and local control of environmental quality. However, even though statutes such as the 1972 Clean Water Act (CWA) were passed calling for strict enforcement of uniform standards based on EPA guidelines, many states continued to operate seasoned programs that differed significantly from the federal mandate. Even now, not every state has received EPA's delegated authority for regulating the environment. While many states altered their programs so that they fit the national mold, others continued to march to a different drum, leaving the EPA no choice but to oversee the mandated programs.

In the evolution that followed the rise of national control, former state and local programs for environmental action have provided a stem onto which federal control was grafted. Even those states that lack EPA-delegated authority to run the national programs have modified their approaches when managing environmental quality. In every case, the legal environment of water quality control has made a move toward uniformity.

Today, after twenty-five years of experience with national control, there is growing concern about the effectiveness of top-down, command-and-control regulation that typifies all national programs. There is recognition that homogeneous solutions applied to heterogeneous problems

225

often yield high costs and weak results. As a result, we find renewed interest in returning environmental control to the states. Indeed, major federal statutes and programs now leave considerable space for state action. With such change in the works, questions naturally follow regarding the evolutionary process and where it will take us.

The move to environmental federalism is not without critics. Indeed, some feel that a return to state control will simply toss away twenty-five years of environmental progress and begin an inevitable race to the bottom of the environmental trough. Some less informed critics hold the view that environmental protection began with the EPA; the states simply provided no formal protection before 1970. Those who cling to this view understandably oppose actions ending federal control.

Others see a move to environmental federalism as breaking the yoke of a monopoly regulator that has followed congressional mandates to prescribe costly uniform rules for widely diverse situations. To these, a return to state control offers opportunities to reinvigorate significant state protection and to stimulate innovative and competitive institution building. The proponents of federalism argue that the experience gained in the past twenty-five years will not be tossed away but added to the pre-1970 experience. Following this evolutionary logic, state statutes and common-law rights will likely be strengthened; market forces will be used more frequently to generate a new family of property rights–based outcomes that will generate more environmental protection at less cost.

We count ourselves among those who favor an evolutionary path that combines the learning of the past twenty-five years with the long history of environmental protection that preceded the period of national law. We believe that those closest to problems are better equipped to manage water quality problems, that those who receive benefits should bear the costs of beneficial actions, and that competition among states for investment, citizen goodwill, and environmental quality can generate more effective outcomes. Instead of seeing a race to the bottom, we believe the race will be to the top.

How might one test the hypotheses that individual states are prepared to assume control of water quality in their own borders, and that the results could be more effective? What evidence might one assemble to make a case for environmental federalism?

This chapter examines the case for environmental federalism for a sample of eight states west of the Mississippi River, each representing a distinct region or tradition. The eight states are Arizona, California, Idaho, Kansas, Louisiana, New Mexico, Oregon, and Texas. In what follows, we focus on water and water pollution control.

Initially, we seek to put at rest the notion that these representative states paid no attention to water quality prior to the advent of national legislation. The next major part of the chapter examines the pre-EPA period for each of the eight states. This examination of administrative law shows that western states have a positive history of responding to water-related problems. Our discussion also examines how water quality evolved in the post-EPA period, a period that pushed toward uniformity. Even here, we find that institutional variety is maintained within the tighter context of uniform federal statutes. We conclude the section with a summary that addresses environmental federalism viability for the eight states.

The next major section of the chapter examines each state's common-law history in protecting environmental rights, searching for empirical evidence of a viable common-law tradition. In this section, we explain how common-law environmental protection works and then turn to the record for the states. The search for actions based on common-law rules that protect environmental rights involves an examination of reported court actions since 1940 that relate either to water- or air-pollution cases. Evidence that a state had a strong tradition of enforcing environmental rights in the prefederal period indicates existence of precedents that can be called on again. The examination of data enables us to assess the states by common-law viability.

After examining the common-law story, we turn to the 1990s' property rights movement and discuss how western states participated in the movement. Seven of the eight states in our sample entertained or passed state property rights legislation that reflects a political commitment to property rights. But closer examination of statistical data on the movement helps us to draw different inferences regarding the viability of property rights–based environmentalism in the eight states. We then consider the three elements of our analysis—administrative law, common law, and property rights—for each of the eight states. Based on these considerations, we offer a forecast for the regulatory behavior of each state if the current national regime for water quality management devolved to the states.

Water Quality Control before and after the 1970 Clean Water Act

A person examining western water law is struck by its diversity and creativity, a clear example of necessity being the mother of invention. The necessity is, of course, water that is in short supply in most western states. In spite of this, these states have experienced large growth in population and agricultural and industrial output, none of which would be possible without some reliable source of water. How to get, keep, and allocate the essential commodity has occupied generations of westerners. The result of this struggle with scarcity is found in an elaborate array of institutional responses, all designed to deal with different aspects of the water problem.

Institutions for managing water quality generally came later but were logically connected to those that focused on water supply. To give a picture of this evolutionary process, we briefly sketch the pre-1972 (pre-Clean Water Act) responses of Arizona, California, Idaho, Louisiana, Kansas, New Mexico, Oregon, and Texas. As we discuss each state's experience, we first provide capsule summaries of the evolution of institutions that deal with water rights, followed by a discussion of administrative law that developed for managing water quality.

Arizona

Water Rights

Arizona is an appropriation state. Its water law is based on the uniquely American notion that the person who first makes beneficial use of a water source, whether or not that person is a riparian owner, has legal, usufructuary rights to that water. A shorthand form of this doctrine is "first in time; first in right." The territorial supreme court in Arizona adopted the prior appropriation doctrine in the 1888 case of *Clough v. Wing*.[1]

Arizona is also a public-trust jurisdiction. Its statutes deed all "natural channels, lakes, ponds, and springs" in addition to "water in definite underground channels"[2] to the citizens of the state as common property. In the pre-EPA period, most surface water and some groundwater was controlled by the state as guardian for the people. Controlling water involved monitoring and distributing water resources to appropriators, resolving water-related disputes, controlling water quality, and protecting Arizona's contractual rights to water use under interstate and international compacts.

Administratively, Arizona had, by the early 1970s, developed a sophisticated institutional arrangement for handling its many water concerns. Ultimate administrative authority over water resources rested with the land commissioner (Dewsnup and Jensen 1973, 104). The office of the commissioner approved or denied requests to appropriate water resources, monitored the distribution of these appropriations and settled disputes involving water rights.

Water Quality Control

In 1967, Arizona passed a state water pollution control code.[3] Arizona's pre-EPA water quality control was handled by both the Department of Health and the Water Quality Control Council. The council set water quality standards and issued and enforced water quality regulations (Dewsnup and Jensen 1973, 106). The Department of Health issued regulations to control water pollution.

To some extent, the Arizona agencies followed the logic of common law where a public defender acts against producers of public nuisances. Either government agency could seek an injunction against a person violating their orders. Although traditionally concerned with the effects of economic development on water quality, the two agencies also handled issues related to recreation and wildlife (Dewsnup and Jensen 1973, 107).

In the pre-EPA period, Arizona developed a multidimensional institutional approach to water problems. This included an office to oversee water appropriation and distribution, two offices with authority over water pollution control, offices to protect contractual rights to "interstate" waters, and agencies to manage electricity generated from interstate waters. Furthermore, Arizona developed a rich body of case law discussing water-related claims. At the time EPA was emerging on the national scene, Arizona systematically regulated water quality in its borders.

The Post-EPA Period

The primary water pollution legislation in Arizona today is found in the 1986 Environmental Quality Act.[4] Administratively, the Department of Environmental Quality (DEQ) has ultimate regulatory authority for water pollution control in Arizona. The DEQ administers a revolving fund for financing water quality improvements and oversees regulatory units that set and enforce surface water and groundwater quality standards.[5] The agency also sets navigable water quality standards, monitors water quality standards, issues water quality certificates, and coordinates the federal EPA's National Pollution Discharge Elimination System (NPDES), but lacks EPA approval to issue NPDES permits.

The state water quality agencies also administer programs that include a safe drinking water program, wellhead protection that guards the quality of groundwater, and a program that focuses on prevention of groundwater pollution.

Arizona provides tax exemptions for purchases and use of nonpolluting equipment, and rights to water use may be bought and sold in Arizona. Finally, Arizona recently completed volunteer efforts to monitor the Santa Cruz River on a monthly basis to assess instream water quality improvement from the Nogales wastewater discharge.

California

Water Rights

In the pre-EPA era, California had a complicated set of water rights laws, which combined riparian and appropriation doctrines, adding pueblo water rights to the mix.[6] Many of California's early non-Spanish settlers arrived in the state to mine, and miners on public lands used the appropriation system to acquire water rights.[7] However, the state also recognized the common law of riparian rights. When rights to water use came into conflict, California courts held that appropriative owners had superior rights to riparian owners, if those riparian owners did not hold vested rights.[8]

After passage of the 1866 Mining Act and its amendments, the California legislature passed a statute establishing a procedure for acquiring appropriative rights. This procedure was expanded, as were regulations implementing the appropriation process, by statute in 1913.[9] In 1928, the state amended its constitution, requiring all riparian (as well as other) users to put water to a "reasonably beneficial" use, after a supreme court case in which a riparian owner was held to have superior rights to an appropriator, even though the riparian owner was "wasting" water.[10] The *Herminghaus* ruling restricted riparian owners to the reasonably beneficial-use requirement, but did not do away with vested riparian rights, which existed side-by-side with appropriative rights throughout the prefederal era. This mixture of water rights law is known as the "hybrid system" or "California doctrine." Unlike most states that follow the system, California follows the traditional common-law rule that recognizes riparian water rights, even when the rights are not used for productive purposes (Getches 1984, 203).

California created an office of water commissioner in 1868,[11] and a state engineer's office in 1878. Originally, water commissioners helped resolve private water disputes. With passage of the 1913 Water Commission Act, the duties of the engineer expanded, and a six-member water commission was created. The commission was responsible for implementing the newly created system for appropriating water, issuing appropriations permits, investigating water rights issues, and helping adjudicated water use conflicts.

In 1921 the commission, and its powers, were transferred to the Department of Public Works, which in the 1930s oversaw the Central Valley water project in California. In 1956 the state created yet another water office, the Department of Water Resources, and a water rights board.[12] Responsibilities of the department were broad, while those of the board consisted of administering the appropriative rights acquisition process and making water rights determinations. In 1967, the water rights board joined forces with the water quality control board to form the Water Resources Control Board. Thus, in the years before passage of the CWA, California had three agencies handling water-related problems: the Department of Water Resources, the Water Resources Control Board, and the California Water Commission.

Water Quality

In 1949 California passed a water pollution control law, known as the Dickey Water Pollution Control Act,[13] which created a state water pollution control board and nine regional water pollution control boards. The boards catalogued industrial dischargers and adopted water discharge requirements that set levels of effluent quality and quantity (Sokolow and Hanford 1986, 7). The Dickey Act, which made no provision for enforcement against people violating discharge levels, was amended in 1959 to allow the regional boards to issue cease-and-desist orders against violators. Of key interest, California did not take a uniform, one-size-fits-all approach to water pollution control, focusing instead on demand and supply conditions in each water basin and setting water quality objectives for each of them.

California's Water Resources Control Board was given primary policy-making and enforcement powers for water pollution control. The agency directed research on water pollution issues, maintained a statewide data bank, sponsored public information programs, dispensed funds to the regional boards, and regulated and enforced the cleanup of oil pollution (Dewsnup and Jensen 1973, 137). Based on its history of issuing and enforcing water discharge requirements, California became the first state to receive EPA delegation to administer the NPDES program, yielding strong evidence that California was clearly not a pre-EPA water pollution wasteland. Long before passage of the CWA, California's regional water pollution control boards were required to weigh the costs of water pollution against the benefits of economic development when setting discharge limitations, a bit of logic that was lost when the federal government assumed control of water quality.[14]

The Post-EPA Period

The primary water pollution control legislation in California now resides in amendments to the Porter-Cologne Water Quality Control Act of 1969.[15] The current program maintains the outlines of the earlier state system, which includes the Water Resources Control Board (WRCB) and nine regional water quality control boards.

Over the past four years, California has experienced significant controversy regarding its Water Quality Control Plan for Salinity for San

Francisco Bay/Sacramento–San Joaquin Delta (Beck 1994, 251). Parts of the WRCB's plan for these waters was rejected by the EPA in 1991. Following a 1993 lawsuit, the EPA was required to issue regulations for this estuary, and recently, water quality control decision making has rested largely in federal, not state, hands.[16]

Idaho

Water Rights

Idaho has been an appropriation state since 1881, when the territorial legislature accepted appropriation as the state's official water use policy and allowed for water distribution by water masters.[17] Guarantees of the right to appropriate unappropriated water were a part of Idaho's 1889 constitution.[18] Like Arizona, Idaho has a public trust doctrine, which declares that rivers, streams, springs, and lakes are the property of the citizens of the state. However, rights to use these waters, including groundwater, could be obtained by valid appropriation.[19]

Idaho's pre-EPA administrative arrangement vested ultimate authority for water use policies under the Department of Reclamation (Hutchins 1968, 90). This department was responsible for evaluating and for deciding water use claims and requests. The department also had primary responsibility for distributing appropriated water in the state. This job was delegated to water masters, who had statutory powers to distribute water within various water districts.[20] The agency also took charge of monitoring and allocating groundwater withdrawals.

Water Quality

Prior to EPA, Idaho water quality control rested with the Board of Health. This office had the power to establish water quality rules, and regulations required "to preserve and enhance the quality of water for all beneficial uses" (Dewsnup and Jensen 1973, 262). The board had broad powers to create effluent standards and to create and monitor an effluent permit system. In addition, the board oversaw the drinking water system in Idaho and enforced rules and regulations concerning water supply and other public water supplies.

Before passage of the CWA, Idaho's water policy was more focused on economic development than on explicit environmental protection. An exception to this general rule is legislation from the late 1960s and early 1970s, in which the state legislature gave the park department authority to take, as a trust, a number of natural springs that were thought especially beautiful or useful for recreational purposes. At this time, Idaho's code also allowed the governor to take certain scenic lakes in trust to maintain their unique qualities.[21] Idaho's pre-CWA code did not reflect a strong water quality emphasis.

The Post-EPA Period

In Idaho, the administrative structure for water quality control places primary responsibility with the Department of Health and Welfare's Division of Environmental Quality (DEQ). The DEQ writes rules and regulations, although, as of 1995, these rules and regulations must be approved by the Board of Health and the state legislature. The DEQ also sets surface and groundwater quality standards.[22]

Idaho does not have primacy to issue NPDES permits, although the Water Quality Bureau in Idaho is responsible for certifying that federal NPDES, and other federal permits, will not violate Idaho water quality standards (Beck 1994, 6:331). The state provides tax exemptions for non-polluting equipment.

As of 1995, the focus of Idaho's water quality program shifted from nonpoint source pollution control (primarily agricultural and timber harvesting runoff) to creating and monitoring total maximum daily loads for its waters. This effort will require the state to (1) identify sources of pollutants, (2) establish loads of pollutants that troubled streams can handle, and (3) establish load levels for individual polluters. Idaho is expecting to rely heavily on voluntary cooperation to implement its total maximum daily load program.

In addition to protecting surface water quality, Idaho has a program to protect groundwater, which provides 90 percent of the state's drinking water (Benjamin and Belluck 1994, 233). A special groundwater council develops and monitors groundwater plans and sets groundwater quality standards (Benjamin and Belluck 1994, 234).

Kansas

Water Rights

In the mid-1870s, the Kansas Supreme Court declared that common-law riparian rights governed the use of waters in the state,[23] and this doctrine stood (although the court had conceded that riparian and appropriation regimes could coexist) until 1945, when the state legislature changed the states' water law to the appropriation model.[24] Rights to water in Kansas before passage of the CWA were distributed in the following manner: unappropriated water was appropriable, rights to appropriated water vested, no matter whether those rights had been acquired by means of the riparian or appropriation doctrine, although people with vested rights under riparian rules were required to obtain a permit to preserve these rights.[25]

The Board of Agriculture had ultimate authority over the water resources of Kansas, with primary responsibility for these resources resting in the Division of Water Resources. The board had authority to approve all rules necessary to control and allocate Kansas water. Kansas deeded its unappropriated water to the use of its citizens in 1945.[26]

Water Quality

Water quality control was the responsibility of the Board of Health. In the pre-CWA era, the board administered a water quality control act,[27] which created a council to aid the board. The council made recommendations for rules and regulations concerning both water quality and solid waste disposal systems. The board had authority to adopt rules and regulations concerning pollution of surface water and groundwater by gas, oil, saltwater injection wells, and sewage. More broadly, the board could establish water quality standards to ensure the beneficial use of the state's water resources.

Acting before many other states, Kansas passed legislation in 1963 calling for the creation of a state water plan that embodied long-term goals for water use, including environmental concerns.[28] Thus Kansas demonstrated an early concern for water quality.

The Post-EPA Period

Today, primary responsibility for controlling pollution rests with the Department of Health and Environment, Division of Environment. The department enforces Kansas water quality control law. Other related offices include the Bureau of Water and the Offices of Pollution Prevention and Environmental Remediation.

The Division of Environment writes and enforces regulations, sets water quality standards, and monitors dischargers. The EPA has delegated authority to Kansas to administer the federal NPDES program.

Louisiana

Water Rights

Unlike some states in our sample, Louisiana has an abundance of water, and its legal framework reflects this difference. Moreover, because of its early history, Louisiana applied a modified version of the French civil code notion of *res communes* to water, which means that state waters cannot be owned privately. However, the state determined that by segregating portions of running water, these portions could be reduced to ownership. Generally speaking, running water and the water and beds of both navigable and nonnavigable waters are common property.[29] As of 12 August 1910, waters not otherwise "owned" became the property of the state.[30] Louisiana is considered a kind of riparian law state, which imposes a "reasonable use" requirement on riparian owners.[31]

In the pre-EPA period, Louisiana had no state administrative institutions designed specifically to monitor or distribute private water rights. Rather, the state itself sold and distributed water through state agencies, such as the Bayou Lafourche Fresh Water District, the Iatt Lake Water Conservation District, the Sabine River Authority, and the Bayou D'Arbonne Lake Watershed District. Not surprisingly, because no administrative network existed to monitor private water rights, no administrative system existed to adjudicate water conflicts. Louisiana state courts handled private water use conflicts.

Water Quality

Louisiana water quality control emerged through court interpretation of a 1910 statute. The first action came in 1912, when the state supreme court decided an early water pollution case in *State v. Hincy*.[32] The court ruled that the discharge of salt water from oil wells into a freshwater stream violated Louisiana State Act 183 of 1910, which prohibited knowing or willful discharges of noxious substances into streams of the state (Silverstein 1972, 739). Although it would seem from the *Hincy* case that Louisiana had fairly early statutory protections against the intentional tort of nuisance, the court subsequently undercut this protection by denying an injunction to abate a nuisance based on a balancing calculus.[33]

In 1940 Louisiana created the Stream Control Commission to monitor the quality of the state's waters and control pollution levels in those waters.[34] Water conservation districts within the state were given similar powers. The commission had broad powers to establish water pollution standards for public uses of the state's waters, establish streamflows, control the discharge of wastes into the state's waters, and prohibit unreasonable discharges or discharges contrary to public interest.[35] Working thirty years later under the 1970 Clean Water Act, the commission required applicants to obtain permits prior to discharging wastes into state waters.

Because no state administrative body existed to monitor private rights, state actions concerning violations of pollution control rules and regulations were left to the attorney general. A person accused of intentionally violating pollution standards, as of 1970, could be subject to both civil and criminal sanctions.[36]

Louisiana presents a unique case. Rather than create a multilayered administrative response to the problem of water use control among private parties, Louisiana rejected administration law and relied instead on its court system to adjudicate water use conflicts. Further, Louisiana developed a fairly complex system of state agencies to sell water resources to citizens of the state. Other state agencies managed public works connected with water—an elaborate system for levees, canals, spillways, drainage control, flood control, and river improvement. Louisiana created drainage districts, levee districts, levee boards, and waterworks districts to aid in the effective control of its waters. The state also used "police juries" to monitor causeways, dikes, and dams, to establish water conservation policies, and to provide water for irrigation. While it is not surprising, given the scope and diversity of the water resources of the state, that Louisiana developed creative solutions to water problems, it is interesting that the state followed an almost pure common-law approach to water quality management, never establishing an administrative body for settling disputes and managing the various boards.

The Post-EPA Period

Following the passage of federal statutes, Louisiana developed a bureaucracy for administering water quality standards. The agency with primary responsibility for the task is the Department of Environmental Quality (DEQ), which was not created until 1983 (Beck 1994, 6:396). Responsibility for administering and enforcing water quality control legislation, as well as for regulating the discharge of pollutants into the states' waters, rests with the Office of Water Resources. The DEQ has regulatory powers and sets and enforces water quality standards. The state may seek injunctive relief and impose civil or criminal penalties, and obtain cleanup costs from polluters.

Other state agencies with functions related to water quality control include the Department of Transportation and Development, which is in charge of flood and drainage control, the Department of Natural Resources, the Commissioner of Conservation, and the Office of Coastal Restoration and Management (Beck 1994, 6:396).

Louisiana state courts apply the public trust doctrine broadly, based on a Louisiana Supreme Court ruling in *Save Ourselves, Inc. v. Louisiana Environmental Control Commission* that held that

> A public trust for the protection, conservation and replenishment of all natural resources of the state was recognized by art. VI, §1 of the 1921 Louisiana Constitution. The public trust doctrine was continued by the 1974 Louisiana Constitution, which specifically lists air and water as natural resources. . . .[37]

The court went on to say that the 1974 constitution creates a positive obligation for state agencies to protect the environment in accordance with legislative enactment implementing the public trust/environmental protection policy embodied in the case.

Unlike the other states represented in this study, Louisiana has a fairly limited, rather confusing administrative framework for managing water quality issues. In its early history, the state avoided many administrative procedures, relying instead on rules of law and court action. The federal mandate changed this. Again, we note that Louisiana has not faced the scarcity constraints of the other states in our sample and presents a dramatic contrast to the western states under consideration.

New Mexico

Water Rights

Two legal regimes govern water rights in New Mexico. On the one hand, the state recognizes pueblo rights to water, that is, water rights historically held by Indian pueblos. These rights predate all other waters uses in New Mexico (Beck 1994, 6:530). Cities that were pueblos in the past may claim rights to all the water they need based on this status. On the other hand, like its neighbor Arizona, New Mexico is a prior appropriation state.[38] New Mexico has recognized appropriative rights since its early days as a territory (Dewsnup and Jensen 1973, 511). Appropriative rights to water use were established by creating and maintaining a beneficial use of water. In 1907, the state created a permitting system, and thereafter, appropriative rights were created by permit approval.

As in Oregon, the state was divided into water districts, monitored by water masters (Dewsnup and Jensen 1973, 512). An interesting twist to western water law involves the use of both public and private eminent domain to protect water rights. In the prefederal period, public entities could acquire water rights by means of eminent domain (Dewsnup and Jensen 1973, 511), and in one case a private party used the eminent domain doctrine to exercise a right to water use.[39] Municipalities, counties, and state universities could acquire long-term rights to use more water they needed at a given time, so long as this excess water was used within forty years (Beck 1994, 6:530).

Water Quality

New Mexico passed water pollution control legislation establishing a water quality commission in 1967.[40] The commission had authority to create water quality standards for all interstate streams and issue regulations to control water pollution. Unlike later federal rules, state standards were either general and applied to the entirety of a stream, or special and applied to certain sections of a stream or to the chemical quality of a stream. The water quality commission could bring suit to prevent or restrict water pollution seeking injunctive relief only. In most cases, agencies preferred voluntary efforts over litigation to prevent pollution.

The Post-EPA Period
New Mexico is, along with Texas, in the rather unusual position of having more than one agency responsible for water quality control issues. The Water Quality Control Commission has primary responsibility for implementing the state's water quality programs, but this commission does not have a full-time administrative staff (Beck 1994, 6:530). Powers of the commission include the ability to make policy decisions concerning water pollution and adopting water quality standards and regulations. Because it lacks a full-time staff, the commission delegates the responsibility for implementing and monitoring water quality standards and regulations to the Environmental Improvement Division of the Health and Environment Department, which has regulatory powers. New Mexico does not have primacy to administer the federal NPDES program. The federal permitting program is administered by the EPA.

Oregon

Water Rights
Like California and Kansas, Oregon has undergone a change in its water law regime from riparian rights to the hybrid California system of water rights. Under Oregon law an appropriation regime governs, although vested riparian rights that existed when the state shifted to the appropriation system were preserved. The Oregon Supreme Court accepted the doctrine of riparian rights in 1876 in *Taylor v. Welch*.[41]

In the early 1900s, the court issued opinions limiting traditional riparian rights to those people who made some substantial beneficial use of their rights. In 1909 the state legislature passed a statute declaring appropriation the more suitable legal doctrine for Oregon, rejecting further reliance on riparian theories.[42] Thus, by the early part of the twentieth century, water law in Oregon was moving away from a strict riparian regime and toward a mixed riparian and appropriation system.

Under state law, Oregon's water supply was monitored by a state engineer who was responsible for appropriating water rights, distributing water, and adjudicating water conflicts. The state engineer was empowered to divide Oregon into water districts and appoint water masters to oversee each district.[43] Masters were responsible for dividing and regulating the use of surface water and groundwater by private rights holders. During droughts, masters regulated wells and reservoirs. When persons using water from a ditch or reservoir had a conflict over distribution, the master had the authority to divide the water resources to settle the dispute.

Water Quality

Oregon passed a water pollution control statute in 1939[44] and established an environmental quality commission in the 1940s.[45] This commission dealt with water and air quality. It was authorized to create water quality standards and to promote voluntary cooperation to improve Oregon's water quality. Long before the days of EPA, the commission oversaw studies concerning water quality. It also managed relations with other states, the federal government, and industry on water pollution topics.

Charged with the responsibility of managing waste discharge, the environmental quality commission established a permit system that rationed on the basis of volume and pollution concentration (Dewsnup and Jensen 1973, 623). Following traditional common-law remedies for public nuisance, the commission could bring legal actions for injunctive or abatement relief against offenders. Oregon went even further than other states, giving its water pollution control agency the right to sue for damages to fish or wildlife that resulted from pollution.[46]

Discharge of oil and other refuse into the waters of Oregon was also regulated. Additionally, Oregon created a system of tax incentives to promote installation of pollution abatement devices.[47] Thus, it appears that Oregon had common and statute law for protecting environmental quality before the passage of the CWA.

The Post-EPA Period

The Department of Environmental Quality is in charge of water quality control in Oregon, which is managed by a citizen group called the Environmental Quality Commission. The commission has typical regulatory powers that include setting effluent standards and monitoring water quality standards.

Importantly, the Department of Environmental Quality does have primacy to issue NPDES permits within the state, and is authorized to monitor compliance with the CWA. Point source discharges into navigable waters require NPDES permits, while discharges into nonnavigable waters require state permits (Beck 1994, 6:710). The department, along with other government units, has created voluntary programs for managing nonpoint source pollution. Finally, we note that since 1987 Oregon has employed the total maximum daily load system, allocating effluent limits and monitoring water quality. Generally speaking, Oregon water quality standards are more stringent than federal requirements.

Oregon divides its waters into basins and has developed a water quality management plan that specifies minimum water quality standards for each basin. The basin plan also provides for a review process for proposed projects in the basin areas (Beck 1994, 6:710).

Texas

Water Rights

Conservation and development were driving concerns in Texas in the prefederal period.[48] Like California, Oregon, and Kansas, Texas is a hybrid water law state. For a time, Texas courts recognized riparian rights, but Texas recognized appropriated rights to water and vested beneficial use riparian rights. Recognition of riparian rights was significantly curtailed by the Texas legislature in 1895.[49]

Water rights controversies were common in Texas throughout the late nineteenth and twentieth centuries, thanks in part to land grants made while Texas was a part of the Spanish empire, then a part of Mexico, as well as to the nature of riparian rights under civil law codes (Dewsnup and Jensen 1973, 700). Between 1845 and 1889, common-law principles of riparian rights controlled water law decisions. Thereafter, Texas passed an irrigation law that adopted appropriation for irrigation purposes. This act was amended in 1895, and the state expanded its use of the appropriation principle. Statutes in 1913 and 1917 further increased the impact of appropriation. However, it was not until 1931 that Texas passed legislation imposing the appropriation doctrine across the state.[50] Waters in Texas may be appropriated by permit, and unused riparian rights have, since 1953, been canceled by the state.

Texas water law is complicated, and so too was the administrative system created to manage these rights. At least three different administrative agencies had, at times, authority to issue permits for water appropriation: the Board of Engineers, the Water Commission, and the Water Rights Commission (Dewsnup and Jensen 1973, 702). In the period immediately preceding the promulgation of the CWA, the Water Rights Commission was in charge of issuing and monitoring appropriation permits.

Water Quality

Shortly before the 1972 Clean Water Act, Texas had two agencies with primary responsibility for water pollution control. These agencies were the Water Quality Board, created in 1967,[51] and the Railroad Commission, which had existed for decades before (Carssow 1970, 1035). Additionally, the health department had authority to engage in some regulation of the state's waters primarily having to do with waste disposal and sewage plant operators (Carssow 1970, 1035). Before creation of the board, in 1967, the Department of Health was in charge of much of the water pollution control effort in Texas. The Parks and Wildlife Department also played a part in water quality control, by bringing suit against people illegally discharging or otherwise affecting aquatic life and wildlife in the state, although such actions required Water Quality Board approval. The Water Development Board created long-range water use and development plans, while the Railroad Commission had sole authority to manage oil and gas waste in the state.

Texas adopted state water quality standards for interstate waters in 1965. In 1967, under the State Water Quality Act, Texas expanded water quality standards to all waters of the state (Dewsnup and Jensen 1973, 702). In sharp contrast to the federal approach, Texas water quality standards were based on intended water use. State waters were classified by zone, with some specified as "protected."[52] In this way, the board decided not only how much total pollution a given water could handle, but how much pollution an individual could contribute to the water (Dewsnup and Jensen 1973, 705–6). Polluters were required to obtain an effluent permit from the board.

Local governments were empowered to investigate the water quality of streams and prosecute violators of water quality standards for civil penalties (Janks 1970, 1293). Responsibility for enforcing pollution standards rested with the board of engineers and the state attorney general. Although enforcement through negotiation and cooperation was preferred, the board could conduct formal hearing and issue orders. Parties who failed to comply with orders could be prosecuted by the attorney general and subject to both civil and criminal penalties. Thus in Texas, a system for establishing water quality standards as well as a permitting system for effluent discharge existed before the CWA was passed. Of key interest, the system recognized local interests in setting quality standards and relied on suits by public defenders to keep polluters in line. The approach was far different from the federal approach.

The Post-EPA Period

In 1991, Texas passed legislation combining the functions of several agencies that dealt with environmental regulation into a new agency, the Texas Natural Resources Conservation Commission (TNRCC).[53] Primary responsibility for water quality control rests with the commission.[54] In the administrative shuffle, some functions that traditionally rested with the state Department of Health (concerning drinking water standards, wastewater treatment, solid waste management) have moved to the TNRCC. The agency acts as liaison between other states and the federal government.

The Texas Natural Resources Conversation Commission does not have primacy to issue NPDES permits. However, the Texas water quality program has received federal EPA approval. This means that Texas issues state effluent discharge permits certifying compliance with state water quality standards. Point source dischargers must apply for federal permits with the EPA. Texas has chosen not to follow the EPA's technolo-gy-based standards, and has focused instead on water quality standards (Beck 1994, 6:795).

Conclusion

As we noted at the beginning of this section, the states in our sample display significant diversity when it comes to protecting their waters from pollution. Some states have long-developed and elaborate admin-istrative mechanisms to control and prevent water pollution (Arizona, California, Oregon), while other states have much less elaborate water quality programs (New Mexico). Some of these differences reflect the fact that pollution posed greater threats in some states than in others, and thus was addressed earlier or more fully in affected states. Some differences may indicate that special interest groups have played an im-portant role in developing water quality control programs For example, in Texas the Railroad Commission regulates water quality affected by oil or gas, and in Oregon, environmental groups appear to have influenced the high level of regulatory protection of the state's waters.

In addition to diversity among the regulatory programs of these states, we also note that a small amount of experimentation has taken place re-garding the use of waters. Examples of this include California's limited market in water rights, created in the 1980s, Oregon's water conserva-tion program, and Texas's emphasis on water quality standards as op-posed to technology-based standards. In addition, California, Kansas, and Oregon have conformed to EPA's mandates and gained delegated author-ity for operating the federal programs, while the other five states con-tinue to operate alongside EPA, which manages a federal regulatory component.

Based on this review of administrative law, what can we say about the potential viability of water quality management by this sample of states? Our conclusions are based on two considerations: the extent to which viable water quality management existed prior to the advent of EPA and the adjustments that have taken place since the national take-over of water quality programs.

With respect to the first consideration, the evidence suggests that peo-ple will logically and systematically take action to protect environmen-tal assets when those assets are threatened; our survey of early history says nothing less. However, the evidence also indicates that individual states will do things quite differently. Environmental concerns and rela-tive scarcity vary across states. The second consideration leads us to con-sider the rise of elaborate state bureaucracies that were driven partly by

EPA mandates. Given devolution of control, the three states with full EPA approval for water quality management would likely continue to mimic EPA controls. But based on their earlier history, we would predict gradual adjustment to more flexible and innovative regulation. The states without EPA approval would more likely continue their somewhat unique water quality management approaches, which suggests significant differences in response across the eight-state sample. But given the long history of concern for environmental quality we would expect to see tighter standards where the benefits are higher and more relaxed control where environmental quality is more abundant and the biological envelope is less threatened.

Common Law, Property Rights, and Environmentalism

Having assessed the administrative law component of the legal environment within which water quality management has emerged, we now turn to the other component, the common law. With the exception of Louisiana, which followed French law, common-law rules that addressed the environmental rights of property owners provided a core element of environmental protection for the states in our sample. This less formal, judge-made law, which reflected the norms and customs of people in various regions, was gradually supplemented by state statutes and regulations. But all along, the common law has survived as an element in the environmental protection process. As we assess state control, evidence of strong common-law viability brightens the prospects for protection of environmental rights and therefore a more effective system of environmental protection.

Common-law protection of environmental rights is fundamental to a market-based environmental policy. Indeed, prior to the formation of EPA and the rise of national regulation, the common law was a far more essential mechanism for protecting water and air quality rights than it is today. At common law, private parties held alienable rights to the quality of water, air, and other environmental features of their land. Any unwanted invasion of pollution can be an actionable tort with pleadings based on nuisance or trespass.

Consider how water quality was managed under this scheme. The common law holds that downstream owners of land have the right to the beneficial use of water that passes their land. In addition, the law holds that no upstream right holder can unreasonably diminish the quality of water to downstream right holders. Where common law operates, market transactions address the problem that might be faced by an upstream discharger. The party upstream can purchase environmental rights from downstream parties; that is, they contract around the rule.

The remedy for nuisance or trespass can be as simple as it is extreme, at least by today's standards. Private parties damaged by pollution can bring action under the private-nuisance doctrine. Public defenders are called on when pollution damages affect a large number of parties, the so-called public nuisance problem. Common-law remedies call for the offending party to stop polluting, and more often than not, pay damages. When granted, injunctive relief often means that a polluter must cease the polluting activity or at least install equipment that eliminates the damaging discharge. Common law accommodates mass tort suits that might be brought by a public defender against a polluter as well as private nuisance suits brought by one party against another. Where a federal question or state diversity is at issue, common-law suits are heard in federal courts, which often look to precedents in state law for guidance. All other cases are heard in state courts. As a result, each of the states developed a unique body of common law.

As indicated in our survey of administrative law in the previous section, states often institutionalized common-law protection when statutes were passed establishing administrative agencies. These agencies carried out traditional common-law functions when pollution was a public nuisance that affected a large number of similarly situated people. While common-law courts continued to hear cases involving water pollution, access to regulatory agencies for redress made it less likely that common law would be the principal means for protecting environmental rights.

Examples of Common-Law Protection

To illustrate how common-law remedies were used to protect water quality, we offer some vignettes from a number of states and jurisdictions.[55] In our first case, the Carmichaels owned a 45-acre farm in Texas, with a stream running through it that bordered on the state of Arkansas. The city of Texarkana, Arkansas, built a sewage system to which numerous residences and businesses were connected. The sewage collected in the city was deposited "immediately opposite plaintiffs' homestead, about eight feet from the state line, on the Arkansas side." The Carmichaels sued the city in federal court in Arkansas.[56]

The court found that the "cesspool is a great nuisance because it fouls, pollutes, corrupts, contaminates, and poisons the water of [the creek], depositing the foul and offensive matter . . . in the bed of said creek on plaintiffs' land and homestead continuously . . ." thereby "depriving them of the use and benefit of said creek running through their land and premises in a pure and natural state as it was before the creation of said cesspool. . . ." The Carmichaels were forced to connect their property to a water system to obtain water for "their family, dairy cattle, and other domestic animals, fowls, and fish."[57] The cost of the water hookup and use was $700; they claimed the value of their property was reduced $5,000, the reduced enjoyment of their homestead over the past two years was valued at $2,000, and the dread of disease was valued at $2,000. Besides the claim for damages, the Carmichaels also sued in equity for a permanent injunction against "said open sewer, cesspool, and nuisance."

The judge found that the city was operating properly under state law to build a sewer system, but that there was no excuse for fouling the water used by the Carmichaels, regardless of how many city residences benefited from the sewer system. Citing other cases, the court found that the action at law for damages was proper as was the request for an injunction. The court stated:

> If a riparian proprietor has a right to enjoy a river so far unpolluted that fish can live in it and cattle drink of it and the town council of a neighboring borough, professing to act under statutory powers, pour their house drainage and the filth from water-closets into the river in such quantities that the water becomes corrupt and stinks, and fish will no longer live in it, nor cattle drink it, the court will grant an injunction to prevent the continued defilement of the stream, and to relieve the riparian proprietor from the necessity of bringing a series of actions for the daily annoyance. In deciding the right of a single proprietor to an injunction, the court cannot take into consideration the circumstance that a vast population will suffer by reason of its interference.[58]

The judge held: "I have failed to find a single well-considered case where the American courts have not granted relief under circumstances such as are alleged in this bill against the city. . . ."[59]

A New York case also illustrates how strictly riparian rights could protect the water quality rights of one citizen. In *Whalen v. Union Bag & Paper Co.,*[60] a new pulp mill polluted a creek. A downstream farmer, Whalen, sued the mill for making the water unfit for agricultural use. The trial court awarded damages of $312 per year and granted an injunction, ordering the mill to end harmful pollution within one year. The appellate division denied the injunction and reduced the damages to $100. The court noted that the mill was an important economic asset to the area. It cost over $1 million to build and employed five hundred people, which was worth far more than the water was to the plaintiff. However, the Court of Appeals (New York's highest court) reinstated the injunction:

> Although the damage to the plaintiff may be slight as compared with the defendant's expense of abating the condition, that is not a good reason for refusing an injunction. Neither courts of equity nor law can be guided by such a rule, for if followed to its logical conclusion it would deprive the poor litigant of his little property by giving it to those already rich.[61]

To make clear that its decision went beyond a case involving serious destruction of water quality, the court cited an earlier Indiana holding involving a similar situation:

> The fact that the appellant has expended a large sum of money in the construction of its plant, and that it conducts its business in a careful manner and without malice, can make no difference in its rights to the stream. Before locating the plant the owners were bound to know that every riparian proprietor is entitled to have the waters of the stream that washes his land come to it without obstruction, diversion, or corruption, subject only to the reasonable use of the water, by those similarly entitled, for such domestic purposes as are inseparable for and necessary for the free use of their land; they were bound also to know the character of their proposed business, and to take themselves at their own peril whether they should be able to conduct their business upon a stream . . . without injury to their neighbors; and the magnitude of their investment and their freedom from malice furnish no reason why they should escape the consequences of their own folly.[62]

These holdings did not mean that there could be no pollution. They meant there was no excuse for uninvited pollution that significantly reduced water quality. To avoid water rights litigation, polluters could have contracted for riparian rights from downstream landowners or bought all the land along the stream. This was, in fact, common practice.

The concept of a federal common law controlling water pollution was considered by the Supreme Court as early as 1906.[63] In that case, Missouri sued Illinois for allowing Chicago to dump sewage into Lake Michigan, which emptied into the Mississippi River, the source of drinking water for St. Louis, where about two hundred people died each year from typhoid. The federal courts had jurisdiction because the dispute was between two states and involved navigable waters of the United States. As noted by the Court, the issue was whether there was scientific evidence that typhoid bacteria could live in the river until it reached St. Louis. Under common-law nuisance standards, if harm could be shown from the pollution, injunctive relief could be obtained against the dumping of sewage. The evidence presented showed that bacteria could not survive the trip. Illinois was not responsible for typhoid in Missouri; injunctive relief was not granted.

International Paper Co. v. Maddox[64] shows how the common law accommodated the transfer of rights among polluters and receivers of waste. International Paper had a plant built in the 1930s on a Louisiana bayou. Recognizing the rights of downstream landowners, the mill had paid forty landowners for the right to discharge effluent into the stream, at a cost of several hundred thousand dollars. Plaintiff Maddox operated a fishing camp on the bayou, some twenty miles downstream, and had not sold rights to the mill. He claimed his livelihood was threatened by the water pollution and sued for damages or, failing that, an injunction. Expert witnesses in the case testified that the mill had installed superior water pollution control devices, but that the mill's effluent still caused damages. The court awarded Maddox $8,000 in damages for the loss of value of his business and reduction in property values. The case was appealed[65] and the appeals court upheld the lower court's decision.

The last major federal case was decided before passage of the Clean Water Act of 1972 when the Supreme Court reasserted that a federal common-law basis exists for water pollution actions. In this case, Illinois sued Milwaukee for sewage pollution of Lake Michigan, the source of Chicago's drinking water.[66] The Court noted that federal common law, which looks to states for guidance, can be invoked to abate a public nuisance in interstate waters. The Court's response addresses the question of racing to the bottom: "While federal law governs, consideration of state standards may be relevant. Thus, a State with high water quality standards may well ask that its strict standards be honored and that it not be compelled to lower itself to the more degrading standards of a neighbor."[67] The Supreme Court held that an injunction could be issued by the federal district court.

Months after this case, the Clean Water Act was passed. Milwaukee then returned to the courts asking it to vacate its order. The Supreme Court held that the act generally displaced federal common law, which meant that federal common law could not be used to impose more stringent effluent limitations than those set forth in the statute.[68]

The decision of the Court was reaffirmed in a 1992 interstate water pollution case when the Supreme Court noted that the EPA was granted jurisdiction by Congress over water quality from all point sources.[69]

Hence, a state's assertion that its water quality standard is being violated is legally irrelevant if the EPA says that it is not being violated. The states are little more than EPA agents in water quality issues.

Finally, in a break from U.S. case law, we provide a vignette on a common-law case involving a British angling association and discussed by Brubaker (1995, 282–84), which sheds light on how common-law suits protected water quality for anglers. In *Pride of Derby and Derbyshire Angling v. British Celanese Ltd and Others*,[70] action was brought by a fishing club, Pride of Derby, and its association, Derbyshire Angling Association, against the borough of Derby, British Celanese, and the British Electricity Authority. The three defendants respectively discharged untreated sewage, industrial waste, and heated effluent that polluted and raised the temperature of the River Derwent damaging the environmental rights of the anglers. Pride of Derby and Derbyshire Angling owned a fishery in the river. The suit by the fishing clubs requesting that the polluters be enjoined was joined by the Earl of Harrington, who owned land along the river, giving him riparian rights to undisturbed water quality.

The lower court issued an injunction restraining the three defendants from reducing the quality of the river's water, but then suspended the injunction for two years to allow time for the defendants to alter their operations. On appeal to the Chancery Court, the court upheld the injunction. The Chancery Court rejected the argument by the Borough of Derby that it had statutory authority to pollute provided by Parliament when the borough was authorized to build a sewage treatment works. The court noted that the statute did not authorize pollution and in fact prohibited discharge that "shall be a nuisance or injurious to the health or reasonable comfort of the inhabitants [in the region]" (Brubaker 1995, 283). The borough also asked the court to substitute damages for an injunction because the community could not easily rebuild its sewage treatment plant. Rejecting the petition, the court noted, "In the present case, it is plain that damages would be a wholly inadequate remedy for [the angling club], who have not been incorporated in order to fish for monthly sums" (Brubaker 1995, 284). The common-law injunction required the borough to redesign its sewage system, Celanese to change its discharge practices, and British Electricity Authority to reduce its discharge of superheated water.

Common-law remedies moved to the back of bus after 1970 when new federal statutes seized the pollution control territory. Thereafter, suits were brought under statutory law, and because ownership of affected land was no longer necessary for standing, the number of potential litigants and hence pollution cases expanded dramatically.

An Examination of the Record

Court reporters record suits brought in state and federal courts, and automated databases like Westlaw and Lexis contain the record of all cases reported. Recognizing that these databases are not exhaustive, we used Westlaw to count the number of cases reported for all water and air pollution actions that included common-law pleadings—nuisance and trespass—for each state in our sample for state and federal courts for the years 1945 through 1994.[71] To account for general growth in transactions in the economy, we divided the number of annual cases by real gross domestic product (GDP) to give a transaction weight to the cases. Similar count and calculation for all water and air pollution cases irrespective of pleadings allows us to examine the ratio of common-law cases to all cases. States with a higher proportion of common-law pleadings are stronger common-law and property rights states and therefore are the more viable candidates for environmental federalism.

Figure 7.1 shows the total number of common-law cases adjusted for GDP for the years 1945 through 1994. The low activity of federal cases in the pre-1970 period indicates the paucity of actions involving a federal question; in short there were no federal statutes and there were few controversies involving multiple-state matters. Later, there is an explosion of federal cases reflecting the large number of federal statutes, and regulations that emerged. For state courts, there is an increase in the early 1970s followed by a leveling.

Figure 7.2 shows the share of all water and air pollution cases that contained common-law pleadings, 1945–94, in total and by court system. Obviously, the share falls systematically. But notice the share of federal court cases. In the pre-1970 period, there were wide oscillations reflecting the diversity of federal questions and the infrequency of pollution issues. After 1970, the share of federal cases that contain common-law pleadings begins to stabilize.

What about the eight western states? Do they follow the same pattern? We examined the same time series of data for the eight states in our sample and found two distinct patterns. Arizona, Idaho, Kansas, Louisiana, and New Mexico fall into one pattern. In these cases, there is a low level of common-law activity in the pre-1970 period. After passage of statue law, activities accelerate. California, Oregon, and Texas show a reverse image. Common law flourished in the pre-1970 period and diminished after that.

What can we infer from these data? Because common-law viability requires precedents based on property rights, trespass, and nuisance, the states with the stronger pre-1970 experience are more likely to provide

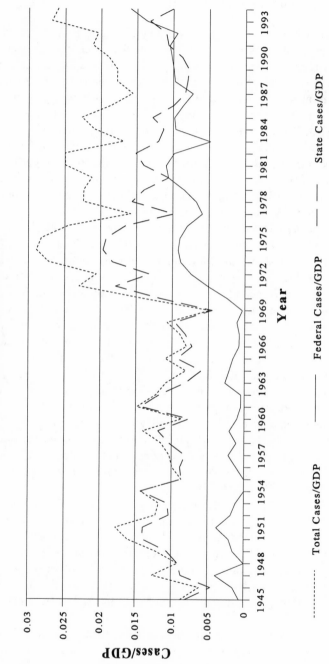

Figure 7.1
Total Air or Water Divided by GDP

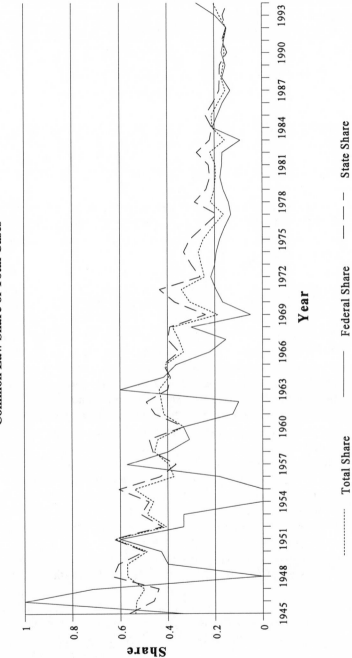

Figure 7.2
Common Law Share of Total Cases

common-law protections than those with a weak pre-1970 record. California, Oregon, and Texas show promise; Arizona, Idaho, Kansas, Louisiana, and New Mexico are less promising.

Evidence of Free Market Viability:
The Property Rights Movement

The continuing 1990s' property rights movement is itself strong evidence that ordinary people nationwide are more than just concerned about federal encroachments on private property rights.[72] The fundamental issue that galvanizes the movement is as simple as the words of the Fifth Amendment: "Nor shall private property be taken for public use, without just compensation." For our purposes, the effort to regain property rights protection is consistent with a desire to recover local control of environmental protection in ways that are consistent with free market environmentalism.

In the East, the property rights movement is inflamed by regulatory takings associated with enforcement of the Endangered Species Act and the control of wetlands inspired by the Clean Water Act. Added to these are federal designations of historic corridors, wild and scenic rivers, and other regulatory actions that have brought unwanted control of land use to the holders of private rights. Among western states, these issues are joined by federal actions that limit access to vast holdings of federal land and revisions of long-standing grazing rights. Some see the federal government as out of control, disregarding the sanctity of private property rights, always deferring to the interests of environmentalists in an effort to shut off gainful uses of land by private citizens. Others see the federal government as their only avenue for accomplishing vital and unappreciated environmental goals that will restore and preserve nature's sanctuary for future generations. But it is not so much the differences in viewpoints that matter to property rights advocates as it is the means for accomplishing the goals of environmentalists. If land rights are desired by any group, the property rights advocates say, then those who want the land can obtain it by simply buying it.

Concern over property rights protection led to failed efforts in the early 1990s to gain federal legislation. Later, the 104th Congress added property rights protection to its Contract with America. Again, no final action was taken. Disappointed by the failed effort to gain federal legislative protections, property rights advocates moved to the states. By September 1995, property rights bills had been introduced in forty-three states and passed in eleven of them. At the time, every state west of the

Mississippi except Arizona, Oklahoma, and North Dakota was either debating or had passed legislation.

Boudreaux, Lipford, and Yandle (n.d.) analyzed the effort to introduce state property rights legislation and developed a statistical model that predicts which states would entertain such action (Clegg 1995; Pendley 1995). The ordering obtained from the model ranks state property rights protection from strongest to weakest as follows: Idaho, California, Oregon, Kansas, New Mexico, Louisiana, Texas, and Arizona.

What does this mean for the viability of state-managed water quality programs? When we combine this information with our earlier assessments of administrative and common law, we find an interesting pattern. California, which has by far the largest and most diverse economy of any of the states considered, has a strong record of administrative law and common law, and a strong commitment to property rights. Oregon is similar. These two states appear to offer the brightest prospects for environmental federalism based on flexible rules that embody market forces. By contrast, Arizona has a weaker common law and property rights record, suggesting a continuation of EPA-like programs if devolution occurs. Kansas is a stronger common-law state, has approval for operating EPA programs, and shows less affection for property rights, which implies a more bureaucratic system of administrative law. This combination of traits suggests that Kansas would continue to follow the EPA blueprint in the event of devolution.

We lack evidence to make strong predictions about the remaining four states: Idaho, Louisiana, New Mexico, and Texas. Texas has a strong record on property rights but has a weak common-law tradition. New Mexico is a strong common-law state but has a weaker bureaucracy and attachment to property rights. Louisiana has its own peculiar form of administrative law and shows little attachment to property rights, and Idaho is a weaker common-law state but a stronger property rights state.

Conclusion

In 1970, the management of environmental rights long held by citizens, communities, and local and state governments was nationalized. For some states, highly developed bodies of state administrative law teamed with enforcement of common-law rights were replaced by a fresh arsenal of complex federal statutes. For others, the emerging federal law meant building an administrative mechanism that did not fit their pattern of evolving water quality control institutions. Now, some twenty-five years later, there are possibilities that states will again manage the destiny of water quality in their borders.

We will never know how water pollution control would have matured among the states in the absence of the federal interruption. However, our review provides evidence that some states would have formed multistate compacts for water quality control. They and others would have developed river basin management, perhaps with tradable rights. Some would have relied heavily on common law, which itself would have matured in unknowable ways. Others would have likely moved in the direction of setting performance standards that varied on the basis of community characteristics and the purpose of watercourses. Still others might have developed regulatory systems much like the ones that emerged under federal mandate. While we cannot know how state management of water quality would have worked out, there surely would be more variety, experimentation, and reliance on some estimation of costs of benefits.

Notes

1. *Clough v. Wing*, 2 Ariz. 371, 17 Pac. 453 (1888).
2. Dewsnup and Jensen (1973, 103); see Ariz. Rev. Stat. § 45-101 (1988).
3. *Act of March 16, 1967*, ch. 106, Ariz. Sess. Laws 534 (1967).
4. Ariz. Rev. Stat. § 49-201–361 (1988).
5. Ariz. Rev. Stat. § 49-281–287 (1988).
6. Pueblo rights were a part of Mexican law, as created by the king of Spain. Under this doctrine cities and towns (pueblos) were given preferential rights to use the water of streams on which the towns were located. When California was taken from Mexico these rights were protected by treaty. Pueblo rights remain an exception to the system of appropriative rights in California. See Fischer and Fischer (1990, 24).
7. See *Irwin v. Phillips*, 5 Cal. 140 (1855).
8. See *Lux v. Haggin*, 69 Cal. 255; 4 P. 919 (1884).
9. 1913 Cal. Stat. c. 586.
10. See *Herminghaus v. Southern California Edison Co.*, 200 Cal. 81; 252 P. 607 (1926).
11. *Pico v. Colimas*, 32 Cal. 578 (1867).
12. 1956 Cal. Stat. 1st ex. sess., ch. 52.
13. *Dickey Pollution Control Act*, 1940 Cal. Stat. ch. 1549, 2782.
14. Cal. Water Code § 13241 (1992).
15. Cal. Water Code §§ 13000–999.10 (1992).
16. Beck (1994, 252). We note that the EPA approved California's water quality standards for this area in May 1995. See *Water Law Newsletter* (1995, 5).
17. 1881 Idaho Sess. Laws, pp. 267 and 273; see also Dewsnup and Jensen (1973, 259).
18. Idaho Constitution, art. 15, sec. 3.

19. 1911 Idaho Sess. Laws 1911, ch. 230, § 1; Idaho Code § 42-201–224 (1990).

20. Idaho Code § 42-605 (1990).

21. Idaho Code §§ 67-4301–4306 (1990).

22. Idaho Code §§ 39-101–130 (1993).

23. *Schamleffer v. Council Grove Peerless Mill Co.*, 18 Kan. 24 (1877).

24. Kansas Stat. Ann. § 82a-701–725 (1989).

25. Vested riparian rights had to be of some beneficial use at the time of, or within three years of, the passage of Kansas's 1945 water law act.

26. Kansas Stat. Ann. § 82a-701 (1989).

27. Kansas Stat. Ann. § 65-3301–3416 (1989).

28. Kansas Stat. Ann. § 82a-901; 82a-903 (1989).

29. Beck (1994, 6:390), citing Louisiana Civil Code, art. 450.

30. Louisiana Rev. Stat. § 9:1101 (1991).

31. One commentator notes the following: "A 1984 study concluded that the Louisiana statutes defined riparian rights 'so vaguely and contain so many gaps that the rights of landowners, nonriparian, and "the state" with regard to withdrawing or using surface water—or restricting such use—are neither clearly delineated nor adequately protected by law'" (Martin 1984, 6:390). Martin is citing the Office of Public Works, Department of Transportation and Development, and the Louisiana Water Resources Study Commission's Report to the 1984 Legislature.

32. *State v. Hincy*, 58 So. 411 (1912).

33. *Busby v. International Paper Co.*, 95 F.Supp. 596 (1951); and see Silverstein (1972, 739).

34. Louisiana Rev. Stat. § 56:1431–1445 (repealed 1979).

35. Louisiana Rev. Stat. § 56:1439 (repealed 1979).

36. 1970 Louisiana Acts 405, p. 997.

37. Beck (1994, 6:393) citing *Save Ourselves, Inc. v. Louisiana Environmental Control Commission* 452 So.2d 1152, 1154 (La. 1984).

38. New Mexico Constitution, art. 16, sec. 2.

39. See *Kaiser Steel Corp. v. W. S. Ranch Co.*, 81 N.M. 414, 467 P.2d 986 (1970).

40. *Water Quality Act*, ch. 190, 1967 New Mexico Laws 1109.

41. *Taylor v. Welch*, 6 Or. 198 (1876).

42. Oregon Rev. Stat. § 537.010–.990 (1988).

43. Oregon Rev. Stat. § 468.745 (1992).

44. *Act of December 1, 1938*, ch. 3, 1939 Or. Laws 9.

45. Oregon Rev. Stat. § 468.010 (1992).

46. Oregon Rev. Stat. § 468.745 (1992).

47. Oregon Rev. Stat. § 468.150–.155 (1992).

48. Texas Constitution, art. 16, sec. 59(a) (1984), adopted 2 October 1917.

49. 1913 Texas Gen. Laws § 5.0001.

50. 1913 Texas Gen. Laws ch. 171, p. 358.

51. Tex. Rev. Civ. Stat. Ann. art. 4477-1 §§ 1–24 (1966).

52. "Protected uses" included: contact and noncontact recreation, domestic raw water supply, industrial supply, propagation of fish and wildlife, aesthetics,

mining and recovery of minerals, hydroelectric, irrigation cooling water, and navigation (Greene, Kyle, and Watson 1970, 1052).

53. *Act of August 12, 1991*, ch. 3 §§ 1–11 (1991).

54. Texas Codes Ann. Water Code § 26.001–.256 (1988).

55. The discussion that follows is taken from Meiners and Yandle (n.d.).

56. *Carmichael v. City of Texarkana*, 94 F. 561, W.D. Ark. (1899).

57. *Carmichael v. City of Texarkana*, 94 F. 561, W.D. Ark. (1899) at 562.

58. *Carmichael v. City of Texarkana*, 94 F. 561, W.D. Ark. (1899) at 573, citing 2 Add. Torts, § 1085.

59. *Carmichael v. City of Texarkana*, 94 F. 561, W.D. Ark. (1899) at 574.

60. *Whalen v. Union Bag & Paper Co.*, 208 N.Y. 1, N.E., 805 (1913).

61. *Whalen v. Union Bag & Paper Co.*, 208 N.Y. 1, N.E., 805 (1913) at 805.

62. Citing *Weston Paper Co. v. Pope*, 155 Ind. 394 (1900).

63. By federal common law we mean the application of common-law principles by the federal courts when they resolve interstate issues. The first Supreme Court case applying common law to water pollution was *Missouri v. Illinois*, 200 U.S. 496 (1906), which is discussed here. This holding was of peculiar interest to water. The Supreme Court recognized the right of states to obtain an injunction against air pollution sources that imposed damage on another state. Evidence of damage to vegetation in Georgia as a result of sulphur dioxide from a Tennessee company was held sufficient to allow Georgia to move for an injunction. *Georgia v. Tennessee Copper Co.*, 206 U.S. 230 (1907).

64. 105 F.Supp. 89 (W.D.La. 1951).

65. *International Paper Co. v. Maddox*, 203 F.2d 88 (5th Cir. 1953).

66. *Illinois v. Milwaukee*, 406 U.S. 91 (1972).

67. *Illinois v. Milwaukee*, 406 U.S. 91 (1972) at 107.

68. *Milwaukee v. Illinois*, 451 U.S. 304 (1981).

69. *Arkansas v. Oklahoma*, 112 S.Ct. 1046 (1992).

70. *Pride of Derby and Derbyshire Angling v. British Celanese Ltd and Others* (1953) 1 Ch. 149.

71. We used both water and air pollution actions because the two were often combined.

72. On this, see Yandle (1995).

References

Beck, Robert E. 1994. *Waters and Water Rights*. Vol. 6. Charlottesville, VA: Michie Company.

Benjamin, Sally, and David Belluck, eds. 1994. *State Groundwater Regulation*. Washington, DC: BNA Books.

Boudreaux, Donald J., Jody Lipford, and Bruce Yandle. n.d. Regulatory Takings and Constitutional Repair: The 1990s' Property Rights Rebellion. *Constitutional Political Economy*, forthcoming.

Brubaker, Elizabeth. 1995. *Property Rights in Defence of Nature*. London: Earthscan.

Carssow, Tim. 1970. Water Pollution Control in Texas. *Texas Law Review* 48: 1032–35.

Clegg, Roger, ed. 1995. *Farmers, Ranchers and Environmental Law.* Washington, DC: National Legal Center for the Public Interest.

Dewsnup, Richard L., and Dallin W. Jensen, eds. 1973. *A Summary-Digest of State Water Laws.* Arlington, VA: National Water Commission.

Fischer, William R., and Ward H. Fischer. 1990. Appropriation Doctrine. In *Water Rights of the Fifty States and Territories*, ed. Kenneth R. Wright. Denver: American Water Works Association, 23–30.

Getches, David H. 1984. *Water Law in a Nutshell.* St. Paul, MN: West.

Greene, D. Scott, John B. Kyle, and John A. Watson. 1970. The Texas Water Quality Board. *Texas Law Review* 48: 1047–85.

Hutchins, William. 1968. The Idaho Law of Water Rights. *Idaho Law Review* 5: 1–129.

Janks, W. Thomas. 1970. Local and Regional Water Pollution Control in Texas. *Texas Law Review* 48: 1286–384.

Martin, Patrick. 1984. Louisiana. In *Waters and Water Rights*, ed. Robert E. Beck. Vol. 6. Charlottesville, VA: Michie, 389–98.

Meiners, Roger E., and Bruce Yandle. n.d. Common Law Environmentalism. *Public Choice*, forthcoming.

Pendley, William Perry. 1995. *War on the West.* Washington, DC: Regnery.

Silverstein, Iri R. 1972. Comment: Water Pollution in Louisiana: An Attempt at Control. *Loyola Law Review* 18: 734–45.

Sokolow, Alvin D., and Priscilla L. Hanford. 1986. Small Community Responses to Water Quality Requirements in Nonmetropolitan California. California Water Resources Center, Sacramento.

Water Law Newsletter 28(3). 1995. Denver: Rocky Mountain Mineral Law Foundation.

Yandle, Bruce, ed. 1995. *Land Rights: The 1990s' Property Rights Rebellion.* Lanham, MD: Rowman and Littlefield.

Chapter 8

Why States, Not EPA, Should Set Pollution Standards

David Schoenbrod

The solutions to most local environmental problems are no longer in the hands of the state and municipal officials elected by the people most directly concerned. Instead mandates issue forth from Washington in tax code-like abstractions, their terms dictated by the complex interplay between Congress, the White House, the Environmental Protection Agency (EPA), the federal judiciary, and various special interest groups, including the self-described public interest groups. Just who is responsible for which aspect of any given policy remains a mystery to the local citizenry. Even if they did know, it would be hard to pin responsibility on officials who are accountable at the polls. And even if the responsible officials did have to face reelection, any local concerns would count for little in the welter of issues in national elections. So, as a practical matter, a federal aristocracy imposes environmental controls on localities, regardless of local wishes.

The nationalization of environmental policy is both radical and recent. Washington sets mandatory environmental quality goals, specifies standards for categories of pollution sources, and dictates deadlines and procedures for states and cities by which to implement them. Yet the regulation of pollution was almost entirely the province of state and local governments before the early 1970s.

The early 1970s were a time of panic, not just about the environment, but also about Vietnam, urban riots, and the ability of government at any level to respond to the needs of human beings. The desperate times pro-

This chapter previously appeared in *Regulation*, 19, 4 (1996). Reprinted by permission of the author, Cato Institute, and *Regulation* magazine.

duced martial measures. The response to Vietnam was war, the response to poverty was called a "war," and the response to environmental degradation was sufficiently warlike that national politicians could boast that they had won the fight before it began. A federal chain of command was established in which Congress gave instructions to the EPA about how it should give instructions to the states about how they should deal with all environmental problems. The statutory and regulatory instructions take into account every conceivable contingency and also order the states to submit voluminous plans and reports to the EPA to ensure that the primary instructions are carried out. There was little thought that the ecowar would be run from state capitals rather than Washington; after all, the federal government itself had caused many of the most controversial problems of the day (e.g., nuclear power plants, big dams, stream channelization, federal highways, overgrazing of federal lands). Similar problems came from nationally marketed goods, which states could not regulate without subjecting manufacturers to a maze of requirements (e.g., new cars, lead in gasoline, DDT). But the federal government did not stop with correcting its sins of commission and omission—it decided to declare war on all aspects of the environmental problem, no matter how local.

After a flurry of federal statutes, environmental quality improved and the panic ebbed. From this, many people, such as Gregg Easterbrook (1995) in his book *A Moment on Earth: The Coming Age of Environmental Optimism*, concluded that the national takeover was necessary to clean up the environment.

Rationales for Environmental Mandates

One rationale given for why Washington should take over was that pollution can cross state boundaries. "Everything is connected to everything else," went the mantra. States will not set reasonable standards for interstate pollution because, in regulating local polluters, state officials have little political incentive to take account of the harm that pollution causes out of state. However, the first and largest single step in the national environmental takeover, the Clean Air Act amendments of 1970, failed to deal with interstate pollution. The heart of the Clean Air Act is the federally required state-implementation plans whose function is to achieve the mandatory national ambient air quality goals. The statute requires the EPA to disapprove a state's implementation plan if it would fail to achieve the national goals instate or allow pollution to significantly interfere with a downwind state's ability to achieve those goals. The EPA has repeatedly enforced the *instate* requirement but, over the past quarter-century, has not enforced the *interstate* requirement, despite complaints from downwind states. As an environmental law textbook concludes, "The control of interstate pollution provides an easy rationale for federal regulation of air pollution. . . . Despite this . . . the control of interstate pollution would still have to be considered an unfulfilled promise" (Percival, Miller, Schroeder, and Leape 1992, 818). Other federal environmental statutes also focus on intrastate pollution. Under the Resource Recovery and Conservation Act and the Superfund statute, the federal government sets comprehensive standards for the disposal of toxic wastes and the cleanup of contaminated sites, primarily to protect subterranean water and soil, which usually do not cross state lines. Similarly, the Surface Mining Control and Reclamation Act aims primarily at restoring landscape contours, a quintessential local issue, and only secondarily at controlling the runoff of mining wastes into streams and rivers, which can contribute to interstate pollution. Likewise, the Safe Drinking Water Act deals with the local distribution of water. Thus, the national takeover of environmental law must be defended, if it can be defended at all, on the basis that Washington should regulate *local* pollution.

The sponsors of the Clean Air Act amendments of 1970 also argued that Washington must take over because the states had failed to protect the environment. But it was the federal government, not the states, that had been the laggard. With the emergence of the environmental movement in the 1960s, state and local governments responded to public sentiment by enacting broader pollution control laws. According to Robert W. Crandall (1983), pollution was reduced twice as much in the 1960s as in the 1970s. Yet, the federal government's first substantive steps toward regulating air pollution thwarted aggressive state regulations.

In the early 1960s, the automobile manufacturers, concerned that many states might impose strict and differing emission limits on new cars, sought advice from Lloyd Cutler, an eminent Washington lawyer, former New Dealer, and later counsel to President Jimmy Carter. Cutler suggested that the manufacturers get Congress to give the secretary of Health, Education, and Welfare (this was before the creation of the EPA in 1970) the authority to regulate emission standards for new cars. He reasoned that the companies would be able to keep the secretary from imposing expensive pollution reduction measures and that this national authority would be a powerful argument against state regulation. Congress obliged the auto manufacturers in 1965, and in 1967 it actually prohibited most states from regulating new car emissions. The 1967 statute was designed to help electric utilities by requiring states to regulate their emissions through a complicated process that was likely to delay and weaken any controls applied to them.

In comparison, the federal government neglected the air pollution issues with which it was particularly well suited to deal. It did little to control emissions from new cars, as Cutler predicted, and totally failed to remove the lead from gasoline. In 1970 the political winds shifted in Washington. Earth Day and a series of acute air episodes on the East and West coasts made air pollution a hot-button, national issue. In addition, Ralph Nader (1970) accused Senator Edmund Muskie of selling out to polluters. Muskie had hoped to ride his environmental record to the presidency in 1972. A bidding war commenced in which President Richard Nixon, Muskie, and other legislators seeking the 1972 presidential nomination vied to be the environmental champion by proposing the toughest air pollution laws in history.

The resulting statute, a 1970 amendment to the Clean Air Act, regulated new cars with vigor and also, as the first step in the national takeover, required the states to regulate stationary sources to achieve national air pollution goals. As the Supreme Court put it, "Congress took a stick to the states."[1] The EPA later claimed that this federal stick radically reduced pollution from stationary sources. But according to Crandall, "Assertions of the tremendous strides [the] EPA has made are mostly religious sentiment."[2] The belief that it took the federal government to make the states act comes from federal officials who claim credit for what state officials had already been accomplishing.

EPA officials call the national takeover "a dynamic state and federal partnership" (Patton 1996, 16), suggesting that in Washington "dynamic" means "heads I win, tails you lose." Given the palpable unfairness of this condescending partnership, elected state officials often resist federal environmental mandates. In the ensuing drama, state officials are cast as the environmental bad guys, rounded up by the EPA cavalry and, if need be, hauled before a federal judge. That such typecasting is a function of the structure of the federal statutes, rather than some peculiar environmental insensitivity of state governments, is made clear by one federal environmental statute in which federal officials bear responsibility for most cleanup costs—Superfund. Then the shoe is on the other foot; state officials perennially call for cleanups that cost more than federal officials are willing to pay. In sum, the record does not show that federal officials are more environmentally sensitive, just that they have the power to act more opportunistically.

EPA's Chain of Command

Even though the federal takeover was unnecessary, is there anything to be gained by returning authority over pollution to state and local governments? Yes, indeed. For starters, we could dispense with the entire federal chain of command—its bulk defies belief.

At its pinnacle is a thick volume of statutes in fine print. Under this volume is a stack more than two feet high, also in fine print, of EPA regulations. The EPA regulations are so lengthy, in part, because those who write them respond more to pressures from the agency to enlarge and protect its power than to the public's need for clear, concise rules. The problem is not that the agency is oversolicitous of environmental quality; it is that it is oversolicitous of itself. So the regulations construe the agency's power overbroadly and then react to the obvious instances of overbreadth by providing narrowly defined exceptions. Thus, under a statute regulating the handling of hazardous wastes, the agency takes seventeen pages to define the concept of "hazardous waste"—the definition reads as if written by Monty Python's John Cleese.

This is still just the tip of the pyramid, for the agency copiously supplements its regulations with "guidance" documents. (You can see why guidance is necessary.) For example, one subset of the guidance documents for Superfund cases fills thirteen loose-leaf notebooks. There are probably twice as many guidance documents for that particular statute, but no one knows for sure because the agency itself has been unable to assemble a complete collection. The various mandated state plans and returned state reports provide still lower levels of the pyramid, each exponentially larger than the one before. The entire pyramid would be unnecessary in a system not run from Washington; so would many of the EPA's 17,000 employees and the state, municipal, and private sector employees who participate in the federal rule-making proceedings and perform the paperwork required by the federal rules.

States and localities, if left to their own devices, would not adopt such a compulsive style for making environmental policy. Instead of trying to reason from cosmic first principles to comprehensive solutions, local officials could assess particular problems as they arise and decide what should be done, just as sensible human beings handle issues that arise in their lives.

Butler and Macey speak for many liberal and conservative scholars in concluding that the "command and control regulatory strategy . . . has not set intelligent priorities, has squandered resources devoted to environmental quality, has discouraged environmentally superior technologies, and has imposed unnecessary penalties on innovation and investment" (Butler and Macey 1996, 1). And no wonder. People sitting in Washington are trying to choreograph all of the environmentally related activities in the United States in the face of wide disparities in local conditions and ceaseless changes in pollution control technology. Moreover, EPA officials must respond to elected officials, and the federal courts have jurisdiction over EPA regulations. As Stewart (1988, 153) put it, the federal chain of command is a "self contradictory attempt at central planning through litigation."

The framers of the Constitution envisioned states serving as laboratories in which different policies would be tried and compared. State-by-state experiment, however, disappears with federal mandates. Yet experiment is what we need. Scholars holding diverse political perspectives have suggested pollution taxes, emissions trading, greater reliance on the common law, and other radical alternatives to Washington's command-and-control approach. Others, such as former EPA administrator William Ruckelshaus, have criticized the federal approach under which there are separate regulatory schemes for air pollution, water pollution, and so on. They suggest, instead, that plans be looked at holistically because this approach often can produce better overall environmental quality at lower costs, implying flexibility at the local level. Such innovation, however, threatens the EPA with its worst nightmare—loss of control. So, while the EPA feels compelled to experiment, it hedges innovative programs with so much red tape that flexibility is largely illusory. States, on the other hand, are more open to real experimentation, and it makes more sense to experiment on the state level.

Accountability

With the national takeover, democratic accountability goes by the boards for three reasons. First, the massive job of controlling the nation's environment from Washington encourages Congress to delegate its policy-making responsibilities to the EPA. As a result, environmental policies are made by bureaucrats rather than officials who are directly accountable to voters. Second, voters cannot effectively hold national officials accountable for how they resolved local environmental disputes. Third, federal mandates give federal legislators and the president the means to take credit for the benefits of environmental programs while placing blame for any ensuing costs on state and local officials.

Popular revulsion at such federal opportunism resulted in the passage of the Unfunded Mandates Reform Act of 1995. The act is an attempt to keep Congress from imposing mandates on state and local governments without providing the necessary funds to implement them. In other words, if Washington politicians take credit for the benefits promised by a new mandate, they must also take responsibility for ensuing costs. But, as is well known, the act leaves in place all preexisting mandates, including the entire corpus of federal environmental law.

The national environmental laws are chiefly regulatory mandates and sometimes tax mandates. For instance, Title V of the Clean Air Act amendments of 1990, which require air polluters to secure permits from states, turns out to be a mandate to tax. Under Title V, states must charge permit fees at a level that the EPA deems sufficient to fund the bulk of the state's air pollution control program, not just the cost of issuing the permit as the EPA suggests. Prior to 1990, most polluters did not have to get permits, yet they still had to comply with emission limitations. Before the statute, state pollution officials had to get approval for their budgets from state legislators who also had to take responsibility for the taxes needed to fund the budgets. After the statute, unelected federal officials supplanted much of the budgetary and taxing authority of elected state officials. The State and Territorial Air Pollution Program Administrators Association and the Association of Local Air Pollution Control Officials, whose funding comes partly from the EPA, vigorously supported the federal mandate for permits and support federal mandates in general.

The Rise of the National Class

The national takeover of environmental policy is not an isolated event. Wiebe (1995) argues that the single most striking change this century in American government was the rise to power of a nationally oriented, elitist, antidemocratic group that he calls the "national class." As he tells the story, the heyday of democracy in America (for white men anyway) was the nineteenth century, when power resided in a large middle class oriented around the "Main Streets" of America. The Main Street middle class believed in democracy. Voter self-education was prevalent, and voter turnout was much higher than in the twentieth century.

Around 1890 a new national class began to emerge—it was urban, educated, and believed that its expertise and highly rationalized means of analyzing problems were engines of progress. While the Main Street class was to be found at the village school board, the Rotary Club, or behind the counter at the local bank, the national class gathered in the higher counsels of government, nationally oriented groups like the American Bar Association and nationally oriented corporations. Thinking that experts like themselves should not have to be accountable to "lay people," the national class restructured elections and governmental processes to insulate policymakers from electoral accountability. A prime example was delegating lawmaking power to administrative agencies, often thought of as a pet project of the New Dealers. Wiebe shows, however, that the haughty mind-set of the national class was entrenched at the national level with the election of Herbert Hoover, who ran for office as the "Great Engineer." Its methods of trying to insulate decisions from the voters also included federal mandates and the turning of questions of policy into questions of "rights," including environmental rights.

Wiebe's description of the national class is not the same as how the national class defines itself, for such aristocratic pretensions are hardly compatible with its self-image of reasoned tolerance. So each one of its institutional innovations for blunting popular control of policy issues comes with a set of less aristocratic-sounding rationales. In the case of the national takeover of environmental policy, the rationale was that states would not make good decisions on intrastate pollution because, in competing to lure employers, each state would set ever lower environmental standards, so all states would end up with the poorest possible environmental standards—a "race-to-the-bottom" argument.

It is true that a state is likely to set lower environmental standards than it otherwise might in order to attract industry from other states. But sellers of goods set prices lower than they otherwise might to attract customers. The question is, why isn't such competition between states, as with sellers, a good thing? In the early days of the New Deal, many policymakers believed that competition among sellers was inherently disastrous because sellers would engage in a race-to-the-bottom price that would lead most of them to bankruptcy. This thinking resulted in the New Dealers' attempts to control all prices. Soon, however, economists showed that price competition does not lead to a race to the bottom, except in rare circumstances. The proponents of a national takeover of environmental regulation never thought much about what conditions would be necessary to produce a race to the bottom among states regulating pollution. They knew that there was a race to the bottom because they wanted more stringent regulations, and they knew themselves to be reasonable.

Revesz (1992, 1244) concluded that "race-to-the-bottom arguments in the environmental area have been made for the last two decades with essentially no theoretical foundation." Revesz has not proven that there never could be a race to the bottom, but he has shown that it was not the real reason for the national takeover. The clincher is that the national government has taken control of many environmental issues for which a race to the bottom is impossible because the facility in question is not portable—for example, abandoned waste sites.

The race-to-the-bottom argument does not justify the continued national control of intrastate pollution. The argument focuses upon just one determinant of state environmental policy—the competition to attract employers—ignoring other determinants such as the competition to avoid pollution, which goes by the name NIMBY—that is, "not in my back yard." NIMBY is a race to the top. The national class deplores both race to the bottom and NIMBY. In one thing it is constant: people like themselves should shoulder the experts' burden of supplanting the decisions of the communities affected. Moreover, the logic of the race-to-the-bottom argument suggests that all aspects of state and local government that would tend to affect industrial location should be taken over by a government with broader jurisdiction and, in an increasingly global economy, that government should be international in scope. This is an argument for the nascent "international class." Even if enough scholars could torture economic models long enough to produce some set of assumptions under which there would be a tendency toward a race to the bottom, it is implausible that its impact would be sufficient to offset the benefits of getting rid of the federal chain of command.

In rejecting the race-to-the-bottom argument, I own that some states will end up at the bottom relative to others. This is anathema to environmentalists who are fervent enough to think that any pollution is too much and naive enough to think that environmental standards divide purity from danger. In fact, between purity and danger is a huge gray area entailing risks smaller than those we face crossing the street. Where to set standards in that gray area is a question of policy, not rights. One of the virtues of allowing states to set their own environmental policies would be that electorates with different environmental values could set their own standards for intrastate pollution; those who dislike the balance struck in their state could move to another one.

It is also possible that some states will fail to deal with pollution hotspots that present real dangers; however, the national class exaggerates this potential because it looks down on ordinary voters. If pollution is starkly dangerous in a locale, it will be the stuff of reports by associations of state regulators, the news media, medical associations, and the EPA. Informed voters know what to do. Indeed, federal laws requiring firms to make public their emissions of toxic pollution have caused firms to reduce emissions on their own and have led states such as Louisiana, often thought of as a polluter's haven, to tighten regulations. And if worse comes to worst, people can move or sue. Although there are many obstacles to redress under common law, there are significantly less when a threat is defined and imminent.

Finally, the federal chain of command has failed to respond to egregious threats for years on end; you can look it up in the congressional testimony of environmental groups.

A Proposal to Reform the EPA

The Environmental Protection Agency should be stripped of its power with four exceptions. First, it should gather and publicize information on pollution and its consequences, on both the national and local levels. Second, it should propose to Congress rules of conduct to control types of interstate pollution that are not adequately addressed or that require special protection, such as the Grand Canyon. Third, it should propose to Congress rules of conduct for goods, such as new cars, when state-by-state regulation would erect significant barriers to interstate commerce. Fourth, it should draft model state environmental laws and conduct policy studies that states could use when considering whether to enact such laws. States, however, should be free to amend or reject federal proposals in favor of different approaches to pollution control.

I first suggested such a radical reduction in the national role for pollution control at a conference attended in large part by EPA officials, and former-EPA officials, whose law practices are built upon their knowledge of the agency's inner workings. Threatened with rustication from the national class to mere Main Street status, they reacted as if I had released a mouse to run around the room. For all their yelping, they came up with only three arguments to keep their privileges, each of which reveals much of what is wrong with the federal environmental aristocracy.

First, they argued that many state pollution control agencies are short-staffed. Of course their concept of the "work that needs to be done" is based on the paper-pyramid model of the federal chain of command—they actually think it is useful. Much of federal environmental officials' time is spent telling state and local officials what to do and checking that they do it. Under my proposal, we could dispense with a large portion of the EPA's 17,000 staffers. Perhaps some of them could be sent to the states, but that may not be necessary once the paper pyramid has been composted. Even now, state and local governments mount the vast majority of enforcement actions.

The EPA loyalists further argued that it takes the national government to stand up to locally powerful industries. Sometimes, of course, the neighbors of a plant are reluctant to see it regulated to the point of purity for fear that it will go bankrupt or move. As loyal members of "the best and the brightest," the federal environmental aristocracy wants the power to "bomb the village to save it." On the other hand, a plant might get its way because it has greased some palms. As Schlesinger (1995) observed in arguing against devolution of authority to the states, local government is controlled by the "locally powerful." The premise of his argument is that the national government is controlled by the virtuous rather than the powerful. Concentrated interests buy "access" in Washington just as they buy "clout" on Main Street. The difference is lost on me. While the state and local political playing fields are not perfectly level, at least people know the score. It would be hard to find an Arkansan who does not know that the Tyson poultry folks have clout in Little Rock. But at the federal level, the workings of concentrated interests are shrouded by the remoteness, size, and complication of the federal government.

Finally, the EPA loyalists argued that state governments are not competent to produce sound regulations. But, being the folks who took part in writing the EPA's contributions to the *Federal Register*, they were throwing stones from a glass house. The language that the EPA produces is—and I mean this—worse than the babble that comes from the Internal Revenue Service. It is opaque, arcane, elliptical, repetitive, and evasive. The policies are often dumb and sometimes perverse. EPA staffers explain that such problems derive in part from the legislative and administrative constraints under which they operate. True enough, but the federal house is still glass, regardless of who built it. In the downsized EPA that I propose, the EPA, stripped of its fiat power, could retain its leadership role only by convincing states to adopt its regulations by the quality and sensibility of its policies. That is how the private organization that proposes the Uniform Commercial Code and other uniform laws to the states attains its influence. We need an EPA that succeeds by earning its leadership, not by bringing the states down to mind-numbing mediocrity.

Notes

1. *Train v. Natural Resources Defense Council*, 421 U.S. 60, 64 (1975).
2. Quoted in Brimelow and Spencer (1992, 59–60).

References

Brimelow, Peter, and Leslie Spencer. 1992. You Can't Get There from Here. *Forbes*, July 6.

Butler, Henry N., and Jonathan R. Macey. 1996. *Using Federalism to Improve Environmental Policy*. Washington, DC: AEI Press.

Crandall, Robert W. 1983. *Controlling Industrial Pollution: The Economics and Politics of Clean Air*. Washington, DC: Brookings Institution.

Easterbrook, Gregg. 1995. *A Moment on Earth: The Coming Age of Environmental Optimism.* New York: Viking.

Nader, Ralph. 1970. Foreword. In *Vanishing Air*, John C. Esposito. New York: Grossman.

Patton, Vickie L. 1996. A Balanced Partnership. *Environmental Forum*, May/June.

Percival, Robert V., Alan S. Miller, Christopher H. Schroeder, and James Leape. 1992. *Environmental Regulation: Law, Science, and Policy.* Boston: Little, Brown.

Revesz, Richard L. 1992. Rehabilitating Interstate Competition: Rethinking the "Race-to-the-Bottom" Rationale for Federal Environmental Regulation. *New York University Law Review* 67: 1210–54.

Schlesinger, Art, Jr. 1995. In Defense of Government. *Wall Street Journal*, June 7, A18.

Stewart, Richard. 1988. Controlling Environmental Risks through Economic Incentives. *Columbia Journal of Environmental Law* 13(2): 153–69.

Wiebe, Robert H. 1995. *Self-Rule: A Cultural History of American Democracy.* Chicago: University of Chicago Press.

Index

271

About the Political Economy
Forum and the Contributors

The Political Economy Research Center (PERC) is a nonprofit research center located in Bozeman, Montana, that focuses on market solutions to environmental problems. For more than fifteen years, PERC has been a pioneer in recognizing the value of the market, individual initiative, and the importance of property rights and voluntary activity. This approach is known as the new resource economics or free market environmentalism. PERC associates have applied this approach to a variety of issues, including resource development, water marketing, chemical risk, private provision of environmental amenities, global warming, ozone depletion, and endangered species protection.

In 1989, PERC organized the first of an ongoing program called the Political Economy Forum aimed at applying the principles of political economy to important policy issues. The purpose of this forum is to bring together scholars in economics, political science, law, history, anthropology, and other related disciplines to discuss and refine academic papers that explore new applications of political economy to policy analysis.

The papers in this volume emanate from the Political Economy Forum held in June 1996. The research was partially supported by a grant from the E. L. Wiegand Foundation that provided funding for David D. Haddock, Dean Lueck, Robert H. Nelson, Barton H. Thompson Jr., and Bruce Yandle. They were joined by other authors and participants who discussed the prospects and pitfalls of devolving natural resource management and environmental regulation to lower levels of government and to individuals. The policy implications of the papers in this volume provide a refreshing antidote for command-and-control regulation originating in Washington, D.C.

Terry L. Anderson is professor of economics at Montana State University and executive director of PERC (Political Economy Research Center), in Bozeman, Montana. Anderson is the series editor of PERC's Political Economy Forum Series published by Rowman and Littlefield. (This book is the tenth volume in the series.) He is author, coauthor, or editor of nineteen books, including *Free Market Environmentalism* and *Enviro-Capitalists: Doing Good While Doing Well*, and has published numerous articles in professional journals and popular publications as diverse as the *Wall Street Journal* and *Fly Fisherman*. Anderson has been a visiting scholar at Oxford University, the University of Basel (Switzerland), Canterbury University (New Zealand), Stanford University, and Cornell University Law School. He holds a B.S. in business administration from the University of Montana and an M.S. and Ph.D. in economics from the University of Washington.

Karol Ceplo is a research associate with Clemson University's Center for Policy and Legal Studies and a doctoral candidate in history at the University of Georgia. Ceplo has been a faculty member at Clemson University and holds undergraduate and graduate degrees in English. She received her J.D. degree from the University of Virginia. Her research and publications focus on environmental and international law.

Sally K. Fairfax is professor of natural resources law and policy in the Department of Environmental Science Policy and Management and in the Department of Environmental Planning at the University of California, Berkeley. She has a master's degree in political philosophy from New York University and a master's degree in forestry. Her Ph.D. in political science is from Duke University. Fairfax is a student of public resource administration, focusing primarily on federal–state relations as they affect land management. She is coauthor, with Carolyn Yale, of *The Federal Lands*. She is also author of the second edition of Samuel Trask Dana's classic text, *Forest and Range Policy*. Her most recent work concerns state school and trust lands. Her book, *State Trust Lands*, coauthored with Jon Souder, was published by University Press of Kansas in 1996. In addition to her academic work, Fairfax has an extensive record of administrative service.

David D. Haddock was an E. L. Wiegand Adjunct Scholar at PERC while completing the chapter that is published here. Concurrently, he is professor of law and economics at the Northwestern University Law School in Chicago. Haddock holds a Ph.D. in economics from the University of Chicago, and previously taught economics at UCLA, Ohio State University, and Emory University. More recently he has held visiting positions at the University of Chicago and Yale University law schools.

Peter J. Hill is professor of economics at Wheaton College, where he holds the George F. Bennett Chair. He is a senior associate of PERC, and in addition to this book, has coedited three previous volumes of the Political Economy Forum Series. His research and articles, especially on the evolution of property rights in the American West, helped found the new resource economics, which is the basis for free market environmentalism. He is coauthor, with Terry L. Anderson, of *The Birth of a Transfer Society* and, with Joseph L. Bast and Richard C. Rue, of *Eco-Sanity: A Common Sense Guide to Environmentalism*. As an economic consultant, he has worked with the Bulgarian government in its attempts to privatize agricultural lands. Hill has a B.S. from Montana State University and a Ph.D. from the University of Chicago.

Dean Lueck is associate professor in the Department of Agricultural Economics and Economics at Montana State University. Lueck received his B.A. in biology from Gonzaga University and his Ph.D. in economics from the University of Washington. He has conducted research in law and economics and natural resource economics and published articles in such journals as the *American Economic Review*, the *Journal of Law and Economics*, the *Journal of Legal Studies*, and the *RAND Journal of Economics*. In 1994–95 he was John M. Olin Faculty Fellow in law and economics at Yale Law School, and in 1995–96, he was an E. L. Wiegand Adjunct Scholar at PERC. His current projects include agricultural organization and contracts and economic petroleum conservation.

Andrew P. Morriss is associate professor of law and associate professor of economics at Case Western Reserve University, Cleveland, Ohio. He received his law and masters of public affairs degrees from the University of Texas at Austin and his Ph.D. in economics from Massachusetts Institute of Technology. While a graduate student at Texas, he worked for the Texas Department of Agriculture's pesticide regulatory office. Morriss also worked on several pesticide exposure cases while an attorney with Texas Rural Legal Aid. He has written several articles using empirical methods to analyze the law.

Robert H. Nelson is professor at the School of Public Affairs of the University of Maryland. From 1975 to 1993, he was a member of the economics staff of the Office of Policy Analysis of the Department of the Interior. His writings include *Zoning and Property Rights*, *The Making of Federal Coal Policy*, *Reaching for Heaven on Earth: The Theological Meaning of Economics*, and *Public Lands and Private Rights*. Nelson is a senior fellow at the Competitive Enterprise Institute and was an E. L. Wiegand Adjunct Scholar at PERC in 1995–96. He previously served as senior economist of the Commission on Fair Market Value Policy and Federal Coal Leasing and as senior research manager of the President's Commission on Privatization. He has been a visiting scholar at the Brookings Institution and the Woods Hole Oceanographic Institution. Nelson earned a Ph.D. in economics from Princeton University.

David Schoenbrod is professor at New York Law School and an adjunct scholar of the Cato Institute. He is author of *Power Without Responsibility: How Congress Abuses the People through Delegation* and coauthor of *Remedies: Public and Private.* He also has published articles on remedies, environmental law, and the law and politics of regulation in scholarly journals as well as the editorial pages of the *Wall Street Journal, Legal Times,* and the *New York Times.* After graduating from Yale College, he attended Oxford University as a Marshall Scholar gaining a graduate degree in economics and then completed Yale Law School, where he was an editor of the law journal. As an attorney at the Natural Resources Defense Council from 1972–79, he was in charge of the litigation to get lead out of gasoline.

Barton H. Thompson Jr. is the Robert E. Paradise Professor of natural resources law at Stanford University and was an E. L. Wiegand Adjunct Scholar at PERC in 1995–96. He is coauthor of *Legal Control of Water Resources* and the author of numerous articles on water policy and on constitutional issues in the environmental and natural resources field. Thompson received his law degree from Stanford Law School, after which he clerked for then-Associate Justice William H. Rehnquist on the U.S. Supreme Court.

Bruce Yandle is Alumni Distinguished Professor of economics and legal studies at Clemson University and PERC Senior Associate. In 1995–96, Yandle was an E. L. Wiegand Adjunct Scholar at PERC. Yandle received an A.B. from Mercer University and a Ph.D. from Georgia State University. He served as senior economist on the President's Council on Wage and Price Stability and as executive director of the Federal Trade Commission. Yandle is the author of *Environmental Use and the Market* and *The Political Limits of Environmental Regulation,* coeditor of *Taking the Environment Seriously,* and editor of *Land Rights: The 1990s' Property Rights Rebellion.*

Jonathan Yoder is a doctoral student in the Department of Agricultural and Resource Economics at North Carolina State University. His dissertation will focus on the economics of wildlife damage to agricultural property. He received a B.A. in biology from Indiana University and an M.S. in economics from Montana State University. His master's thesis is a study of the impacts of spotted owl litigation on the U.S. lumber market. He currently holds a research assistantship and teaches introductory economics at North Carolina State University.